Praise for *Walking Home*

*"Sonia Choquette's book **Walking Home: A Pilgrimage from Humbled to Healed** is real, raw, and honest. As she walks an ancient pilgrimage to work through her devastating loss, grief, and abandonment, she finds the way back to a place of genuine forgiveness and healing. As we, the reader, walk with her, we find the same for ourselves."*

— **Jack Canfield**, co-author of the
Chicken Soup for the Soul® series

"Brilliant! Sonia Choquette takes us on a pilgrimage of the heart. She introduces us to places and people that offer timeless wisdom and sacred teachings for our own life journey."

— **Robert Holden, Ph.D.**, author of
Happiness NOW! and *Loveability*

*"Sonia's book **Walking Home: A Pilgrimage from Humbled to Healed** is grounded and inspiring, and her courage in making this arduous pilgrimage helps others live by their authentic voice and spirit."*

— **Chaz Ebert**, publisher of Ebert Digital, president of Ebert Productions, and vice president of The Ebert Company

"Sonia Choquette has a pilgrim's ardor. Join her on the trail to an authentic self. Witness her passion and her humility. Prepare yourself to be inspired. Every footstep, every word, is a blessing."

— **Julia Cameron**, author of *The Artist's Way*

CHEMINS DE SAINT-JACQUES

WALKING
HOME

ALSO BY SONIA CHOQUETTE

All of the above are available at your
local bookstore, or may be ordered by visiting:

Hay House USA: www.hayhouse.com®
Hay House Australia: www.hayhouse.com.au
Hay House UK: www.hayhouse.co.uk
Hay House South Africa: www.hayhouse.co.za
Hay House India: www.hayhouse.co.in

WALKING
HOME

A Pilgrimage from Humbled to Healed

SONIA
CHOQUETTE

HAY HOUSE, INC.
Carlsbad, California • New York City
London • Sydney • Johannesburg
Vancouver • Hong Kong • New Delhi

Published and distributed in the United States by: Hay House, Inc.: www.hay house.com® • *Published and distributed in Australia by:* Hay House Australia Pty. Ltd.: www.hayhouse.com.au • *Published and distributed in the United Kingdom by:* Hay House UK, Ltd.: www.hayhouse.co.uk • *Published and distributed in the Republic of South Africa by:* Hay House SA (Pty), Ltd.: www.hayhouse.co.za • *Distributed in Canada by:* Raincoast Books: www.raincoast.com • *Published in India by:* Hay House Publishers India: www.hayhouse.co.in

Design: Tricia Breidenthal
Interior photos: Courtesy of the author

Library of Congress Cataloging-in-Publication Data

Choquette, Sonia.
 Walking home : a pilgrimage from humbled to healed / Sonia Choquette. -- 1st edition.
     pages cm
 ISBN 978-1-4019-4451-3 (hardcover : alk. paper) 1. Choquette, Sonia. 2. Spiritual biography. 3. Pilgrims and pilgrimages--Spain--Santiago de Compostela. I. Title.
 BL73.C393A3 2007
 204.092--dc23
 [B]
                                        2014011698

Hardcover ISBN: 978-1-4019-4451-3

10 9 8 7 6 5 4 3 2 1
1st edition, September 2014

Printed in the United States of America

To my father, Albert Paul Choquette,
and my brother, Bruce Anthony.
Thank you for helping me find my way home.

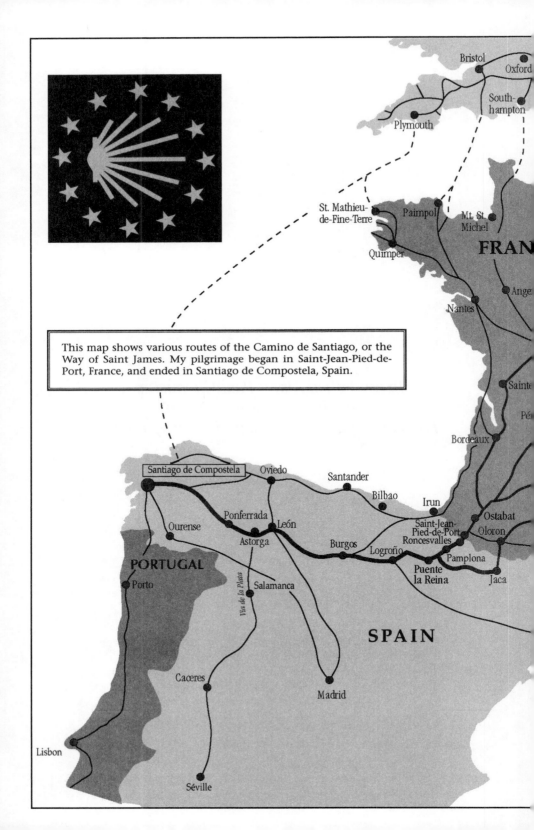

This map shows various routes of the Camino de Santiago, or the Way of Saint James. My pilgrimage began in Saint-Jean-Pied-de-Port, France, and ended in Santiago de Compostela, Spain.

CONTENTS

PREFACE

My name is Sonia Choquette, and I have been an intuitive coach, guide, and spiritual mentor for most of my life. From the time I was a teenager, I have helped lift people up, show them the way out of problems, and guide them toward solutions. It's been my gift, passion, and purpose to do this for others; and over the course of 35 years, I've had the honor of serving tens of thousands of people through one-on-one consultations, workshops, my website, and more than 20 books.

Drawing from my own life challenges, and the benefit of having masterful mentors from an early age, I've sharpened my five senses to a high degree and also awakened my sixth sense, which has served me well. Whether teaching or coaching, I am guided by intuition as well as my own past experiences. I don't draw from theory, but rather from what I've learned in the trenches.

I have traveled the world over sharing tools and techniques to help others overcome obstacles, heal heartache, find their passion, activate and follow their intuition, and succeed in their goals. And I have loved every minute of it, feeling profoundly grateful for the blessing of being able to be of service in a way that is so fulfilling and satisfying to me.

I've never allowed a thing to stop me, slow me down, get in my way, or trap me in a corner—and have taught others to do the same—fearlessly meeting life head-on rather than running away or letting it overwhelm me. That is, until suddenly, in the course of six weeks, both my father and brother unexpectedly died . . . and my life fell apart. All that I thought I had risen above, outsmarted, or refused to be bothered by came crashing down on me at once; and I was buried alive in an avalanche of sorrow, grief, and pain.

None of the tools I had used in the past helped me to feel better or find my ground.

Overcome with shame and a sense of personal failure, I found I could no longer teach or counsel others. Instead, I had to return to the state of novitiate—to confront all of the unhappiness and pain I thought I'd left behind and relearn from scratch the fundamental lessons of humility and compassion. I was able to achieve this through the practice of pilgrimage—specifically, by walking the Camino de Santiago, a more than 800-kilometer (500-mile) trek over the Pyrenees and across northern Spain. It was only through this process of sacrifice and self-abnegation that I was able to reconnect with my authentic self and recover a sense of inner peace.

Here is my story.

PART I

THE HUMBLING

1

Death

On August 19, 2008, I received a frantic call from my older sister Cuky (pronounced "Cookie") at just after seven in the morning.

"Oh my God, Sonia," she said, as if she had just been punched in the stomach. "Bruce died!"

"What?" I said, shaking myself out of the deep slumber I was in only moments ago.

"Bruce died."

"No!" I responded in shock. "When? How? What do you mean?" I pummeled her with question after question, confused and disbelieving.

"He died in his sleep last night. In Durango."

"You're kidding. I can't believe it," I responded, completely in shock.

Breathing deeply, and now speaking more calmly than ever, but still clearly shaken, she assured me it was true. "Yes, honey. He died in his sleep."

"Oh no! Bruce!" I cried, realizing my brother had slipped out of my life forever. "I just talked to him two days ago. He asked me for the Rolling Stones documentary *Shine a Light* for his birthday. I just ordered it for him. He can't be gone."

"I know. It's unbelievable," she answered, sounding as stunned as I now was.

"How did you find out?" I asked. "Who told you?"

"Noelle called. Bruce's girlfriend called her and let her know. She was afraid to call Mom and Dad."

"Do they know yet?"

"Yes, Noelle went over there and told them in person about an hour ago."

Poor Noelle. She was always the kid in the family to do the hard things like this.

"How are they?" I asked, suddenly afraid for them, especially for my mom. They were not young. How would they take this news? They were both so devoted to taking care of Bruce.

"I'm not sure. I'm going to call now and check on them. Call Noelle."

I hung up the phone and stared into space. My brother had had a difficult life. He'd struggled with schizophrenia, bipolar disorder, addiction, and depression, as well as a whole slew of physical ailments ever since he was a teenager. But he always seemed to hang in there and had recently seemed to be doing much better.

He was a difficult brother to have, because of both his illnesses and his stubborn temperament. We all loved him very much and tried our best to support him, but he was willful and did things his own way, which at times was self-serving and shortsighted, causing an awful lot of drama in the family, especially for our parents.

At heart he was mostly just a kid. He was a drummer and played in bands for much of his life. That's what led to his drug problems more than anything. It was part of his rock-and-roll world. He was also an artist, a poet, and a great cook. He loved music; food; friends; his family; and, of course, his kitty cat, Winter Girl. He had a huge heart and never shut himself away in spite of his challenges.

Bruce's finest achievement was graduating from college with a degree in computer design, which he had only recently completed. Because of his mental illness, it was difficult for him to concentrate, and yet he was determined. Only months earlier, he had walked with all of the other graduates of the University of Colorado, Denver, to receive his diploma. It was a glorious moment in his life, and we were all so proud of him.

Over the years, my parents supported him in every way. While he lived with his girlfriend of many years, it was my parents who made sure his life was on track. Especially my dad.

Because Bruce didn't drive, Dad drove him to school, to his doctors' appointments, and to get his groceries. He also helped Bruce pay his bills and take care of the house that his girlfriend owned and in which he lived. He was endless work and wearied us all.

Both parents checked in on Bruce every day, several times a day, and had for years. In fact, my father's biggest worry was wondering who would take care of Bruce after he died, even though we reassured him that we all would and not to worry. He did worry, though. A lot. Bruce was a handful, and Dad questioned whether we would be able to handle him with the same patience that he had.

Recently we were all feeling very optimistic about Bruce. After what seemed like a lifetime of drama and trauma, he seemed to be feeling and acting better than ever before, and more self-reliant in every way.

His long-standing girlfriend had been transferred from Denver to Durango, Colorado, and he had decided to spend the summer there rather than be apart from her. She had secured a decent job in a pharmacy after also having had a fair amount of emotional and financial setbacks. My family was relieved and encouraged to see each of them standing more and more on their own two feet for a change.

Underneath his illness and drug use, Bruce had a sweet nature. He had the best smile in the world, and to experience it made you immediately smile right back. We were very close when we were young, as he was only a year older than me. We played and plotted as only siblings can do, and managed to get into a lot of trouble while growing up.

That started to change around the age of ten, when he got his first drum set. I was left in the dust for rock-and-roll. Bruce played in a band with my other brother Neil, and then went on to play with many other bands over the years. Unfortunately, along with that world came a lot of drugs, which scared me to death. I ran away, and he dove in. He tried them all, and some grabbed hold of him, ravaging his mind and body.

Eventually Bruce broke down and needed medical care and treatment, mind and body, to keep him alive and healthy. But once he decided to get well, he stayed the difficult course and seemed to be slowly succeeding, particularly with the help of my father.

We were encouraged and even excited when he decided to move to Durango. That showed he felt strong and confident because he was stepping away from my parents' daily support.

Once there, he took up yoga to pass the time and keep fit. He lost more than 35 pounds, which was great because he had gained so much weight in his stomach due to the drugs he was taking for his ongoing mental problems. He was proud of this and seemed happier than he had been in a long time.

In fact, I'd just had perhaps the most rewarding conversation in years with him only two days earlier, and so hearing that he was dead was almost impossible to absorb.

Sitting in silence, I prayed for Bruce's spirit and his peaceful transition. Then I picked up the phone and made a reservation to fly to Denver. It was time to go home and lay him to rest.

The funeral was surreal. My parents, although shattered, were strong and dignified. My dad was mostly quiet and very emotional. He hardly spoke as he fought back the tears, as most men of his generation did. My mom vacillated from being wildly optimistic that Bruce was now in heaven to being genuinely confused and overwhelmed that he had died. She was clearly in shock, and it wasn't wearing off.

My brothers and sisters and I surrounded them both and did our best to comfort and blanket them from the pain they were no doubt suffering. All I could think of was that he was at last free of a life of physical torment. I was glad for that.

Six weeks later, I traveled to Japan to teach a workshop. It was a quick trip, and I returned home after five short days. When I landed, I received a message on my voice mail that my husband, Patrick, would be meeting me inside the terminal, which was something he never did. If anything, because I travel so much, if he picked me up at all, he usually just pulled up to the curb at the airport and I jumped in the car once I had my bag. Sometimes I just took a cab home. Coming inside to meet me was all wrong, and so was his voice. Suddenly I was scared.

I retrieved my bag and quickly skirted through customs. Once I walked out from behind the customs hall doors and into the terminal, I saw Patrick standing there waiting for me, his face completely white.

I walked directly up to him and asked, "What happened?"

He shook his head and grabbed my hand and said, "I'm sorry, Sonia. Your dad died this morning."

2

Humpty
Dumpty

Shortly after Bruce and my father died, my life started to come apart. Not my professional life. If anything, that was the one area of my life where I found solace, even strength. Whether it was working with clients one-on-one, teaching workshops, or speaking at live events, when I was in the flow of service to others, I was at one with my spirit and a million miles away from my own increasing heartache and emotional unhappiness. When I was working or teaching, I was peaceful. The problem was that I couldn't work 24/7, although there were days when I almost succeeded.

As the initial shock and sadness over my losses wore off, I found myself consumed with anger. Top of the list of targets for my ire was Bruce. My brother had introduced so much pain into my family for so many years because of his addictions that his death was just one more bullet in our hearts. I had tried to be kind and loving to him during his life, but his addictions and self-absorption had made it difficult to do.

Over the years, I ignored most of his obnoxious behavior, telling myself the spiritual thing to do was to love and support him in spite of his actions. After all, he was not physically or emotionally well. I did my best to be a good sister, but he had been so manipulative and self-centered with his drug use that it disgusted me many times over.

But I never told him. Instead, I just tried to love and accept him as he was. I managed to do that while he was alive. So I was appalled that suddenly I couldn't do it anymore. I had so much pent-up anger toward him that it took my breath away.

It also shamed me. I was not supposed to be angry with him. He was dead, for God's sake! I was supposed to have unconditional love for him and be glad he was at peace.

But this didn't deny the chaos, drama, and manipulation that his behavior so often, and for so long, brought to the family—that's what made me so angry. Why did he get to be such an asshole and not have anyone expect anything of him? Why did he get to live with impunity from all the ways in which he had inflicted pain on the rest of us?

The unspoken family rule (or maybe my own) was that as the stronger, more fortunate one, I was to be kind, loving, giving, nonjudgmental, and accepting—and not have a single negative reaction to his endlessly crappy behavior. And while he was alive I had more or less managed that. But now, apparently, I was having an intensely delayed negative reaction toward him that I couldn't shut off.

I prayed for these feelings to go away, but they didn't budge, and for that I was also disappointed in myself. Being this angry with my now-dead brother didn't fit in at all with my self-image as a spiritual teacher and guide, and that left me feeling embarrassed.

If I let slip to anyone that I did harbor these feelings, especially to any of my spiritual or professional peers, I was immediately chastised. I was told things like: "Forgive him." "Don't judge." "It was your karma to have a brother like this." "Be grateful it wasn't you." "I'm surprised that you feel this way given that you should know better." Essentially, I heard the same words I had told myself for all the years he was alive. Now those words only made me angrier.

I slipped away in shame, and seethed all the more in silence when alone.

I was especially angry with myself for confiding my conflicted feelings to my husband, Patrick.

His response when I was reacting to Bruce's past behavior was often to agree with me about how unacceptable his behavior was all those years rather than simply listening to me. All I wanted to hear was, "I'm so sorry, Sonia." But it never came.

I was so angry that he failed to comfort me when I was in so much pain. Why couldn't he just put his arms around me and reassure me that everything was going to be okay? Why couldn't he see that this much loss all at once was suffocating me with confusion and grief? Instead he withdrew, leaving me to struggle in pain on my own.

To add to that nightmare of angry emotions, I was also furious with my father. All my life I had been a "good girl" and done everything I could to love and be present with him. But for many years—for reasons I could not for the life of me understand—he seemed to resent me, and he let me know it. When I was a child, he often lost his temper and smacked me around; and when I got older, he told me that I wasn't wanted because I upset my mother. When I became a published author and began to work in the public sphere, he told me that I was not to speak of my work when I went home to visit them. I wasn't allowed to talk about my books or my workshops or any of my successes, because he feared it took the spotlight off my mom.

I never understood these conditions, but agreed to them anyway. Only now they enraged me. What kind of weird control was he exercising over me all those years? It was as if he banished my light, and it hurt me terribly, although I never let him or my mother know. I simply respected his unreasonable and extremely painful request, and tried to be loving toward him anyway.

Now I was furious with my father for refusing to see and welcome my gifts. But worse, I was angrier with myself for suddenly having these immature feelings toward my father, and so soon after he was gone. I hadn't felt those feelings for years, and some I had never allowed myself to feel.

Come on, Sonia. Really? Haven't you worked out your childhood wounding yet? I admonished myself. *How pathetic of you.*

My father loved my mother so much that he completely doted on her and thought she was the center of the Universe. He did not want anything, including me, to outshine her. I thought I had come to peace with, and even achieved sympathetic appreciation for, his devotion to her. After all, how many great loves does one witness such as his for my mother?

My father met my Romanian mother in the small town of Dingolfing, Germany, toward the end of World War II. She was a newly released prisoner of war, and my father was an American officer stationed there. Soon after they married. He was 20, and she was 16.

He brought his pregnant bride to America, and they proceeded to have seven children. He felt responsible for her in so many ways, and circled her with dedication and loyalty that was near heroic. He was a true knight in shining armor. But as a knight, he often considered anything that took attention off of her as the enemy.

I was named after my mom—and I was most like her. I was convinced that my father didn't like this about me. There was to be only one of her. Somehow I accepted that while he was alive, and even took no offense. So why now, as soon as he passed, did my feelings of anger toward him erupt?

It was not as though he was never there for me. When Patrick and I bought our first house, a dilapidated two-flat in Chicago, just after I became pregnant with our first daughter, he spent over a month with us, tirelessly helping us renovate the house before the baby was born. At that time I felt he truly loved me and wanted to show me in the best way he could.

So it's not as if I hadn't tried to move beyond and heal my childhood wounds before this. I thought I had. I went to healing workshops, saw a therapist, read a ton of books on the matter, and studied with master teachers explaining that all that transpired in one's life was part of one's karma and life lessons, and that no one was ever a victim.

And I absolutely accepted and believed all that to be true. I lived by those principles, and for the most part was at peace with this understanding of life and my difficult relationship with my father.

He was devoted to my mom, and she was his great love. If the power of that love blinded him to the hurt he caused me by pushing me to the side, I accepted and understood that, and even thought it sweet. I had a nice relationship with him in the last years of his life and knew him to be a patient and loving man, clear to his last breath.

Yet the minute my father died, right on Bruce's heels, all sorts of ancient, denied, or ignored feelings erupted inside of me like a volcano I couldn't contain. I was blowing up inside, and I was horrified that this was happening. I remembered the father I was frightened of, the one who would lose his patience and beat me for the slightest infraction. The one who was depressed and angry and felt threatened by me. Why on earth were these feelings poisoning my life all of a sudden?

Now, of all times, I needed to be mature and compassionate and helpful to my mom, and instead all I wanted to do was take someone down because I was so outraged. Although I tried to hide how I felt, I was less and less successful by the day.

Perhaps inevitably, my anger at Bruce and my father infected my already frustrated feelings toward Patrick.

In a book called *The Seven Principles for Making Marriage Work* by John Gottman, I once read about the four apocalyptic horsemen that kill a marriage: criticism, contempt, defensiveness, and stonewalling. We were embroiled in all four, and it was getting worse by the day. While these problems were not new, after my dad and brother died, I found I no longer cared about working to solve them.

So the battles raged on between us—over what I felt was his defended stance and lack of sympathy for my losses and pain, and his anger toward me for running away to work even more than ever. For neither of us being what the other wanted.

He called me crazy. I called him cruel.

He told me I was a fraud. I told him it was his projection and that he was a child.

He iced me. I fried him.

It got to the point where the air he breathed infuriated me, and I told him so.

I had to get away.

Consequently, I accepted every single invitation to teach or speak that came my way, even though I was exhausting myself. At least when I was traveling and teaching, I didn't have to be around him.

Truthfully, in my own sneaky way, I had been using this ploy to run away from him for years. When we were first married, I invited him to join me in teaching my students in small groups, but not long into our arrangement we found ourselves fighting on the way to and from workshops. It broke my heart. I loved my work, and he was stealing away my joy. So one day, after yet another argument, I simply told him I couldn't work with him anymore. He was shocked and furious. I was relieved.

Once I stopped working with Patrick, I started to hire other people to take his place and help me at the workshops. Only that just brought into my life a series of others who, while I appreciated their efforts and talents, also let me down and left me feeling as disappointed and unsupported as Patrick had in the end. What I didn't see then but was beginning to see now was that I didn't need support at work. I needed support in my life. I needed love. I needed witnessing and kindness. I needed care and reassurance, and I paid these people to offer it to me.

Looking back, I blamed myself for these failed relationships. *What was wrong with me? Why were the people I attracted to me so wrong?*

Finally, I reached my limit. I was nearing a nervous breakdown. I could not keep up with my work demands while my emotional life was so turbulent and unhappy, and my wounded self was bleeding to death. I was sad. I was hurt. I was lonely. I was ashamed. I was angry and tired. All the dark feelings and unfulfilled emotional needs that I had danced around or spiritualized away over a lifetime came back with a vengeance and demanded attention.

One day, Patrick started yet another petty argument with one of our daughters—over something that I thought was silly. I felt he was being controlling and mean-spirited, and I just hit the wall.

I told him enough was enough and that I couldn't live with him anymore.

He couldn't believe it. I was the kind of person who always bounced back, stayed in the game, and kept on trying. Quitting wasn't like me.

I couldn't believe it either.

Like Humpty Dumpty, however, I felt as though my life had been slowly cracking and crumbling apart, and on that day, what remained just shattered. I had felt it coming but didn't realize it was so close. I could not put it back together again. I didn't want to.

I didn't like Patrick. I didn't like my unhappiness. I didn't like my unbridled anger and resentment. But most important, I didn't like *me*. And I didn't want to continue being the unhappy person I had become.

As much as it scared me to do so, as loyal and devoted to my family as I was, I needed to stop. I was no longer living by my own values, and I needed to admit it.

Patrick moved out two months later and went to Breckenridge, Colorado.

I moved inward.

3

Spiraling Downward

After Patrick moved out, I went into mourning and shame.

I was embarrassed to be in this situation, knowing that if my clients and readers knew the painful circumstances of my life, they would no doubt accusingly ask, "If you are so intuitive and spiritual, why didn't you see this coming? Why didn't you stop it?"

I *did* see it coming. I just didn't want to believe it. I felt like a failure in so many ways.

Looking back over the past 30 years of my marriage, I had honestly tried to get along with Patrick. When on adventures together, we had a lot of fun and our relationship worked. But at home, we mostly just fought. It often felt as though we weren't an adult married couple at all, but rather were two combative, angry siblings battling each other for control. While that didn't surprise me, as we were both from big, dysfunctional families and had to battle to get our needs met while growing up, to continue as we had for all these years was ridiculous and exhausting.

I felt demoralized, disappointed in myself, and ashamed that I had ended up in this place. I, who espoused unconditional love, forgiveness, and understanding, working with spirit guides for help and trusting intuition for guidance, had found none of these tools and beliefs helped me one bit in healing my broken relationship and finding some peace with Patrick. We had some kind of intense karma between us, and we had failed to work it out.

I vacillated between feeling indignation, rage, sorrow, and fear as I considered what had happened between us and to our family and what lay ahead. I was alternately furious and devastated. And deeply sick at heart.

I was done with my frustrating, unhappy marriage. What I didn't realize was that I was also done with my life as I knew it.

I began to pray in earnest. I needed a divine intervention to help release me from the old, miserable patterns of relationship I had long held on to and which had had such a debilitating stranglehold on my life.

I also wanted the noble crusader in me to die, the one who fearlessly rushed in to defend a cause no matter the personal cost. I was depleted as a result of all these battles, and the only aspect of my feminine nature left over had been funneled into endless caretaking and rescuing at the expense of all other more refined and receptive—and genuinely joyful aspects—of my femininity.

It was time to put the inner fighter in me—this dominant male energy that was constantly guarding, watching, saving, and working—to rest, and allow my quiet feminine self—the side that could receive, allow, and relax—to emerge. I knew this self to be my authentic spirit, and I wanted God to help me bring her home.

I knew in my heart that this was the reason why my soul was facing this crisis. It was time to reach deep inside and allow myself to surrender to what was happening in my life.

One day I just fell to my knees and prayed. I asked the Holy Mother God and all my invisible divine helpers to release me from these negative patterns that I had carried, and remained so attached to, and was now so ready to surrender. I could feel an intense energy burrowing into the back of my head and into the very center of my heart as I voiced my request, as if she were questioning my sincerity and resolve. Did I know what I was asking? Was I certain that this was what I wanted?

I took a breath and knew it was.

"Please, Holy Mother God," I whispered in prayer, "help me cut the invisible cords that bind me, and set me free. Give me the inner strength to let go of all that I have created up until now, on every level, and which no longer reflects the highest path for me, and for those I love and serve. Help calm my more masculine energies so I can settle into my own divine feminine nature and cool the angry fires of hurt and fear that have burned in my heart for so long."

After making my prayerful request, I got up and lit a candle to the Divine Mother, to say "thank you" for hearing me. I was ready to surrender. I knew it was time to release control over my life and let God take over.

I spoke my intention aloud: "This life of mine is now finished. My present way is no longer serving me or allowing my greater Spirit to express through me. I ask for the cocoon to break open and free my true divine light. I surrender all attachments on all levels to the past and am now ready for what the Universe has in store for me. And so it is."

At that moment time stood still. I knew my intention was heard and registered by the heavens, and that my request would be honored and met with divine support. I sensed an inner shift take place in me. I didn't feel euphoric. I didn't even feel happy. Rather, I felt somber and quiet in spite of the thousand sounds swirling around me, the Universe saying, *Okay, get ready.*

The next morning, I suddenly had a powerful intuitive hit from my Higher Self that said, "Sonia, it is time to heal your life, and the only way to do that is to walk the Camino de Santiago. And go alone."

4

A Pilgrimage?

Shortly after my father and brother died, a woman showed up to one of my workshops using a cane and wearing a cast over what apparently was a seriously injured foot.

She sat near the front of the room, and as the class was assembling, I asked her what had happened. She said she had injured her ankle while walking the Camino de Santiago and had to quit before she completed it. She then asked me if I knew about the Camino, which I admitted I didn't.

"Oh Sonia, if anyone should walk the Camino it's you," she gushed.

"Really?" I answered, intrigued. "You think so?"

"Absolutely," she reassured me, without going into why she thought that.

"I'll look into it," I responded. But then after the class began, I didn't think about it again. At least not for a while.

About six months later, I was teaching a workshop in Australia and another student came up to me and asked if she could show me some photos she took while walking the Camino.

"I don't know why," she said, "but I feel that I must show you these."

While the photos themselves weren't terribly remarkable, seeing them nevertheless had a strange impact on me. As she gave them to me, one at a time, I had the strangest feeling I had been there before. In fact, it was such a strong feeling of déjà vu that I had a difficult time concentrating on my class for the first few minutes.

I meant to talk to the woman more about the Camino after class, but as soon as it ended, she disappeared. That night I had intended to look up information on the Camino on the Internet, but as is so often the case after teaching a class, once I had dinner, I went to my room and immediately fell asleep.

I thought more about the Camino on the flight home the next day. Still feeling the impact of those photos, I decided that it was something I would put on my bucket list to do someday.

When I got home, I looked into it a little more, but still not too seriously. I was so busy with other things that it kept getting pushed to the back of my mind.

That's why I was taken by surprise when I woke up and received this intuitive directive. I literally said out loud, as if to my Higher Self, or my spirit guides, or the Universe at large, or whatever spiritual influence was sending me this message, "Okay. I hear you. I'll go."

Only I didn't know what I was agreeing to.

So I got online and started to learn what I could about the Camino.

The Camino was one of the three major pilgrimages in the Catholic religion. There was the pilgrimage to Rome, the pilgrimage to Jerusalem, and the Camino to Santiago, Spain, where it is believed that the bones of James the Apostle are buried.

In the Middle Ages, this path, also known as the Way of St. James, or simply The Way, was traveled by over a million Catholic "peregrines," or pilgrims, who walked it as a plenary indulgence to be forgiven their sins and made new in the eyes of the Lord. Or at least the Church. Due to this it had also become known as The Way of Forgiveness, which is clearly the way I was seeking.

As I read about the Camino, chills ran through my entire body. I knew in some deep part of my being that I had already walked this path once before. The sensations were vague, but unwavering. I simply knew it was true but could not access more than this overwhelming feeling.

19

Legend has it that the apostles, after the death of Christ, were sent off all over the known world—India, Egypt, Africa, Armenia, Persia—to spread the word of Christ. Catholic documents say James the Apostle was sent to Spain to convert the nonbelievers. He wasn't that successful, however. He only managed to convert seven people in twelve years.

In A.D. 42 he returned to Jerusalem, where his luck changed and he began to convert people by the scores, including a known sorcerer named Hermogenes. This impressed the crowds and drew all the more converts to him but angered a Judaic monarch, Herod Agrippa, who had St. James arrested and executed, then had his body thrown over the city walls where wild animals could devour it.

But his loyal followers recovered his body and sent it back to Spain in a rudderless stone boat, where it eventually landed on the Galician coast in northwestern Spain, surrounded by scallop shells.

All seven of his original converts received his body and took it inland for a proper burial. That was the last anyone heard of St. James for another 800 years.

Then one day, a hermit named Pelayo, who led a quiet, isolated life, was awakened out of his daily routine when he noticed a brilliant star overhead.

He then heard celestial music, which caused him to rush to the local bishop and report what had occurred. He was followed back to where he'd had his vision by a group of local peasants who, armed with picks and shovels, discovered a tomb deep inside a dark cave near the site. In the tomb lay a body and a letter that said, "Here lies James, son of Zebedee and Salome, brother of St. John, beheaded in Jerusalem. He came by sea, born of the disciples." This location where the tomb was discovered became known as the Santiago de Compostela (St. James Field of the Star). A church was soon constructed on this site.

Spanish bishops and kings were very excited, even ecstatic, over this discovery, and began encouraging pilgrims to walk to Santiago. Soon they came by the millions from all over Europe.

The Catholic Church, a vast power at the time, sent a group of highly religious and fearless Crusaders, known as the Knights

Templar (or Knights of the Temple), to protect the pilgrims from thieves as they made their way to the shrine.

Their service as protectors of pilgrims expanded across Europe, from Jerusalem to Spain and Portugal. In support of the protection of pilgrims, the Knights Templar created what was to become the first banking system, allowing pilgrims to deposit their money with them in one city and collect it in another, so they could travel without worry, no longer making the pilgrims easy prey for robbers while on the road.

Because of their impeccable credit and upright means of protecting money, the Knights Templar became both extremely wealthy and powerful, often rivaling the power of kings.

They built several cathedrals and castles, which served both as monasteries and military posts, their powers increasing with time as the reigning popes exempted them from taxation and other oppressive jurisdictions enforced upon ordinary citizens.

Their rise in power eventually led to jealousy and accusations of being lovers of power and money by their enemies, in part due to their increasingly secret requirements for those who sought to join their ranks, coupled with their financial sovereignty.

As they became more powerful, they began to ask knights applying to join their ranks to take secret tests to establish their sincerity. These ceremonies and tests were never publically revealed, which ultimately led the Templars' downfall. Because of their secrecy, the Knights Templar came under extreme suspicion and were subjected by their enemies to the most outrageous accusations, from heresy to idol worship to sodomy and more, some of which the accused confessed to after being arrested and made to endure horrific forms of torture.

On October 13, 1307, Philip the Fair, king of France, a manipulative man who was greatly indebted to the Knights Templar and both unable and unwilling to pay back what he owed, put out secret orders to round up all the Knights Templar across Europe and try them for crimes against both God and the Church in order to take away their power, thus leading to the infamy of the date, Friday the 13th.

Due to extreme torture used against the wrongly accused Knights, many of them made false confessions, including the grand master of the Knights himself, a man named Saladin. Some of these innocent men were sentenced and burned at the stake in Paris; others were killed elsewhere. Those in Spain and Portugal escaped this fate and were not accused of any wrongdoing, although all were eventually retired.

As I read this, my feelings of déjà vu intensified. I had had, ever since childhood, recurring dreams of being part of some sort of secret Catholic society, rife with extreme rituals, and devoted to the protection of people. The more I read about the Knights Templar who protected the ancient pilgrims, the more I was overwhelmed with a sense of knowing and, surprisingly, grief and sorrow.

I had written about these dreams in my first book, *The Psychic Pathway,* 13 years earlier and had spoken about them on many occasions to both my family and my students. I had spontaneously mentioned, almost without thinking, many times that I had once upon a time been a Knight Templar myself, and felt an intensely strong connection to Crusaders and the medieval Catholic Church.

Funny how those dreams had faded in the past few years, having been such a big part of my life since I was a child. And yet, as I was researching the Camino, I felt the same eerie, ominous feelings I had in all those dreams.

I had long been considered and called a warrior, and had even been laughingly referred to as Joan of Arc by some of my closer friends for my fearless ability to confront and fight whatever I considered to be an affront to my spirit or the spirit of someone I loved. And yet, it was that very same warrior self that I longed to leave behind.

I was done protecting and defending the inner world—the world of spirit, intuition, and authentic personal power—and standing up to those who denigrated my work, and my world. I was also tired of fighting for the underdog and the oppressed at my own expense, and carrying those who I feared could not carry themselves. I was especially done fighting the "enemy" in my husband, or anyone else for that matter.

All of this flashed across my mind as I discovered more and more about the history of the Camino. I knew in my heart that perhaps this was one of the greatest reasons why I had to make this pilgrimage: to bring closure to an ancient story and identity that I no longer resonated with. Inside my being was a dark, heavy, patriarchal energy suffocating my inner feminine.

The self I yearned to be and express no longer resonated with the warrior essence. While I loved my strength, my fire, and my courage, I was war weary and needed to lay down my defenses and open my heart to a different kind of strength.

That is why I had to walk the Camino. I knew it in my heart.

5

Making
the Decision

Once I made up my mind to listen to my inner guidance and go on this pilgrimage, I had to massively rearrange my life. It was no small assignment, as I would have to take at least a month and a half off of work and be out of communication with my world for that entire time. That was a long time to disappear, especially in the face of a divorce and massive professional responsibilities and commitments.

I knew it wouldn't be easy. But obstacles had never stopped me from pursuing anything else in my life. In fact, it almost seemed a prerequisite for me that things be difficult if I were to undertake them. The challenge was what made life interesting.

First I told my daughters. To my surprise, they were all for it and fully supported my plan.

"Go for it, Mom," said my oldest daughter, Sonia. "You've been saying you needed a change for some time. This is obviously a great way to begin making changes in your life."

A born empath, Sonia had suffered along with me for the past several years, which only made me feel all the more guilty and depressed.

My other daughter, Sabrina, was my optimistic cheerleader. "You can do this, Mom. I know it's important, so if that is what your Higher Self told you to do, you have to trust your spirit and go for it."

Relieved that they understood and supported my intention without question, I now had to tell Ryan, who managed all my business affairs and to whom I would be leaving a mountain of responsibility and work while I was gone. I wasn't sure what he would think.

I called him a few days later to tell him I was going to walk the Camino.

"What's a Camino?" he asked, almost laughing when I told him that I needed to take more than a month off. I wasn't surprised by his reaction. He knew me well and had seen me do other crazy and unexpected things before, but never of this magnitude.

"It's an over 800-kilometer spiritual pilgrimage starting in France at the foot of the Pyrenees, and ending in Santiago, Spain," I answered.

"You mean the Pyrenees *Mountains*?" he asked, not sure he had heard me correctly.

"Yes, the mountains."

"How are you going to do that, Sonia? You just had knee surgery a few months ago!"

He was right. I did have knee surgery, and I was not yet fully recovered.

"I don't know, Ryan. But I am being guided to do it, so I have to."

"Are you sure you are being guided correctly?" he asked. "I'm not aware that you are much of a hiker."

"I know. It's crazy, isn't it?" I answered, laughing myself. "I'm not a hiker at all. But I guess I'll become one."

"How long does a Camino take? You have so many speaking commitments coming up this year. I'm not sure you have the time."

"I don't know. I've read it can take anywhere from a little over a month to two months, depending on how fast you walk," I replied, now laughing even harder. "If I have to, I'll run."

"Across Spain? You are ridiculous." I could picture him shaking his head on the other end of the phone.

"I know. It does sound ridiculous. But, seriously, Ryan. I have to go. I don't know exactly why, but I trust my vibes."

"Well, that I know. Okay. Let's see what you have ahead for the year."

We discussed my teaching schedule and discovered a window of exactly 38 days in May and June when I would be free to do the walk. Then I would have to show up in Vienna to teach a workshop.

"Put it on my calendar, Ryan," I said to him.

"Okay," he replied. "I've inked it in: WALKING ACROSS SPAIN."

Hanging up the phone, I could feel my heart was pounding with excitement. I couldn't believe I had just allowed myself to commit to this. I was going for it, and now there was nothing in my way.

6

Getting Ready

It was only two weeks before I was to leave, and I hadn't prepared at all for the long trip ahead. What was I thinking? This was just like me. It wasn't that I was intentionally procrastinating. It's just that I rarely plan or prepare in advance. I prefer to act on impulse and intuition and leave the thinking and preparing part to sort itself out along they way. That always drove Patrick crazy. Rather than plan ahead, I just dive in and go for things in life, trusting all will work out in the end. And for the most part, aside from some occasional extreme stress, it has, at least for me. That made Patrick nervous because he didn't blindly trust the Universe like I did. If anything, he was just the opposite, always preparing for the worst-case scenario, which annoyed me to no end.

Except this time, as I found my way to the REI store, with my "things to buy for the Camino" list in hand, I felt slightly annoyed at myself for having waited so long to get ready. Walking more than 500 miles across a country required a little more than good luck. I needed good boots, and it would have been better if I had broken them in first. Oh well. There was no time to do that now.

I was nevertheless optimistic. I knew I would make it because I intended to, but the effort might have been more comfortable had I picked up some boots earlier.

In fact, I thought, all I really wanted, more than anything else at this point in my life, was to be comfortable and comforted. "Funny way to seek comfort, Sonia," I said aloud to myself. "Choosing to do one of the hardest things you can possibly think of. That's smart of you."

I laughed out loud. It was so like me to take on difficult things without thinking. I wondered now if maybe that wasn't necessarily the best way to go through life after all.

"Too late now," I said to myself out loud. "You are committed up to your earlobes on this Camino and leaving in two weeks. So I guess you'll soon find out."

My first stop at the store was the shoe department to buy hiking boots. It seemed like an easy enough task until I actually started trying them on. The salesman, a short, red-faced, rotund, and earnest man, was a pro boot fitter, and was not about to simply let me pick a pair that looked good and go merrily on my way. Once he heard what I was doing, he became very serious and said that it was absolutely essential to my success that I get the right boot for the trek ahead, and that I needed to take my time finding it.

"I've helped several people get ready for the Camino," he said, making conversation as he set five or six pairs of boots in front of me to try on. "The last guy I helped was a priest from a parish in Evanston. He was going to walk the Camino to raise money for kids in his parish who needed school supplies and lunches."

I was embarrassed when I heard this. How noble that he had a cause that was so much bigger than personal reasons. Suddenly, walking to heal my unhappy heart seemed silly and self-centered.

"Why are you going?" the boot fitter casually asked as he unlaced the first boot and opened it up for me to try on.

I hesitated. I didn't really know what to say. To share that it was to recover from the end of my marriage and heal my wounded heart seemed way too personal and somewhat selfish compared to saving poor children from going hungry.

I paused. "I don't know," I answered, not quite truthfully. "I'm unhappy and I want to walk my way out of feeling this way, I guess. I know there's a happier, more authentic, grounded me that I want to connect with, a me that has nothing to do with anyone else."

"I think that's why most people go on long hikes. It's a good idea."

I slipped the boot on. It felt fine. "These are good, " I said. "I'll take them."

"Hold on a minute," he answered, laughing at me. "Not so fast. We have to make sure they fit and will be comfortable for the long trek ahead. You haven't even stood up in them yet."

Feeling out of my element, I suddenly felt the urge to simply pick a pair and move on. This was the way I generally made decisions. I was quick. Impatient. Especially when someone was focused on taking care of me. I felt uncomfortable taking the time to make sure what I needed was adequately addressed. I actually worried that I was using up too much of the boot fitter's time and this wasn't fair to other buyers.

While I knew this was crazy thinking, it was apparent that all the buried feelings that I had tried to override with my spiritual education and training were no longer willing to be ignored. They came flying back into my face with a vengeance and made me sweat. It took everything in me not to chastise myself for having these feelings show up.

Stop judging yourself, Sonia, I admonished myself. *Take your time. And accept your feelings. Ignoring them is why you are in the mess you're in. So relax and receive the help you're being given.*

"I like these boots. Thanks for your help. I'll take them," I answered, still trying to make it quick in spite of all my mental coaching.

No such luck. He was going to make sure I got the right boot for the hike, and I had no choice but to slow down and cooperate with him.

"Now stand up and see how they feel," he said, and as I did I couldn't help but notice how unrushed and genuinely interested in helping me he was. I took a breath and attempted to slow down and become as genuinely interested in helping myself as he was.

I did as he said. "These still feel fine." I answered, trying to convince him.

"I'm not sold just yet," he said, shaking his head. "Walk around for a few minutes and see how they feel."

I agreed and walked in a fast, self-conscious circle around the store. Actually, they didn't feel that great once I started walking. They were stiff in the front and hurt my bunions.

"How are they when you walk?" he asked.

"A little tight," I said, "but once I break them in, they'll be fine, I guess," I answered.

"That's not a good start. When are you leaving?" he asked.

"In two weeks," I answered.

"That's not enough time to break them in," he said, shaking his head, "and believe me, you do not want to break them in on the trail. Let's try another pair."

"Okay," I conceded. "You may be right." He was, because the longer I had these boots on the more uncomfortable my feet felt, especially around the front of my foot, where they suddenly burned.

The next pair didn't look as nice as the ones I had just tried on, but they felt a lot better.

"These feel much better," I said, moving my toes. "These are far more comfortable. I'll take these instead."

"Hold your horses," he said and laughed. "Getting the right boots is the key to your success, so slow down and work with me. Now, walk around and see how they feel after at least ten minutes."

I strolled through the store this time, feeling silly as I did. I never quite saw myself as a hiker, spending far more time buying designer shoes at Neiman Marcus, so I felt like a bit of an impostor. But I liked the idea of being a true outdoorswoman, so I slowed down and gave the boots my full attention. After all, I really did want the right boots. And I was in no actual hurry. It was just my habit to be in a hurry. A very old stress-inducing habit.

As I strolled I began to think about the other things I needed to do for the trip besides buying boots and supplies. I also had to show my daughters how to pay the house bills while I was gone. Suddenly it seemed as though I had a mountain of things to do before I left and no time at all in which to do them.

I was responsible for so much. I took care of so much in my home, in my business, for my friends and daughters . . . and to walk away from all of that for nearly six weeks felt risky.

I knew I needed to do it in order to heal. I wanted to, and was ready to in every cell of my being. Still, walking away from so much was so out of the realm of my life as I knew it that it left me feeling vulnerable. I had to trust everyone and the Universe and myself to a degree that I hadn't in a long time. I had to let go of control and let things unfold on their own.

Hmm. I think that's the point of this Camino. Trust and let go. At least that's the point for me, I thought as I looked at wool socks near the shoe section.

The salesman walked over to me. "Well?" he said, "how do these feel?"

"Actually, they feel a lot roomier," I said. "I'll go with these."

"Before you do, how does the front feel, around your toes?"

"Not stiff like the others. I don't feel any pressure there at all."

"How about the heel? Does your heel rise when you walk?"

"A little," I answered, "which is probably why they feel so good."

"That's *not* good," he said, shaking his head. "If your heel is slipping around, you'll get blisters. Here, put on another pair of socks, and see if it still slips."

Another pair?

"Yes, it helps to wear two pairs of socks when you hike. The first pair is called a liner. It's thinner and prevents your foot from getting rubbed raw by the boot. The second one is thicker, and you wear it over the first one. It absorbs the sweat and the shocks to the foot as you walk."

"I see," I said, as I took off the first sock, put on the liner, and then put the thicker wool sock back on, before slipping back into the boot.

"Does that make any difference?"

"It's tighter," I answered, standing up, "but comfortable."

"Now, walk up this incline here," he said, pointing to a small wooden ramp a few feet away. "You want to make sure that the boot still feels good when you walk uphill."

I took a few steps up on it and said, "Yes, it feels fine."

"Are you slipping in the boot?" he asked.

"A little. Not too much."

"That's not good," he answered. "If you slide, you can bruise your toes. And that would be a disaster. Let's try another pair."

I surrendered. "All right. I'm open. What do you have in mind?"

"Give me a minute," he replied, looking at all the models on display. "Okay," he said, as though finding what he was looking for. "I'll get another and be right back."

He then brought out the ugliest-looking hiking boot I've ever seen, as if any were a fashion statement. It was black and gray, and looked big and heavy, and more like a man's shoe than a boot, not at all "trekker-like" in my opinion. Yet once I had it on, it wasn't heavy at all, and felt better than the other two for sure.

I did the obligatory walk around the store, and then walked up the mini-ramp and down, and still they felt pretty good. I put on the two pair of socks and repeated the process, and they still passed the test. "Okay," I said, now sure myself, "these are it. I'll take them."

"What else do you need?" he asked, looking around. "Socks? Liners? Other gear?"

"I need everything," I said, pulling out my list. "I'm embarrassed to say that I haven't done a thing to get ready, and I'm leaving in two weeks!"

"Did you just decide to do this?"

"No. I decided three months ago, but just haven't gotten around to doing the things I need to do in order to get ready until today. I've been so busy, I just let time slip by. I don't really know how it got this late."

"Well, you aren't the first beginner to approach a long hike like this. No worries. We'll get you fixed up and ready to go."

I got socks, hiking pants, hiking shirts, a rain poncho, and a white sun-blocking shirt to protect me from sunburn.

From clothing we moved on to other things I would need on the trail.

I got a water bottle, and a backpack that could carry all my stuff. I also got a tiny green sleeping bag that rolled up into nothing, and a liner for that, as well. I was getting into this.

He gave me the thumbs-up, and kept on moving.

Then he showed me a soft plastic funnel-like object and said, "You might want one of these. It comes in very handy on the trail."

"What is that?" I asked, as he folded it back up, put it in a small pouch, and handed it to me.

"It's a pee cone for when you need to pee," he answered. "You don't have to squat to pee with this thing. You just place it firmly over your privates and pee into it. It funnels it out, like a guy, and you're on your way just as easily."

"Huh. That's interesting," I said. "That's another thing I hadn't thought about, but I guess there are few bathrooms on the Camino, and I'll need to go in the woods. Well, why not? I'll take the pee cone, too."

"PowerBars?"

"Yes."

"Soap?"

"Yep."

"Walking poles?"

"Absolutely."

"Hat?

"Yes."

"What kind?"

"The kind that will keep the sun off my face," I answered.

"This is the best," he said and tossed me a floppy sun hat that looked like a combination French-Foreign-Legion-meets-burka hat, complete with a neck flap, which wrapped around the front of my face and that I could seal with Velcro.

It covered nearly every part of my face and neck, and was perfect. It was a little intense but then again, so was everything about this trip.

"I like it."

Glancing around the store as if to see if there was anything else I might need before I checked out, he said, "I think you've got it all. Let's have a final look at the list."

I handed him back the now seriously crumpled-up list, not realizing that I had been holding on to it for dear life as we worked our way through the store.

Looking it over, mentally checking items off, he looked up and smiled. "I believe we've covered everything!"

We continued to chat as he rang up purchase after purchase, handing me a bill at the end. "That'll be $869.42," he said.

I gasped. "Oh my God. This is so expensive!"

He paused. "Do you want to put any of it back?"

Looking over everything I had just pulled off the shelves, all in hopes of insulating me against the rigors and discomfort of walking across an entire country alone on foot, I said, "No. I can't—I'll need it all." I handed him my credit card.

Man, this was expensive! I thought, lugging my five very heavy bags to the car, throwing them into the trunk one at a time. Suddenly it occurred to me that I would have to carry everything I had just purchased.

"Arrgghh! How am I ever going to do that?" I asked myself out loud, suddenly overwhelmed by the enormity and weight of what lay ahead.

"Well," I answered, "one foot in front of the other, just like the boot guy said . . . that's how."

7

Two Backpacks and Counting

It was just days before I was to leave, and I found myself becoming increasingly nervous about going. I had planned to start at Saint-Jean-Pied-de-Port, a town in the foothills of the Pyrenees in southwestern France that was a historical starting point for pilgrims walking the Camino route. I didn't know much beyond that, and I chastised myself for not learning more. At the last minute, I decided to buy a few books to see if I could glean some useful information that would ease my anxiety and help me feel more grounded before I set off.

The first book I read was *The Pilgrimage* by Paulo Coelho. It was mystical and mesmerizing, and I couldn't put it down. He endured many spiritual tests on the long journey from France across Spain, but he had one thing going for him that I didn't: a guide.

At one point Coelho was attacked by a demonic dog, which sent chills up my spine. I had never considered the possibility of being attacked by wild dogs, and I became sick with anxiety thinking about it.

The next book I read was *The Camino* by Shirley MacLaine. She, too, had her fair share of out-of-this-world challenges, including nearly freezing to death, and to my horror was also met by demon dogs along the way. *Crap*, I thought. *Now I don't want to go.*

The idea of getting attacked by wild dogs was enough to stop me dead in my tracks.

I think it's because when I was six years old, I was attacked by a rabid dog while walking home alone from school. I was minding my own business, only three blocks from my house, when this insane animal, foaming at the mouth, lurched at me from out of nowhere. He cornered me with his vicious growling, barking and repeatedly lunging at me as I screamed for my life. I was trapped for what seemed like an eternity as I wildly fought back, swinging my schoolbag at him and screaming my head off every time he got too close, keeping him far enough away to not bite me.

Miraculously, my older sister Cuky happened to walk by on her way home from high school and saw me cornered by this crazy beast. Dropping her schoolbag, she ran across the street and started screaming and lunging back at the dog with all of her might. As soon as he backed down a bit, she yelled at me to run for my life, which I did.

Home less than two minutes later and thoroughly traumatized, I sat shaking with relief on the front porch, my sister right behind me, equally shaken, saying, "It's okay now. We're safe." We both shuddered in disbelief that we had made it home alive.

That episode burned into my bones a fear of wild dogs. Reading about the likelihood that I would experience one or more of them on the Camino sent me into a tailspin.

Shit! I thought. *Now what? How am I going to protect myself from wild attacking dogs?* And of course, knowing full well from my metaphysical training that we attract what we focus on, and especially what we fear, I was elevating my chances of this happening by the minute.

I needed protection. That was all there was to it. I wasn't about to be caught off guard by a rabid beast as I had been years before. No fucking way!

I was looking online for ways to protect myself when my dog-loving friend Debra, who was staying with me at the time, came in and asked if there was anything she could do to help me prepare, as she knew the hours were counting down before I was to leave and she could sense my rising tension.

"I need pepper spray to ward off wild dogs," I said. "Apparently this pilgrimage is going to be a series of spiritual lessons and tests, and wild dogs will be a part of that because they scare me so much. So can you get me some pepper spray to ward them off?"

"Pepper spray?" she asked. "Are you sure? I don't think that will do you any good."

"It probably won't," I answered, not hiding my irritation, as I was certain that attacking dogs were going to get me no matter what. I knew pepper spray was a pathetic attempt at believing I had a fighting chance against them. But it didn't matter. I wanted it anyway.

"That will only make them mad," Debra continued. "You just have to avoid eye contact and carry a big stick."

"I don't plan on looking them in the eye," I snapped, agitated with her dog-attack prevention lesson. "And I won't have a big stick. Only my walking poles."

"Well, that will work, too," she answered, missing my agitation entirely.

"I need pepper spray! If you don't want to get it, then don't offer," I shot back. She was clearly missing the inevitable bloodbath I was facing ahead.

"Okay," she said, sensing it was time to back off. I had worked myself into such a state of anxiety over the upcoming dog ambush that I was in no frame of mind to hear her out. She wasn't going on the walk, so how dare she tell me how to handle wild dogs, anyway?

My Higher Self was watching me as I found myself tumbling headfirst into the lowest possible vibration I could sink into: fear. It was sucking me in like quicksand, and I struggled to stay afloat.

"Why are you suddenly so afraid?" I chastised myself. "People all over the world have walked this pilgrimage for centuries," I reasoned. "And I haven't read any recent accounts of unsuspecting pilgrims in Spain getting ravaged by dogs." I checked the Internet.

And yet, because my fear of meeting up with wild dogs was so intense, I was convinced that it would be one of the first tests I would have to face while on the path. Coelho and MacLaine were spiritual students, and they both met up with vicious dogs. I'm a spiritual student, so why wouldn't I meet dogs as well? Maybe it was part of the Camino curriculum. Of course, none of this made any real sense. I tried to get grounded and took a breath.

All my life I have prided myself on being a fearless warrior. It wasn't that I didn't feel fear. It was just that I didn't pay attention to it. Feeling fear was a luxury I couldn't afford to indulge in because if I did, I would relinquish my ability to take care of myself and meet my responsibilities. I felt fear standing in front of large audiences when I spoke in public. I felt fear before meeting new clients for the first time. I felt fear whenever I gave interviews. And I certainly felt fear over my upcoming divorce. But, in true warrior style, I ignored my fear. I trusted my spirit, my own wits, my Higher Self, and all my guiding helpers in the subtle realms to watch over and help me, and so I knew I'd be protected. Because of that, I managed to either deny my fear or bury it so deep I could pretend it wasn't there at all.

As a result, the only thing I overtly feared was, well, wild dogs.

So, of course, they would be there to greet me. More and more I could see that this pilgrimage was going to be about facing and feeling all the emotions I had run from all my life. Clear back to when I was six years old. Or even younger.

Fortunately, I had too many other things to focus on to continue to indulge this fearful narrative any longer.

I had to get health insurance in case something went physically wrong (like being attacked by demon dogs), and I had to get trip insurance in case, for some reason, I couldn't make it all the way to Santiago and had to change my flight back home.

These were obtained easily enough, with the help of the Internet and my American Express card. "Wow," I exclaimed as I clicked on the purchase button again and again. "This is becoming one hell of an expensive pilgrimage!"

Another $1,000 later, both travel and medical insurance secured, I sat back and took a breath.

"I need to get on my way. The longer I'm here, building this whole thing up, the more difficult and costly it's becoming. I just need to stop thinking about it, pick up my bags, and get going!"

I didn't like all this precaution and preparation. I was turning into Patrick, preparing for the worst. This was so unlike me. I needed to get back to my spontaneous and trusting self.

"Screw Paulo and Shirley. I don't need demon dogs to teach me lessons either. That was *their* experience. It won't be mine. I've already had my dog lesson, when I was six. My Camino will be a much more peaceful and healing experience," I insisted to the Universe. "I don't need the drama!"

It felt good to shake off the cobwebs of other people's experiences, I thought as I began to cram the mountain of stuff into my backpack. By the time I was finished, I had the equivalent of a dead body in weight in the backpack sitting across from me, with more supplies still on the floor, and no more room.

"I'll never be able to carry this across the street," I thought aloud, "let alone across the Pyrenees. How the heck am I going to do this with my fragile knee?"

As my assistant, Ryan, had reminded me, I'd recently had surgery to repair a cracked kneecap (which I sustained while kickboxing out my frustrations with my life), and I was still on the mend. I was able to walk well enough, but going up and down stairs was still painful some of the time. Suddenly, I worried that my knee wouldn't be able to handle the load.

"You're right," it chimed in with a sudden sharp pain stabbing me out of nowhere, as if refusing the challenge. "This is too much for me."

What to do? I knew there were companies that would transport your bag from town to town if you didn't want to carry it on your back, and I had considered hiring one to carry my stuff for weeks but had not yet committed.

"Is that cheating?" I had asked myself more than once. "Is a true pilgrim only one who schleps her belongings on her back, suffering the journey as she goes?"

"But what if the weight is too much for my knee?" I countered. "Should I power ahead and hope I'll gain strength as I go, or should I wimp out and have someone carry this 50-pound deadweight of a backpack for me?"

I lifted it up and strapped it on, deciding to give it a test run before I made up my mind. The first few steps around the house were easy enough, especially with my poles.

"I can do this, no problem, " I said to myself, feeling like Xena, the Warrior Princess. "Now let's tackle the stairs."

Going down was fine. But when I turned and took a step to go up, my knee buckled in pain and I let out a scream. "Ouch!"

I was on my knees. And it only took three minutes to get me there.

"Now what?" I asked myself. "Is this pilgrimage a bust before I even begin? Am I going to be a fake pilgrim? A designer pilgrim, instead of the real backpack-suffering deal?"

But, then again, I wondered, who I was trying to impress?

"It's *my* pilgrimage," I said out loud to the scoffing, judgmental voices in my head. "Who cares whether or not I carry the backpack myself and break my knee again. Who's judging me anyway?"

I knew God didn't care if I carried my backpack or not. Nor did my Higher Self and my guides. Only my approval-seeking ego did, the part of me who feared being judged. She was coming out of hiding along with my inner child like they were best friends or something, and I could see them more and more in plain sight. I thought about something Patrick had said to me before we had yet another one of our "I hate you" arguments recently.

I told him I was going to do the Camino, and he casually said, "Oh yeah? My good friend Tyson and his 81-year-old mother are going to walk it at the same time as you. And she's carrying her own backpack the entire way! Are you?"

Are you? He knows I cracked my knee trying to kick the energetic crap out of him. What a jerk for asking me if I could keep up with an 81-year-old woman.

I slung the backpack back on and tried again. I walked around the house for a few minutes, my shoulders killing me, and then attempted the stairs once again. Two steps up, and I was down for the count.

"Screw Patrick's insensitive comments," I snarled, throwing my pack on the floor. "I don't care if he or anybody else judges me. I'm not walking to impress a soul, so I'm not going to worry about it if I happen to ask for help. Maybe I need to learn to ask for help. I certainly heard that enough from my daughters and even Patrick over the years. I don't like to ask for help, but I just may have to."

"That settles it," I continued speaking aloud to my inner guilt-tripper. "I'm not going to waste any more time worrying about what other people think. No one cares about this but me. The only voice I need to listen to is that of my body. Ask it to decide. Not my vanity and fear."

"Good advice," I answered, talking back to myself. (Yes, I do that quite a bit, actually.) "What is good for my body?"

I sat with that question for all of 30 seconds and then came up with a great compromise.

"I'll carry two bags," I decided, a backpack and another bag. "I'll carry the backpack on my back every day, with some stuff in it, but not enough to hurt my knee, and I'll send the heavier bag ahead with a transport service. I'll put enough in the smaller one to have it be somewhat heavy, and thus have the true pilgrim backpack experience, but not so much that it trashes my knee and I can't make it."

I was quite satisfied with this solution.

"Perfect," I said to my body, out loud. "Only now I have to go out and buy a second backpack."

8

Taking the Pressure Off

Early the next morning, having decided to have a transport company carry my bag after all, I got online and began to research various companies that could help me. One was a company called Camino Ways, based out of Ireland. This company would not only transport my bag from town to town, but they could also arrange for simple, private accommodations for me in each town along the Camino.

Knowing I would probably make slower progress than many, given my bum knee and my hiking inexperience, I did worry about finding a place to sleep in the shared dormitory-style *albergues* along the Camino reserved for pilgrims. From what I had read they were open on a first-come, first-served basis, and often filled up quite early in the day, and no doubt much sooner than when I would most likely arrive. Maybe booking both transport and a private hostel, in lieu of staying at pilgrims' albergues, would be the smartest option for me, and one that would help ease the pressure I was feeling in so many ways.

I spoke to a guy named Roland who immediately assured me that they could reserve a simple place for me to stay in each town along the Camino, as well as transport my bag to the hostel or inn each day, and even include a pilgrim's breakfast and an occasional dinner.

It wasn't very expensive considering the investment I had already made. Besides, it was my emotional peace I was talking about here. The entire reason I was going on this pilgrimage was to find some emotional peace.

"Can I have a day to think it over?" I asked. "I'll probably go with this, as it makes sense for me, but I want to be sure I'm not cheating by doing so. Some people say not carrying your own bag and winging it from albergue to albergue as you walk the Camino makes you less than a 'true pilgrim,' and I don't want to be that."

"It's *your* Camino," he replied. "Why do you care what other people think or say?"

"True. Okay, I'll think it over and call you back."

A cup of coffee later, I'd made up my mind.

The next day, Roland sent me an e-mail with a full itinerary, complete with the names of the simple hostels where I was to stay in every town, along with downloadable transport tags to put on my bag. It looked as if I would be in very simple one-star accommodations most nights, with the promised pilgrim's breakfast and dinner (whatever that was) included, except for every ten days. Then I was booked into what appeared to be a three-star accommodation with only breakfast included. Sounded good to me. In the e-mail was a message that said, "We will send you a Camino passport book overnight."

The e-mail went on to explain that the passport was a small book in which to get stamps from every town along the Camino, showing that I had walked to that place, in order to get the Compostela or pilgrim's certificate once I arrived in Santiago.

I worried that I might miss the place to get the stamp, but then noticed that Roland had attached the directions to each town's office.

Sighing with relief, I said to myself, *Okay, I guess I've covered just about every single base, haven't I? All I have to do now is show up and start walking.*

At the end of the e-mail, I read, "Buen Camino."

That made me smile. I hoped it would be a "Buen Camino."

9

Packing Up

I can't believe I'm heading back to REI, I thought, as I got back in the car to buy the second backpack. Once I purchased my medium-sized backpack, I drifted back over to the shoe department. I had read a blog on the Camino the night before that said hiking boots were completely unnecessary, and that lightweight Merrell walking shoes were more than enough. The writer made it seem as though the Camino was literally a walk in the park (albeit a long one) and suggested that anyone trying to tell you otherwise was exaggerating to no end, and a whiner. Just as I picked up a pair of the shoes in question, a young salesman approached me and said, "Those are really comfortable. Want to try them on?"

"So I've heard." I answered. "Are they good for long hikes?"

"They can be. Depends on where you'll be hiking."

"I'll be hiking across Spain. I read that shoes like this were more than enough for the trail I'll be on."

"Well, then you should get a pair," he said, clearly having a different attitude than that of my first boot salesman.

"Okay," I said, reverting back to my spontaneous way of deciding things. "I'll take a pair."

Once paid for, into the second backpack they went.

Back home, I pulled everything out of the dead-body backpack and started repacking.

I had to decide what would go into my "I'll carry it myself pilgrim's backpack" and what would go into my "let someone else carry it cheater bag."

Just then my daughter Sonia came in and asked, "Do you have long underwear?"

"No," I answered. "I don't think I'll need them. It's almost June."

"Take these anyway, just in case," she said handing me a pair. "They're mine. Better safe than sorry."

Next, Debra walked in, with pepper spray (*yes!*) and some information from the Internet on what to do if wild dogs surround you.

I took the spray and ignored the papers.

"What else?" I asked myself out loud as Debra and Sonia looked on.

"Did you pack a coat or a windbreaker?" Debra asked.

"No, not really. I have a very lightweight jacket. I don't think I'll need a coat."

"I'm not so sure that's all you'll need. Better take my coat. You never know. You might need it while walking over the mountains," she said.

"Did you pack a warm hat and gloves?" Sonia asked.

"No, I packed a sun hat and a bandana, but not a warm hat."

"Take these, then," she said, handing over a cashmere stocking cap and gloves that a friend had sent me a month earlier to take on the Camino and that I had forgotten to pack.

Glancing around my bedroom, I asked again, out loud, "Anything else?"

Considering the ridiculous mountain of stuff I was taking, all I could see that was left to pack was my bedroom dresser. But then my eyes drifted to my totem, Gumby, sitting on my personal altar, the silly, smiley-faced, rubbery green toy from my childhood.

"Gumby!" I cried. "I have to take you!" I've had Gumby with me ever since I was around ten years old. He was small and silly but always cheered me up and made me laugh. In a way, he represented my alter ego, my inner child, my conscience, and my Higher Self, all rolled into one. He had to go.

"I'll take my pillow, too. Why not?"

Pulling up the final zipper, my daughter asked me, "Are you sure you've got everything you need?"

"I think so. I'm as ready as I can be, but I'm sure I'll think of 20 more things to pack before I actually walk out the door on Monday. Just stop me before I become ridiculously weighted down. I'm supposed to be walking this pilgrimage to lighten my load, and so far, I'm not doing very well."

10

The Last Night at Home

The weekend before my departure for France, I taught a workshop at the Omega Institute in Rhinebeck, New York. My flight from Albany back to Chicago landed at 7 P.M. on Sunday. I had to race home because I was leaving the next day and still had a few final preparations to make.

It was also Mother's Day, and my older daughter had prepared a lovely dinner for me both to celebrate and to send me off in style. I was so touched by her effort, and happy that both of my daughters were there to see me off. I only wished I were more fully able to appreciate their blessings. To the end I was a nervous wreck.

I was leaving all my responsibilities to my daughters and my business partner Ryan to handle while I was away, as I didn't want to focus on anything but the walk. While my Higher Self knew all would be in good hands between the three of them, I was still anxious.

Suddenly I was afraid that they wouldn't be able to manage in my absence. I didn't share any of these feelings with them, of course, but I did realize how much I drew my sense of security from being in charge of everything.

"Am I control freak?" I asked my daughters spontaneously as I helped myself to mashed potatoes. They both laughed. "Maybe a bit," they agreed, "at least when it comes to responsibilities."

"Yet another spark of clarity from the Camino, and I haven't even left yet," I observed.

"Don't worry about a thing, Mom. We've got your back and you can trust us," they wholeheartedly assured me. "And we are really happy you are doing this for yourself."

"Me too."

I knew they meant it. I had been so miserable for the past two years that I'm sure they were sick of me. I had tried to weather the storms I had suffered, and a few I had caused, as well as I could, but between the deaths in my family and the death of my marriage, I was swamped with anger and grief. Every day was a major challenge, and they were the ones who had helped me get through it.

I knew they were spent and had their own grief over their parents' impending divorce to deal with. We all needed this break in order to deal with our private emotions. I was sick over having brought this misery into their lives, and while we were very close and supportive of one another throughout this family nightmare, it was still a personal journey of loss that we each needed time and space to face on our own.

While Patrick and I had endless challenges as a couple, we were both dedicated to the girls. Having our family come unglued like it had filled both of our daughters with heartbreak and anger. And I didn't blame them one bit. I blamed me, unless of course I was blaming Patrick.

I welcomed giving my daughters a break from me. I felt so guilty about everything that I had set in motion that in some ways I couldn't get away fast enough.

And that meant letting go of control.

I was ready and, in fact, I wanted nothing more than to turn the reins of all my responsibilities over to others for a time and take a break. It was all just too heavy. It wasn't my backpack (or two now) that burdened me. It was the responsibility for so many and so much that I felt I couldn't carry on the Camino. It was my life and its endless responsibilities that needed to be unloaded.

I wanted to walk the Camino more than anything to become free of the guilt and anger and shame I was carrying so deep in my heart. I yearned for forgiveness for having all this guilt and resentment. And for failing to be more loving of Patrick and forgiving of him in spite of the fact that I knew it was spiritually the right thing to do.

I trusted my divine support system implicitly and knew I would always receive their support and protection. It was people I didn't trust. Except for Ryan and my daughters. But even while I trusted them wholeheartedly, I had hesitated to ask them for more than was necessary.

I prayed to God as I got ready for bed. Hopefully this would be the beginning of another way of life for me. One that would allow me to relax and receive more support. From the earliest age I was conditioned to believe that asking for anything was selfish and a sin. Giving was better than receiving. It was spiritual. I was to simply be a giver and not complain, and act like a good Catholic girl.

The only place I could look to for help was heaven, and even then I was not to bother too often. I could ask my spirit guides to help me out, and they did, all the time. I just couldn't ask people to help me. That was imposing, and just plain wrong.

This warped message was proving, more and more, to be the great undoing of all of my relationships, but especially my marriage. It made me believe I didn't need much of anything, which was actually not true at all and was why I was so agitated, especially with Patrick, so much of the time. I gave and gave as I was trained to do, while burying my own needs deeper and deeper.

I wasn't aware I was doing that until I would give one ounce too many on any given day and then I would explode, which had happened more and more often since my dad died. His dying sprung open a Pandora's box revealing a lifetime of neglected and suppressed needs in me. And they weren't willing to be hidden away any longer.

I guess I've always needed a whole lot more than I'm willing to admit, I thought as I reflected on the embarrassing amount of stuff I had felt the need to take on this journey. *No wonder I've been so unhappy so much of the time. I'm really needy, and I'm pissed off about it.*

This was one of the fundamental things about myself that I wanted to change, or calm, or get over, or heal while on the Camino. I needed to. I was so angry with so many people and had ended so many relationships because of my over-giving tendencies and subsequent backlog of resentment that I couldn't stand myself anymore.

Unless I got this part of my inner life balanced once and for all, I could never be truly happy in my life or in my relationships.

"That much I know for sure, Oprah," I said, as I headed for bed.

11

Chicago to Paris

I was relieved to get on the flight from Chicago to Paris, to finally be on my way. I had spent so much energy vacillating between anticipating and fearing the experience that it felt good to be getting on with it.

"Okay!" I breathed out a big sigh, probably the first in days and days, as we turned onto the runway. "Here I go," I told myself. "I hope I know what I'm doing."

Once on the ground in Paris, I grabbed both backpacks and headed to a Hilton at the airport to rest for one day and get over my jet lag before I set out.

I woke up early and got ready to leave for Biarritz. Wow. I couldn't believe I was so close to starting. My flight left at one, so I had time for a leisurely breakfast before I set off for the airport. I took out my little purse with all the information I had gathered on the Camino to look over my plan one more time. For walking across an entire country, it didn't seem like there was very much to go on. I had the names of the hostels where I was to stay at the end of each day, and that was it. Not even an address or phone number. Just the name of the town and the hostel.

I guess that's what a pilgrimage is all about, I thought, as I stuffed my little purse back into my backpack. I was to simply follow the signs—which I'd been told were yellow arrows and occasionally the famous scallop shells like the ones found on St. James's body— marking the Camino, and to go on faith. I looked out the window of my hotel room. The skies were nearly black with clouds while thunder and rain crashed down. I laughed as I looked away. *Of course the skies are troubled. They feel the way I do.*

I checked the outside temperature on my iPhone app and saw it was only 45 degrees, which was really cold for the middle of May. I was so glad I had thrown on a heavier windbreaker at the very last minute before I left my house. Looking at the forecast for the days ahead and seeing it was more of the same or worse, I would clearly need it.

I repacked my big backpack, which I had completely emptied the night before, just to make sure one last time that I had had everything I needed, and then went down to breakfast. My head was a bit heavy. I was hungry, jet-lagged, excited, and a little scared, wondering if I was ready to begin tomorrow.

I know when I put my mind to things I always accomplish what I set out to do, so it wasn't a genuine concern. I just wondered what the journey ahead would actually be like and if I was physically up to it. I was healthy and strong but not exactly what I would call athletic. I walked. I danced. I did yoga. I occasionally hit the gym and lifted weights, but not in the past year due to my knee surgery. I took all of this into account when considering I was about to walk across an entire country.

"Well, we'll see," I muttered to myself as I sipped my café au lait.

Perhaps more than anything I was nervous. I am an adventurous spirit and love to leap into the unknown, but I hadn't done it alone, or on as grand a scale as this since I was 20 years old.

The last time had brought me to France, as well.

My parents had been going through many tumultuous collisions at the time and just like now, my family was falling part. In my attempt to help both my mom and dad with their suffering, I found myself in the middle of their emotional struggles, and it took a tremendous emotional toll on me. I couldn't take it anymore. In my mind, they were crazy, and I needed to get away from them.

In addition, I had just abruptly ended a relationship with my first important boyfriend, with whom I had lived for almost 18 months, due to his increasing drug and alcohol use. I wanted the world. He wanted a joint. Even though I knew it was right for me to get away, he was caught completely off guard and was devastated, which left me guilt-ridden and confused. At the same time, I quit college, which also left me feeling ashamed. I was there on a scholarship and was a good student. I wasn't supposed to quit college. No one was supposed to quit college, and yet I was doing just that and without telling anyone or asking anyone's opinion. I was running away from home.

I attempted to find a new life as a flight attendant, but I soon discovered that I was not cut out for that job at all. I felt lonely and completely out of integrity with my spirit, a grand impostor every time I put on my uniform to go to work. Working for the airline felt like working for the army. I was told I was on probation for the first six months and any false move I made would result in termination. Being a good Catholic girl, I was scared to death.

Needless to say, I was not the typical carefree, wild person, who loved to party, was sexually promiscuous, and stayed up all night drinking and doing cocaine, as were most of my fellow flight attendants at the time. I wasn't "cool" like that. I was shy and serious, extremely sensitive, deeply spiritual, and highly intuitive, so this ungrounded craziness, all happening in strange hotels in strange cities while on layovers, left me feeling anxious and stressed and more traumatized than ever.

I felt like such an ugly duckling, a fish out of water, a wallflower in that world that I had to keep running. I was upside down, ungrounded, homeless, and distraught with nowhere to turn for respite and comfort. I often thought of moving to France. Ever since I was a child, I felt drawn there. Although my father was French and was raised in a French-speaking home in the States, he himself never spoke French or talked about France at all while we were growing up. So my attraction to France, and the south of France in particular, did not come from him. It came from a deeper place in me, and I didn't know why.

One day while sitting in a flight-attendant lounge in Cleveland, I mentioned, in a causal conversation with a fellow flight attendant, my dream of going to the south of France. He said if I ever did, he recommended Aix-en-Provence. He then wrote down the address of a place I might check on for a place to stay. And just like this pilgrimage, the minute he handed me that paper with an address in Aix, I decided then and there to go. The next month, without any real planning or information, I took a year's leave of absence from my job and was out the door.

Once I arrived in Aix, things fell into place, and soon I was settled into a rented room on the third floor of an old country house, complete with army cot, small sink, table with a single naked bulb lamp, and a shared bathroom in the hall. It was simple to say the least, but as a person who grew up with six brothers and sisters and had a bedroom that didn't even have its own door, followed by living with my boyfriend, and then with a house full of flight attendants, being alone for the first time in my life, even in such basic quarters, was a relief.

Once settled in, I needed something to do. I found a language school in town where I could learn to speak French for several hours a day, so I quickly enrolled. Other than that I mostly spent my time just wandering through the countryside or the town trying to feel better, mostly to no avail.

While I succeeded in getting physically away from my family, the emotional pain I was in followed me all the way there. I had no idea at the time how to be completely on my own, or process my emotions in a healthy way, so I ended up feeling stressed and afraid and lonely. On top of that I had very little money, so I lived off day-old baguettes and very small amounts of cheese. After three months of that, I suddenly got very sick.

Two days before Christmas the woman who rented the room to me came up to invite me to join the family downstairs for a Christmas aperitif, only to find me on the floor, consumed by fever, and delirious with both severe back and stomach pain.

I vaguely remember her looking at me, panicked, as she put a cool rag over my face. The next thing I knew I was at the local hospital and headed in to surgery for a ruptured appendix accompanied by a severe kidney infection.

I'm convinced my angels sent that woman up to my room to help me at that very moment, as she had never once, in the three months I had lived there, come up before. In fact, I rarely saw her, and when I did I avoided speaking to her because she was, in typical French manner, elegant, aloof, and intimidating to no end. I was so grateful she did.

After surgery, I spent the next 19 days in the hospital recovering, so my holidays were as sad and miserable as the rest of me. And yet, I can now see how perfect it was that this had happened to me. I ended up being nurtured day and night, which on so many levels I needed. The nurses, feeling sorry for me, were very kind and often stayed a few moments longer than necessary in order to reassure me that all would be okay as I recovered. I was so grateful to them for that.

The teachers from the language school where I was a student also came to visit me, some several times during my stay, which both surprised and touched me. They even brought me Christmas and New Year's offerings of candy and figs, assuring me they would still be good to eat after I recovered.

Even the woman who rented the room to me came to visit almost every day. She had softened and treated me with such gentle concern I couldn't believe she was the same person I had been avoiding. These strangers offered me so much love and kindness as I lay there, day after day, that the quiet panic inside me began to settle down.

As I convalesced, I shared a room with a 90-year-old woman who had fallen and broken her leg. She had some form of dementia, which caused her to talk almost nonstop for hours and hours at a time. She wasn't talking to me. She was talking to heaven.

As I listened to her endless chatter, I actually began to understand French. She was talking to angels, departed loved ones, guides, people from her past (some of whom she missed and some of whom she didn't like), and a whole cast of transient invisible characters. I actually found a great deal of it entertaining. She ended up being the best French teacher I'd ever had. By the time

I checked out of the hospital, I had learned enough French to test into the University of Paris, where I would later finish school.

Sitting at breakfast I thought it interesting that this entire phase of my earlier life came rushing back into my consciousness as though it were only yesterday, when I hadn't thought of it for years. Apparently I had been called to the Camino to clear more than just the recent past. I was dredging up the debris of all my ancient emotional wounds, even the ones I had long since forgotten. While swallowing a small morsel of cheese, I wondered if some of those wounds might not even be lifetimes old.

I looked at my watch. It was time to go. Downing the last sip of my coffee and shoving the last bit of chocolate croissant into my mouth, I headed to the checkout desk before I caught the shuttle to the airport. Thirty minutes later I was checked in for my flight and had my boarding pass for Biarritz in hand.

A deluge of mixed emotions flooded through me. One part of me felt like a kid setting off to summer camp. Another part felt as though I were an inmate who had just been released from the prison of my own life. And yet another part of me felt as though I were walking toward something I had long ago known in my soul, a sort of homecoming, or at least a return to something that had begun in another time and now needed to be completed.

My mind was dancing all over the map, but my spirit was excited. I could feel the support of my angels and guides and the spirits of my ancestors cheering me on.

I knew in my heart that no matter what called me to undertake this pilgrimage, something good would come out of it, for me, for my children, for my family, and for generations of my family back and forward.

Settling into my seat for the 45-minute flight, I announced out loud, under my breath, "Let the adventure begin."

12

Get Ready, Get Set . . .

The airport in Biarritz was small, and in no time my two back-packs came sliding onto the baggage claim carousel. I put them both in a trolley and went outside, where I hired a taxi driver to take me to Saint-Jean-Pied-de-Port, 45 minutes away, where I would begin the Camino.

I was immediately taken by how cold it was.

"C'est froid," I said, shivering, to the taxi driver as he placed my bags in the trunk of his car. He immediately agreed and then slid into a tirade on how nasty the weather was that lasted until we arrived at our destination. Turning around the bend of the curved highway, we descended into a charming medieval-looking town backed up against a mountain range. He pulled over.

"C'est Saint-Jean," he said, turning around to show me. "In which hotel are you staying?"

I took out my itinerary and said the Central Hotel. He looked left and right, and then left again in search of it. I searched right alongside him. Neither of us had any luck.

The town wasn't that big, so we strained once more, looking both ways to see where it might be. Finally he suggested that I get out with my bags and simply ask around, as it would be easy enough to find, and he had to get going.

I wasn't exactly happy that he couldn't help me find the hotel, but I knew this was the end of the line for me, and I had to get walking anyway, so I agreed. He jumped out and ran to the back of the car to open the trunk and then soundly plopped my two bags on the ground and asked for 50 euros. The minute he did, I immediately regretted bringing this much stuff and wondered if I could simply walk away from one of the bags and pretend it wasn't mine, as opposed to having to drag both along in search of the hotel.

As he drove off I felt a wave of anxiety. *Now what?*

Slowly I picked up one bag and thrust it on my back, not having a clue as to how I would ever be able to drag a second one along at the same time. When I turned around to arrange the backpack straps, I found myself looking directly at a sign no more than 20 feet away that said "Hotel Central."

I nearly squealed with delight. I immediately ran to the front door of the hotel with the heavier backpack first, now known as my "cheater bag" or simply "Cheater," and dropped it on the front step. Then I dashed back to retrieve the second backpack, now known as the "real pilgrim" or simply "Pilgrim." I left them both outside on the step as I walked into the lobby of the hotel. I thought it would be easier to scope the place out without all that encumbering me. The old hotel was dark, and nobody was at the front desk.

To the left of the reception area was a small dining area, also completely dark. There was a very steep, narrow staircase in front of me.

I saw a small bell on the desk and rang it, hoping it would draw someone from out of the dark. After only two rings a friendly older woman, wearing a dark red sweater, her hair pulled into a tight bun on the top of her head, popped her head out of the kitchen and said, "Bonjour. J'arrive." She emerged seconds later, asking me if I had a reservation.

I said, "Yes, Camino Ways," praying to God that it would be there.

She frowned for a few moments, which was long enough to stir a small panic in me, and then finally said, "Oui."

When I breathed a huge "whew" to her "oui," she started laughing. She then asked for my passport and handed me a key for a room on the fourth floor.

"Do you have any bags?" she asked, as she handed my passport back to me.

"I do," I said, and quickly stepped out to retrieve them. As I dragged in the first, then the second, her brow furrowed.

"I only have you registered for one person," she said, looking at my two huge bags.

"No worries," I replied. "I'm the only one."

Her eyebrow raised in obvious disapproval as I tried to be as nonchalant as possible while pushing Cheater across the floor and throwing Pilgrim over my shoulder.

Looking ahead at the disastrous staircase in front of me, knowing my room was four flights up, I asked if there might be a bellboy or someone around to help me with my bags, ignoring the obvious dearth of humanity.

"Ah, non!" she said as if I had asked for her for the moon. "Pas d'ici!"

Oh, how I love the French. They have such a way of making you feel like an idiot for asking the least little thing of them.

"Okay, pas de problème," I said, smiling, trying to act as pilgrim-like as possible, as if it were no big deal for me to carry the equivalent of a dead body and second backpack up four flights of stairs.

"Bien," she responded, and sat back on her heels to watch me, clearly ready for the entertainment to come.

I decided I would start with Cheater and drag him up first. I took a deep breath, bent my knees, tossed the backpack over my shoulder as if it were a handbag, and like Quasimodo, hunched over and started up the stairs.

I managed to get to the landing and turn to mount the second flight when I heard her snort and walk away.

"AAARRGGH," I silently cried out, dropping my bag on the floor. "I hate you, you stupid Cheater. We are breaking up tonight!"

We struggled for another ten minutes before I had successfully landed him on the extremely dark fourth floor and fumbled around for a light, grateful that no one was around to hear me cursing like a sailor.

I finally found the light switch and opened the door to a dreary, simple room with a single bed and a small connecting bathroom with a minuscule shower in it.

The room was freezing, and there was no heat coming out of the heater. Suddenly I felt very jet-lagged and cold. But I still had to retrieve Pilgrim and drag her upstairs, as well. Fortunately, round two was far easier than round one, and all I could think of was that there was no way I was going to struggle with Cheater like this the entire way across Spain.

Looking at the beast on the floor, I said out loud, "Better get ready to be dumped, Cheater. Unless you prove yourself truly useful to me, and fast, we will soon be parting ways for good."

Cheater was silent.

I looked around the room, which was easy, as it was only eight feet wide. I tested the bed. It squeaked. The pillow was thin.

"Hee hee!" I laughed to myself. "No problem, thin pillow. I have my own!"

I whipped open Cheater and there she was—my fluffy, comforting, inviting, personal pillow beckoning me to lie down.

"Not now," I said, talking to my pillow.

"I have to go into town and find where the Camino starts. I hope it's not too difficult to figure out."

I locked the door and made my way downstairs and across the street. The quaint town was filled with tourist and pilgrim-like shops. The first thing I noticed were countless scallop shells hanging in the windows and at the entrance of nearly every shop.

The ancient pilgrims carried scallop shells and used them as their main tool as they made their way to Santiago. The shells served several purposes. They were used as bowls for food and a means of collecting drinking water from the rivers. They also worked as a mini shovel if the pilgrims needed to dig their way out of trouble.

It then dawned on me that my favorite French dish, "Coquille St. Jacques," a scallop dish in cream sauce, was actually named after the scallop shell of St. James.

✠

As I walked I also noticed to my relief that there were plenty of other soon-to-be pilgrims strolling up and down the street. *At least I am in the right spot,* I reassured myself.

Then I remembered my pilgrim's passport book, which I needed to get stamped while here in Saint-Jean to mark the beginning of my journey. I ran back across the street to the hotel and up the four flights of stairs to retrieve it, finding myself completely winded and out of breath once I got to my room.

"Boy, that's not a good sign. I hope I'll be able to do this," I said to myself. "I've only walked for five minutes, and I'm ready to pass out."

Walking back at a much slower pace, I once again crossed the street and found my way to the pilgrim's office to get my first stamp. When I walked in, I had to sign a paper declaring the purpose of my pilgrimage. I had the choice of *spiritual, religious,* or *adventure.* I chose spiritual.

A skinny, bald, bespectacled man behind a large desk placed a stamp in one of the little squares on page one and handed me a map. He then said he wanted to show me the two ways to get to my first stop on the Camino, which was a town 31 kilometers away in Spain called Roncesvalles. He said that it was supposed to snow tomorrow and he thought it would be better if I took the path along the highway instead of over the Pyrenees, as it could be dangerous traversing the mountains in bad weather.

I had not considered that. I read that the hardest part of the Camino was going over the Pyrenees on the first day, but that it was truly magnificent and that I should just go for it, knowing it was worth it. Now I was hearing that it could be dangerous and I was being encouraged not to go.

I took the map and thanked him. I would decide what to do in the morning, when I had more energy. I then asked for directions to the beginning of the Camino route. The man told me to follow the main street out of town, then just keep following the yellow arrows all the way to Santiago. The last thing he said was, "Buen Camino!"

I walked out of the pilgrim's office, map in hand, greeted by a sheet of pouring rain and a blast of freezing-cold wind in my face.

"Man, this stinks," I said as I tightened the strings on my rain poncho around my face. "I hope it dries up a little tomorrow." I then started to wander around the charming little town, seeing what might be interesting. I happened upon a gourmet chocolate shop, which thrilled me. I treated myself to a small bag of dark chocolate–covered orange jelly peels, which were my favorite, and decided I would allow myself one chocolate at the end of each day, as a reward for all that walking. I had enough for at least the first three weeks, so I was happy. I then wandered into a sports store that featured a pair of rain pants hanging out in front. Given how hard it was raining and how wet my pants already were because of it, I knew I would get soaked if this kept up, so I bought them on the spot.

Feeling very tired and hungry by then, I found my way farther down the street and into a tempting French delicatessen filled with salamis and cheeses, and all sorts of delicious jams and cookies. Still feeling too overwhelmed to focus, I asked the shopkeeper to make me a little cheese sandwich to tide me over until dinner.

Sandwich in hand, I then braved the rain once again and in just a few minutes found my way to the beginning of the path. Great! Now I knew where to start in the morning, if I decided to go over the mountains. I felt grounded with that discovery and started to relax.

I can do this, I said to myself as I headed back to my room, now feeling the full impact of the travel and the pace I had been keeping leading up to the trip.

When I entered the hotel, the same woman who registered me was waiting at the front desk. She said the pilgrim's dinner was included in my hotel reservation and would be served at eight. Looking at my watch and seeing it was only four o'clock, I knew right then I would never be able to stay up long enough to eat dinner. I told her I would not be coming for dinner, glad that I had my sandwich, and that I would see her for breakfast.

"Okay, if you wish," she said, not believing I was passing up dinner.

I slowly walked up the four flights, switched on the light in the dark hallway, and opened the door to my room. It was still raining outside, and inside my room, it was still freezing. I wasn't worried, though. I opened Cheater and found my long underwear and cashmere hat and gloves, as well as my tiny down sleeping bag. Bundled up in all of this, I promptly fell asleep until six the next morning.

PART II

THE
HEALING

Day 1
(26 km; 16 mi)

Saint-Jean-Pied-de-Port to Roncesvalles

Once awake I got dressed. Given how wet and unseasonably cold it was, I was grateful for the long underwear and heavy coat that I had thrown in my bag at the last minute. Without those things, I would be in big trouble. Next I put on a long-sleeve wool shirt and a down vest, then turned to my boots, the most important piece of hiking equipment of the day. Since it was so wet outside I had no choice but to wear the heavy boots. My lightweight Merrells would be soaked and useless in this weather. So they were out. I threw them aside and picked up my heavy hiking boots, remembering the salesman's instructions on how to avoid blisters. I first put on my liner socks, making certain there were no wrinkles in them before putting on my heavier wool socks. Then I slid my feet into my boots. It was a tight fit, but I remember the boot fitter telling me that I didn't want any movement in my boot because that was what caused blisters. I had no chance of getting a blister today, that's for sure.

Next, I packed up Cheater and Pilgrim, and headed downstairs (or rather struggled downstairs) with both in tow. I think I woke up the entire hotel as I clumsily pushed Cheater down the stairs, making enough racket to wake the dead, but he was just too heavy to carry. I met the receptionist at the bottom, glaring at me for all the commotion I was making. Meekly smiling, I asked her if Cheater would be picked up as promised. She assured me that, yes, he would be, at 9 A.M. "Just leave your bag here," she said, which I had no problem with, as I was done moving Cheater for one day.

Greatly relieved to walk away from that heavy burden, I tossed Pilgrim over my shoulder and went into the dining room. There I was I met with a modest buffet of cheese and ham, some warm croissants, and several open boxes of processed orange juice. I ate up and had two cups of coffee; then for good measure, I had one of my own PowerBars as well, which I pulled from Pilgrim, so I was certain I had enough protein to face the day. I had six more with me for later on, so I was covered. Then I drew in a deep breath. It was time to go.

The rain was coming down in sheets, sideways, as I made my way down the Rue de Citadelle, toward the Route de Napoleon and the beginning of the Pyrenees route of the Camino. I wondered if it would be even more difficult to climb in the rain. "Well, I'll soon find out," I said as I headed straight for it. While yesterday I had debated whether or not to walk over the Pyrenees, this morning my body just pointed in that direction and started walking.

I was in such a great rush to get going today that I almost forgot to take a moment to set my intention. This was a true spiritual pilgrimage for me—one that I deeply wanted to heal my body, heart, and soul—and I didn't want to start without acknowledging that truth for myself. I could already see how easily my ego could hijack that awareness by creating a sense of urgency, intimating that if I walked in the rain faster I would get less wet.

But my inner voice nudged me to slow down and remember what I was doing and why before I got under way. I walked over to the ledge of the bridge leading to the path and closed my eyes to pray.

Holy Mother God, creator of the known and unknown Universe, and the Divine Light that oversees this most ancient and holy pilgrimage, watch over and guide me as I make my way this day across the Pyrenees and into Roncesvalles.

As I proceed through this and all the days ahead, help clear my life of all that no longer serves my soul. I humbly ask that my Higher Self oversee this entire journey, and my lower mind release and let go of all that has injured others and injured me as I have traveled this and all my previous lives.

I set my intention to ask for forgiveness and to extend for-giveness to all to whom I am in karmic debt as I journey this way of forgiveness, and to transform my pain into understand-ing and gratitude now and into the future expression of my being.

Amen.

It was a big prayer. Sometimes that is how it works with me. Big prayers come flying through me and remind me of what I came here to do, to learn, and to release. I was committed to my prayer and yet was painfully aware of how far I was from feeling able to do that now.

Opening my eyes and peeking from under my poncho into the sheets of water heading straight at me, I took a breath and starting singing, "I'm Off to See the Wizard." Only this time, other pilgrims flanked me on both sides, heading in the same direction, so I sang under my breath.

Keeping my head down to guard against the rain, I let the rhythm of the song move me forward and toward the eventually more and more and *more* inclining path.

Soon I realized that climbing uphill was all that I could look forward to for quite a while. My mind panicked at first, but with each step it quieted down. Over the course of the day I was met with every kind of weather there was: rain, sleet, and snow, then more rain, then sun and fog . . . then everything all over again, pretty much mirroring my own emotions.

I was confused. I didn't know what kind of thoughts I was sup-posed to have. What were appropriate pilgrimage thoughts? I tried to concentrate on spiritual thoughts, and even prayers, but those slipped out of my mind as fast as they came into it. I tried to think about what brought me to the Camino but that, too, didn't stick.

For a long time I had no thoughts at all, simply focusing on my breathing and taking one step at a time. I was glad that I had had some training in the past in how to breathe properly, slowly into my diaphragm and out through my nose, because that is what helped me to continue onward up the steep incline more than anything else.

I also realized very soon that the only way I was going to complete the 26-kilometer trek I was facing was to go very slowly. It wasn't hard because I didn't have the physical stamina to go any other way. As I walked my butt burned, my back hurt, my knee hurt, and I had to stop a lot to simply catch my breath and take a rest.

I was glad because taking breaks allowed me to fully appreciate the incredible beauty surrounding me. When the sky was clear, the colors everywhere were extraordinary. There were waves of intense green expanses, dotted with small budding yellow flowers fighting the cold, meeting an almost turquoise sky. I also saw what appeared to be giant vultures, or birds of prey of some sort, soaring overhead, lifting my spirit and telling me to look further than right in front of my nose as I walked.

When it clouded over and heavy fog drifted in, which it did often that day, I felt as though I were in a strange dream, being whisked off into another dimension. I didn't know it at the time, but I was.

It took me forever to get to the summit. I was glad that I had packed all those PowerBars (which comprised the greater part of all that weight I was carrying in Cheater) because after a brief stop in Oresson, about 8 kilometers up the mountain, there was no other place to stop until Roncesvalles. I ate five of them as I inched my way along all day.

I don't know what was worse: going up, which just about killed my back and butt; or going down, which equally killed my knees, thighs, and toes. In fact, I banged my toes so much that as I moved along, every step sent a sharp pang that at times made me cry out.

When I first set out in the morning, I was surrounded by other pilgrims and I pretty much just marched along with them, as none of us was going very fast. Soon, however, they all passed me, and I was left to walk down the mountain all alone for hours. I was glad for the solitude. I felt free in a strange and uplifting way.

Going up the mountain, I walked along mostly gravel trails that were easy enough to navigate, but going down, due to the rain and snow and slush, I found myself trudging in thick, sticky mud the entire way. Every time I set my boot down, the ground sucked me in like quicksand, then grabbed onto my foot and held it down. I had to jiggle and twist and struggle to release it, which pained my knee, so I had to do it carefully and slowly. In fact, the entire day was like being in a slow-motion movie as I crawled along.

Once I got into a rhythm and figured out that the only thing I could do from here to the end was put one foot in front of the other, step, push, and breathe, my mind became more and more quiet. Then, after what seemed like an endless inner silence, my thoughts began to drift to my father.

I began to feel the depth of resentments I had held toward my father over the years, and all the justifications I carried for all those resentments. I thought of all the ways in which I felt he hadn't shown up for me, how he lost his temper or was just plain frustrated and beat me, or hadn't supported me or celebrated me, and how he seemed pretty uninterested in me and what I did. I thought about how I had internalized his lack of witnessing me as his rejection of me, and how it was something I had privately kept in my heart as a deep wound.

And yet, as I walked, those thoughts began to give way to thoughts of the challenges my father had faced during his life. I started to deeply consider this, my heart now opening to him as those last endless and difficult kilometers unraveled under my feet.

I remembered him telling me, in one of those rare moments when he shared something personal with me, how as a child during the Depression he'd had a pet pig that he really loved, and how his family had slaughtered it one day for dinner while he was at school, and how his brothers had laughed at him when he cried over that pig after he found out what had happened.

My heart ached as I remembered, as though his spirit were now walking alongside me, sharing that story with me once again. I also thought about all that his family had lost during the Depression and how hard he had to work all his life.

I felt his spirit as I thought about him joining the Army and marrying my mom while he was stationed in Germany, and of him bringing her, then pregnant, back to America and to his family in Iowa—only to have to leave her with them while he went off for another year to finish his tour of duty. And while my mom is incredible, she was and is a handful to deal with, and that must have taken a lot of his energy and attention, as well.

And then there were so many of us to support. Seven kids, in addition to his parents, who lived with us and depended solely on him for support.

With each step I realized just how difficult that must have been. But he took care of all of us and never complained. While we were not rich by any means, we were comfortable enough. We ate well. We had nice clothes that my mother made. We went to a private, albeit humble, Catholic school. And we always had lots of toys under the tree every Christmas. He made sure of that.

My father wasn't emotionally available, nor were most men of his generation, and as a child that was hard to understand. He was serious and said very little most of the time. As I walked I could see how I took that very personally, when in fact it wasn't personal at all.

Eventually I began to realize that his life was not only very difficult when I was a child, but it also never got easier. As we grew up, my brother Bruce became sicker and sicker. This caused my dad so much stress and worry. He tirelessly took care of Bruce, and the demands he made never eased up. So Dad never got to enjoy his retirement at all. In fact, he never really had a day of genuine rest his entire life. Between taking care of Bruce and taking care of my mother, it never let up.

Suddenly I felt sad that I had judged my father so harshly. I also felt the weight of the anger and blame I had carried toward him all these years, and it was so heavy. As I walked, I found myself starting to genuinely rethink all the ways in which I had been disappointed by him or felt I was not appreciated or witnessed by him as a child and beyond. Soon my anger and resentment gave way to something entirely different. I was overcome with sadness for all the ways I had made his life more difficult and was genuinely remorseful. I suddenly realized that I was guilty of treating him the same way I had been so angry with him for treating me. I had failed to witness and appreciate him. I had failed to celebrate him. I had failed to recognize him for who he was. As I walked I could suddenly see it all far more clearly than ever before.

While my dad wasn't that emotionally nurturing, he was there every single day of my life supporting me in the only way he knew how, by providing for my physical well-being and intellectual development. I cried in gratitude for him as I thought of all of this.

"Dad," I said out loud, as I walked, "thank you for doing everything that you did for me—for all of us. I never thanked you."

I wished I had felt before he died what I did now. The Camino was already working its magic on me. Shortly after, I came upon a small marker where a former pilgrim had died while making this trek. It reminded me of how quickly death can come, as it did for my dad.

"I miss you, Dad," I said aloud as I looked at the gravesite. "You always tried hard to do your best."

Roncesvalles seemed to stretch further and further out of reach as I walked toward it, as if the Camino were playing with me. I had to sit down and rest several times because the more I pushed forward, the less progress I seemed to make.

Toward the end, the ground beneath my feet was nothing more than a mud bath, and there weren't any tree stumps or rocks nearby that I could sit on, so I leaned against a tree and rested. As I did, I felt that the tree was breathing with me. I actually stood up and turned around and looked at it as if to say, "Really?!"

Then I remembered where I was and instead I said, "Thank you."

As I took one last breath before setting out for what I hoped would be the final push of the day, it dawned on me how I had internalized my father's lack of witnessing and had been doing the same thing to myself all my life.

It wasn't that I didn't think I was on my path or fulfilling my purpose. I knew my purpose and I had no doubt that I was on my path. It was deeper than that. It's that I did not witness or lovingly acknowledge and celebrate myself in any way, ever. I treated myself the way my father treated me. I just pushed myself to keep doing, keep working, keep giving, quit complaining, and never ask for a thing.

All at once, I felt more compassion for both of us. I also recognized at the same time that the one who had injured me most was not my father at all. Rather, it was me, by treating myself the way I had interpreted him to be treating me when I was a child.

It wasn't his acknowledgment I needed. It was my own. I needed to find to a sense of love and compassion for myself that I honestly didn't feel. I had it for the entire world, but not for myself.

I had read that the Camino gives you a gift every day if you pay enough attention to receive it. This realization was my Camino gift for today. For years I knew I had to have more self-love. For years I knew I had to forgive my father and release myself from this festering childhood wound. This wasn't new information. Yet today, for the first time, there was a new feeling resonating inside my bones.

As I continued, I came upon a sign that said I was in The Sorcieres' Woods, which sent a chill up my spine. Just as I imagined they were in the Middle Ages, these woods were alive with nature spirits and more, and I could feel all their eyes upon me after I passed. I wondered if I had been one of the "sorcieres" burned alive in the Middle Ages, as the Spanish loved to do back then.

"I'm back," I said out loud, spontaneously, "to forgive you." I liked the energy I felt walking through there. The energy was powerful and commanded respect.

Tears rolled down my face as I emerged from the woods and finally walked into Roncesvalles. I wasn't sure if they were tears of exhaustion, pain, surprise that I had made it, compassion for my dad, compassion for me, awareness of my own childhood wounding and undoing, or relief that I could soon stop walking. It was probably all of it combined.

Wow. And this was only day one. My head spun. I felt as though I had entered an alternate reality, and planet Earth and my life as I knew it had disappeared into this mystical new realm.

As I shuffled into town I looked at my watch. It was 4:30 P.M. I had left at 8 this morning, so that wasn't too bad, I thought, given that this day was rumored to be the most grueling of the entire journey. I found my way to the center of town, which wasn't difficult to do, as the Camino spilled right into it and the town was minuscule. I made my way to the Pilgrim's Passport Office, where I proudly received my second pilgrim's stamp.

The next stop was to find my hostel. Thank God that was easy enough, as well. It was very close to the passport office. My feet, back, butt, thighs, and toes all screamed in pain as I shuffle-crawled to the reception desk. On the floor next to it was Cheater, among a few other bags, waiting for me as if to say, "Where have you been all day?"

"You didn't think I would make it, did you?" I silently smirked at him, overjoyed to see my bag was actually there. "Well, ha! You were wrong."

Looking around as I waited my turn to check in, I could see it was a brand-new inn. The receptionist, a young but curt woman, had no trouble finding my reservation and quickly handed me a room key. Third floor!

Looking at it, then at Cheater, I asked her if there were an elevator. She smiled condescendingly at me, as if I had just asked the most ridiculous question of her ever. She shook her head, then finished with gusto: "No!"

Okay then, I thought, realizing once again that Cheater was my responsibility and that my baggage was mine alone to carry. Not sure I could manage to move him given how spent I was, I nevertheless thankfully took the key and headed for the stairway, dragging Cheater behind me.

With one last push of inner resolve for the day, as if channeling Hercules, I lifted the bag and stomped up the stairs without stopping, ignoring all the reasons I couldn't do it, because I had no choice but to.

Five minutes later, I was settled into my brand-new, complete-with-hot-shower-and-blow-dryer, gorgeous, wonderful, welcoming, sunny room—bags and all. I felt as if I had arrived at the Ritz-Carlton. My totem friend Gumby, proudly sitting next to my bag, seemed to agree.

I had never been so grateful for a bed in all my life.

When I checked in, I was told that dinner was served at 8 P.M. If anything, that was early for Spain. I was starving, but there was nothing to be had for hours, so I ate another PowerBar and decided to take a nap.

I woke up the next morning.

Day 2
(22 km; 14 mi)

Roncesvalles to Zubiri

Oh my Gawd—pain! I woke up barely able to move. Every muscle in my body hurt. And I was starving. The honeymoon with the Camino was over. I couldn't believe I had to do this all over again for 33 more days. AAAWWWW!

Once I managed to sit straight up in bed, I eased myself onto my feet and gently walked over to retrieve my hefty first-aid kit. Thank goodness I didn't have any blisters on my feet, but I was so sore I had no idea how on earth I would be able to walk through the mountains for an entire day all over again.

The first thing I reached for was arnica. Many friends had told me it would help with pain. I had never used it before, so I prayed it worked. I had the extra-strength kind, for which I was grateful, and loaded up on that.

Then I began to rub muscle cream all over my calves and thighs. And my butt. I couldn't believe my butt hurt as much as it did. And my toes, which were tender to the touch. I had to rally. I had to be out of my room in the next 30 minutes.

Once the muscle cream started to take effect, I was able to move a little more freely. Thinking about yesterday's wild weather, I chose to put my long underwear on, even though the sun was shining brightly at the moment. I got dressed and then put on my boots. Only once I shoved my foot into my boot, I could barely stand the pressure on my toes. I hadn't planned on this, and so soon into the walk. *So much for my expert boot fitter,* I thought sarcastically. *My boots don't fit at all.*

I sat back and wondered what to do. I had to keep walking. My solution was to take some Tylenol, shove my boots on my feet, and just get up and go, hoping the pain would ease as I walked. I was used to ignoring pain. In fact, I had actually prided myself on how much pain I was able to withstand without complaining. *I'm just like my father,* I realized as I shoved on the second boot. Limping toward the dining room downstairs, I was soon distracted by the lovely breakfast spread laid out before me at the buffet.

There were freshly baked croissants and large pieces of bread with jam. There were slices of apple and pear in syrup, and a bowl of small oranges to the side. There were trays of salamis and ham, and others filled with various cheeses. There was also fresh orange juice and yogurt. All the things I loved to eat. Unapologetically loading up my plate with as much food as it would hold, I was met by a waitress who asked if I would like some coffee. Ordering a café con leche, I happily sat down to dig in.

After stuffing myself to the brim, I headed back up to my room to fetch Cheater and bring him down for transport. Before I zipped up, I reached in and grabbed a few PowerBars to eat along the way. I did some quick math. I had brought 75 bars with me, which allowed for just over two a day. I had already eaten ten since I left Chicago and was only two days into the Camino.

I hope they have a market along the way, I thought, *or I won't have enough bars to last the entire way.*

I wasn't too worried about it, however. I knew I would be passing through several towns and even large cities, and could eventually pick up anything I needed. It's just that I loved my chocolate-mint PowerBars and quite frankly didn't want to run out.

"Conserve, Sonia," I said to myself. "That's the theme for today. Conserve your energy and your PowerBars. Take it easy, and you'll be okay." I walked back to the dining room to fill up my water pack that I wore around my waist before I set off. Once it was full, it was surprisingly heavy. I then also filled up my stainless-steel water bottle and clipped it to Pilgrim. I now had plenty of water until the next watering hole.

Checking to see that I had everything I needed for the day's journey ahead packed away in Pilgrim, including sun hat, warm hat, gloves, sunblock, iPod, camera, rain poncho, neck bandana, and warm windbreaker, I was satisfied. And ready to go.

I sleepily stepped outside the hotel and was promptly slapped in the face with a brisk, stiff wind. Suddenly I was wide awake.

Sunny or not, it was freezing outside. So I stepped back in. I put down Pilgrim, and unzipped her. I then pulled out my neck bandana, the warm windbreaker, and rain poncho and put them all on. I also pulled out my warm gloves and hat and zipped up again. Now I was ready to go.

When I stepped outside this time, it seemed suddenly warmer, until I realized that, duh! It wasn't warmer. I was dressed warmer. Step-by-ginger-step I started searching for the yellow Camino arrows pointing out the way. After only a few yards, I looked up to see a big road sign that said, "Santiago, 790 km." Just past that I saw the yellow arrow.

Before taking another step, however, I paused and said a prayer to set my intention for the day:

> *Holy Mother-Father God,*
> *Please oversee my walk today and help me make it to Zubiri. Guide my attention to the yellow arrows and keep me from getting lost. I also ask for help in keeping my heart and mind open to receiving all Camino blessings throughout this day.*
> *Thank you.*

That said, I was ready to go, and starting singing "I'm Off to See the Wizard" just as I had yesterday. I guess it was the "yellow" thing that inspired me. Yellow brick road. Yellow arrows. It worked for me. I even did a sort of scarecrow jig since there was no one looking. It made me laugh.

I didn't want to think about the 790 more kilometers I had to walk. That felt too daunting for my miserable toes. I decided I would only think about what I had to walk today. That was far more manageable. My destination was a town called Zubiri, 22 kilometers away. After yesterday's trek, that sounded easy breezy. I was optimistic as I started down the path.

It was beautiful outside and I was taken with all the activity going on both above and below me as I walked. The trees were filled with various birds, while mysterious critters I couldn't see rustled in the brush underneath my feet and just out of sight.

Soon enough I found myself surrounded by fellow pilgrims flanking me on either side, some walking alone, others in pairs, some in groups, all undertaking this pilgrimage for reasons of their own, in unison with me.

I quietly observed their different energies as we walked. There were athletic men who almost seemed to run rather than walk down the path. There were chattering young people who seemed oblivious of the difficulties the path laid out before them, their nimble bodies cruising along without the least bit of effort. There were a lot of people riding their bikes on the path, as well. I guess you can ride the Camino on your bike as opposed to walking if that is your preference and still receive a pilgrim's certificate at the end. Given the steep climbs and descents, and the uneven ground beneath my feet, I marveled that bikers would even want to travel the Camino this way. It seemed like a miserable thing to do to me.

Most of the bikers were clearly Tour de France athletic types, as their designer spandex revealed every inch of their ripped bodies. I wondered if the Camino for them was an athletic conquest rather than a spiritual journey. It was still difficult to navigate, in any case, even on a bike.

As I passed several groups of pilgrims, I wondered about their reasons for being here, as well. They joyfully chatted and laughed, and seemed more into each other than the path itself.

Not that I was judging. I was just wondering what the Camino meant to each one.

I had been on the road no more than 30 minutes when the weather abruptly changed and it clouded over and started to rain once again. This created a dense, low fog that shrouded the path, and between the fog and the rain, the route became very slippery and difficult to forge. There were so many wet, uneven stones that unless I kept my head down and watched every single step I took very carefully, I would slip on the rocks and fall down, which I did, several times. Thank God for my hiking poles, as they saved me more than once.

Today was proving to be much more challenging than yesterday. The ground was unstable and shaky, which was the same way I felt inside, too. The expanded and loving state I was in yesterday had completely evaporated, and was nowhere to be found.

I was thrust into survival mode today, and it didn't leave me in a good mood.

Given the difficulty of the walk, I am not surprised that what surfaced in my mind were all the people I had recently ended relationships with, and how difficult these endings had been for me. One friendship that I ended was with a girlfriend I had known since I was 12 years old. Two had been with people I had worked and traveled with. Another was a girlfriend of the past decade, and of course, the big one was my marriage.

Why were so many significant relationships ending at the same time? Was it them? Or was it me? Given my frame of mind at the time, I had come to the conclusion it was them.

All had shown a self-serving side that I somehow had been blinded to up until recently. It is amazing that I can see other people's needs and soul energies so clearly when it comes to my work, and yet still "miss the forest for the trees" in my own personal life. Patrick had always marveled at how I was unable or refused to see obvious "BS" energy in some of the people I had invited into my life over the years. I thought he was unkind and unloving. Maybe he was just clear, and I was delusional.

It's frustrating when you are possessed by a pattern because you can't really see it until it becomes so obvious that it smacks you in the face. I had a long-standing pattern of choosing friends who were really manipulative and ended up tricking me and letting me down. It all started in second grade when my friends Leslie and Stephanie asked me to help them with their schoolwork, then left it to me to do it while they conspired to dump me behind my back as soon as they turned it in. I was so heartbroken that it took years for me to get over it. I guess I was just sensitive.

The names changed over the years, but my pattern and the end result pretty much stayed the same. I created relationships into which I invested my full heart and soul, only to be let down and left behind, blaming myself for whatever went wrong.

All of my failed adult relationships were with people who had not had much success, and because of that felt that someone owed them something. I volunteered myself to be that someone, over and over again.

Maybe it was my karma to do that, to be the fairy godmother to the people whom I now wanted to get as far away from as possible. Maybe in my past lives I was a real jerk and ripped them off and now owed them one. Maybe they were past lives that had to do with the Camino. As I thought of this, something inside me seemed to say, "Yes, it was, and yes, you were."

"Well, at least I am here clearing that karma now," I said out loud to the Universe.

As I walked, I couldn't seem to get into a rhythm. Every step felt dangerous. I kept turning the same ankle and banging my toes. Ouch!

Today the walk felt funky, similar to the energy of some of the people I had just cut out of my life. The more I walked, the more resentful I became. Why did I keep falling into the same trap?

These negative thoughts that were being shaken out of my bones surprised me. I didn't want to think such dark thoughts. I didn't want to think about the friendships I had decided to end. I had already let them go. I guess I could forgive them. I certainly knew in my heart that doing so would be the best thing for my spirit. In many ways I already had and hoped they had forgiven me as well. But I must not have forgiven them enough because right now I still wanted to be angry, and . . . *hmmm, what was it I was feeling?* Disappointed. Yes, that's it. I was so disappointed in them.

I walked with this feeling for a while, slipping and sliding and cursing and catching myself with one of my poles, struggling to keep from plunging down the never-ending descent that was this day's walk.

Disappointed. What an obnoxious energy that was. It reminded me of the grade-school nuns in the Catholic school where I attended, and how they used to shake their heads at me and say— over the slightest infraction, such as laughing in class or not getting a 100 percent on a paper—"I'm *so* disappointed in you." Ugh!

Eventually I began to feel the arrogance of being "disappointed." After all, who was I to have some standard of behavior that others should adhere to? Who was I to be "disappointed"?

I had never openly discussed my expectations with any of these friends. I just assumed that people were supposed to behave in a certain way (determined by me, of course) and, if they didn't, they *greatly disappointed me*.

I began to look at these ended friendships (or "endships," as my friend Mara in Chicago called them) from a new perspective. While still happy to be freed of relationships with these people, I could see how I had no right to be disappointed in them.

They simply were who they were, and I had no right to think I could, should, or would change them. Suddenly I felt arrogant and self-righteous. How obnoxious I must have seemed to them, I realized. Essentially, my attitude was, "Be my friend and live the way I want you to live so I won't be disappointed."

Not that I ever said that or even consciously thought that. I didn't. And yet the more I walked, the more I realized that I did, at least *unconsciously*, imply and expect that. No wonder those friendships blew up in my face. They were not connections based on love and acceptance of others for who they were, or vice versa.

We were all just manipulating and maneuvering one another to get each other to take care of our unmet, unspoken needs, the things we weren't succeeding in addressing ourselves.

I shook my head at this miserable realization when I suddenly flew off my feet and slid straight down the mountain for about ten feet. Sitting in the mud with the wind knocked out of me, I caught my breath.

"I get it. My relationships are like this path today," I said aloud. "Messy, mucky, slippery, and ungrounded."

I was relieved I had let these people go from my life. And humbled to realize they probably felt the same way about me.

I also felt sad that we had ended up apart and feeling bad.

I knew in my heart at that moment that no one was the "bad guy." Or the "good guy." We were just people navigating the muck of relationships given the hidden patterns we were stuck in.

Standing up, I tried to regain my balance and make sure nothing had suffered too much. Knee was okay. Butt was sore but no more than usual. I was fine. The descent continued, as did the slippery ground. It never eased up. I was particularly frustrated that I kept banging my toes on the fronts of my boots, making it nearly impossible to take a single step without feeling excruciating pain.

As I walked, I thought that this was how it felt to be married to Patrick. As much as I wanted to forgive him—and me, for that matter—all I could think of was how much pain I had been in for so many years being married to him. Like the slippery ground under my feet, I had never felt fully safe with him.

I didn't trust him to have my back at all.

I wondered if that was fair. How much of that was me being stuck in a pattern of not asking for or allowing help, and how much was about him not having it to give?

Just as I thought about this my foot slid once again, and I landed in a puddle up to the top of my ankle, the mud now sliding into my boot and through my sock.

"That's an answer for you, Sonia," I said out loud, between cursing. "You took the step into the muck."

That wet foot pissed me off. *When will this end?*

I wanted the pain to end. I wanted the walk to end. I wanted the sliding and muck and mud to end. I wanted to feel solid ground under my feet and trust that I could take my eyes off the path for a second and not get ambushed by unstable, slippery rock and gravel giving way. That's what I wanted, but as far as I could see, it wasn't about to end anytime soon.

There was not much I could do but carry on, so that's what I did. The hours passed and judging by yesterday's pace, I had to be at least halfway to Zubiri by now. I was hungry. And because I drank all the water from both my water pack and my bottle, I had to pee.

Not seeing any sign of a town or village or lone café on the road, I was about to continue on when I remembered my pee cone.

After checking that the coast was clear, I decided to use it.

I pulled it out of my backpack and eyed it suspiciously. *How do I use this thing?* I asked myself.

It was somewhat self-explanatory. I simply had to put it over my "privates" as the sales guy had said, and quite literally go for it. Feeling funny doing this so close to the path, I decided to move a little deeper into the woods for privacy. When I felt I had hidden myself well enough, I looked at the pee cone once again.

"Am I really going to use this thing?" I asked myself.

"Yes. Just use it and stop being such a prima donna!" I snapped right back.

Feeling that standing and peeing like a guy was way too much for me, especially given that I was trying to move away from my "inner masculine," I decided to squat and use the pee cone instead. That way I could ensure that I didn't splatter all over myself, which has happened in the past.

I put my backpack down and struggled to balance under my poncho. I wasn't sure I had everything in its proper place, but before I burst, I just trusted and went.

Afterward, I stood up, pleased that no one had passed by, and somewhat impressed that someone had thought to invent a pee cone. Except when I stood up, I felt way too warm underneath my poncho.

I lifted it up only to see that the stupid pee cone had directed the pee to the back of my pants and my long underwear. My pants, my socks, and my entire backside were covered in pee. I might as well have pointed a fire hose at myself.

Embarrassed and wet, I cursed the pee cone and myself for at least a half an hour. Eventually I started laughing. It is so true that most of what happens to us, we create. *Most of it?* my inner voice challenged.

Walking in my soaking wet pants, I relented. "Okay, all of it."

Funny how this day was completely the opposite of yesterday. Light to dark.

I no longer wanted to feel angry with anyone or myself. I just peed on myself and was tired of being pissed off. It was time to change the channel. I started singing my favorite songs, making up the words whenever I couldn't remember them.

I started with The Beatles, "Can't Buy Me Love," and ended up with Gotye's "Somebody That I Used to Know." I had walked in silence for four hours and had not spoken to anyone on the path over the past two days. In fact, I didn't want to speak to anyone as I walked. But singing was okay.

Several more hours passed, and I found my resentments toward everyone had vanished, at least for the time being. All except the ones I felt toward Patrick, but I was trying. I didn't want to carry the weight of those dark feelings toward him, or anyone, including me. But they wouldn't budge much, no matter what I wanted.

I noticed, even in only two short days of walking, that heavy or negative thoughts made the Camino much more difficult to walk. When I let go of my dark thoughts, I found I could keep on going even when I thought I didn't have another step in me. That's why it was annoying that some of my dark thoughts clung so tenaciously to my mind. They wouldn't let go. The more I tried to make them go away, the more they intensified. I gave up. I let them be.

Finally I stumbled into Zubiri. I looked around to find the town. There wasn't much of one. Only a few sad, empty establishments next to a highway. It didn't matter. I was relieved I had arrived. Once again, all I wanted to do was go to sleep.

It wasn't difficult to find my hostel. It was in a small house directly across from the pilgrims' albergue in the center of town. I knocked on the door and an extremely thin, elderly woman opened it and smiled. In the foyer, right behind her, stood Cheater, as if welcoming me with open arms. I felt so glad to see him.

She started to show me a room just behind Cheater, then put up her hand and stopped me in my tracks, looking down at my mud-covered boots and peed-on pants. She pointed to them and gestured for me to take them off, which I happily did. Mud cracked off of me, and exploded everywhere. I apologized immediately. She simply smiled as if to say, "No problem," took them from me, and placed them in a plastic bag. Once I had stripped down, she pointed to a room behind me. That was apparently my room. Thank goodness there were no stairs to climb today. I was truly too wiped out to carry anything anywhere. The room was very simple. It had a single bed with a small hand shower on the wall next to a toilet separated by a thin wall, and no windows. Perfect.

Once I saw the room and approved, she took me upstairs and pointed to a large sink with a scrub brush and some soap. Then she pointed to the bag with my pants and shoes.

Nodding yes, I realized she was showing me where I could get my boots and clothes cleaned up. Standing in my underwear, I immediately set to it. It was no small effort to get the mud and pee smell off, but I managed. She returned after a few minutes and pointed out a rack on the balcony where I could hang them to dry. Given that it was drizzling fairly steadily, I hoped that they could.

Once my clothes were spread out to dry and I had changed into drier duds, she asked for my pilgrim passport so she could stamp it. I had almost forgotten about that. Then I asked about dinner. She showed me a small map and said I had to walk 2 kilometers into town and could get dinner there after 6 P.M. I looked at my watch. It was already five. My feet hurt so much I wasn't sure I could manage. I was starving, though, and hadn't yet had dinner since I started out, so I rallied.

The problem was my toes. They were so banged up it was hard to walk. Fortunately, I had the lightweight Merrell shoes. They were soft and didn't hurt my toes as much.

I showered, got dressed, and set out to find the place for dinner. I was famished.

Day 3
(20 km; 12 mi)

Zubiri to Pamplona

I woke up at six in the morning, ready to go. I was still unbelievably sore, every single muscle aching like crazy. I think it was not only because of the rigors of the walk, but also because the room had no heat and I was tightly curled up into a frozen ball all night. I slowly unfurled as my eyes opened up, and gently stretched.

Ouch! My toes were so sore that even moving them was excruciatingly painful. I crawled out of my sleeping bag to examine them once I turned the light on. Every one of my toenails was black and blue. No wonder they hurt so much. I had really bruised them.

I popped open the arnica and took two, then a third, for good measure. I then slathered myself in muscle cream, which was the only way I could get moving in the morning. Gumby sat silently watching me as I put on my long-sleeve wool shirt and two pairs of socks. Next I went upstairs to collect my long underwear, pants, and boots. Since my room had no windows, I had no idea what to expect outside. One thing I didn't expect to see was snow coming down in heavy chunks.

My clothes! I ran to the balcony only to find my long underwear, pants, and boots completely covered in snow and still soaking wet. Grabbing them and shaking them off, I could tell this was going to be yet another challenging day.

"Why didn't I bring two pairs of pants? I brought enough of everything else I could think of," I lamented as I scraped off the ice. The boots were a lost cause. I didn't see the thin woman who had greeted me the night before anywhere, but as I began to poke around the salon, I did find a blow-dryer. Yes! I could blow-dry my long underwear and pants. "Thank you, guides," I whispered as I ran downstairs with it before anyone saw me.

It worked. After only ten minutes each, my underwear and pants were toasty dry and ready to go. The boots were another matter. I pulled out the insoles and started drying first one, then the other, then back and forth over the next 15 minutes. I didn't actually manage to get them terribly dry, but I did warm them up a bit.

"Oh well, I'll just wear more socks."

I put on my two pairs of socks, which tortured my toes, and then shoved my feet into my soggy boots. *Ow!*

Taking a deep breath and sucking up the pain, I stood up.

"This is torture," I cried under my breath. "What have I done to my toes?"

Pushing onward, I decided I would dedicate my day to people who suffered around the world. Here I was whining about my toes and cold, wet feet when in some places in the world, this was everyday life. I summoned the good soldier in me and stopped complaining. I then took a moment and put everything back into Cheater, and slammed him shut. How can it be that he seemed to be expanding? I didn't buy a thing, and I even ate a fair number of the PowerBars I brought with me, and yet I could hardly get him zipped. I shoved and punched until I succeeded.

Once that was done, I dragged Cheater into the foyer. Since I still had not seen the thin woman from the night before, I took a marker I brought along with me and marked the name of the next town and hostel on a piece of paper and taped it to the top of Cheater with a Band-Aid, hoping that would be enough to get it to where I was going, which was Pamplona, the town in Spain where they run the bulls.

Opening the front door, I peeked outside and was greeted by a strong, cold wind and a blanket of snow. Breakfast, I was told the night before, was around the corner. I grabbed Pilgrim and dashed out, both hungry and not wanting to get too wet.

It was 50 feet away.

I walked into a small café where an old Spaniard stood behind the counter. Laid out were individually packaged industrial croissants and small cans of artificial orange juice. There were a few packets of butter and jam, to which I could help myself.

The Spaniard asked me if I wanted coffee.

"Café con leche, por favor," I said, disappointed at the bleak "pilgrim's breakfast" before me. He turned and brewed and steamed as quickly as lightning and nearly slid the café over to me before I could sit down. I grabbed it and took it over to the plastic table where I had set down my backpack and poles. The croissant was loveless and the orange juice hard to drink, but the café con leche was heavenly, made by a true maestro. I smiled at him and said, "That's so good!" which seemed to please him. He nodded in response.

I reached into my backpack, took out one of the two PowerBars I had set aside as my day's allocation, and slowly unwrapped it. I would eat half now with this coffee and half on the Camino. I nursed both bar and coffee very slowly, while forcing down the plastic-tasting croissant, thinking I would need the energy even if I didn't like it.

I had a second cup of his delicious coffee before I set out, hoping its warmth would insulate me from the snow that was coming down harder than before. Moments later, fortified as well as I could be, I put back on my heavy windbreaker, gloves, hat, neck warmer, rain poncho, rain pants, and gators over my boots, a last-minute purchase at REI that I discovered in my bag this morning. I was ready.

Outside was beautiful. The snow against the trees was gorgeous, and the fog swirling on the ground made the Camino beckon as if into a magic forest. Looking around for a yellow arrow pointing in the right direction, I saw a young girl weighted down by a huge backpack, wearing plastic bags over sockless feet stuffed into snow-covered canvas tennis shoes. She looked miserable and confused.

I approached her and asked if she was okay. She assured me she was, and then shook her head at the snow.

I nodded in agreement and then pointed to her feet. "Mucho frio!" I said, wondering if she was freezing. Surely she needed some socks, but she shook her head, saying, "No. Okay."

And so I accepted. "Buen Camino," I wished her, as we both started heading for the bridge that would take us out of town and back to the path.

I paused. It was time to pray.

> *Holy Mother God, my toes hurt. Can you work a miracle and help them heal? I can barely walk. I need your help. Remind me why I am doing this because I am really feeling sorry for myself today. Thank you in advance.*
>
> *Amen.*
>
> *P.S. Guardian Angel, please keep me from further hurting my knee and toes today if possible. I want to enjoy myself.*

As I set out, I walked quietly. I wasn't in the mood to sing, and for the longest time, I couldn't even think. The path continued, up, up, up, then turned and went down, down, down, and then up again. My toes were so sore I had to walk very slowly so I wouldn't jam them any more than I had to. What was I going to do about them?

I knew there would be places along the path to get other shoes, and all I could think of, snow or rain aside, was to find some hiking shoes that had open toes, like Tevas. In fact, I daydreamed about Tevas for hours. It helped me navigate the snowy slush I was now literally wading through along the path.

Several hours into the day, I began to actually enjoy the icy cold beauty I was trudging through. I was so glad that I was warm enough. I had overheard in the café last night that a woman from Canada got lost in the Pyrenees the day after I had left St. Jean and was found dead. That was so upsetting. I wasn't sure if it was true, but several pilgrims were animatedly talking with each other about it. I just listened. I knew the path I had just crossed over was difficult, and that they had closed it shortly after I left St. Jean for Roncesvalles. People were talking about it in the pilgrim's office when I went to get a stamp once I had arrived there. But I had no idea it was that treacherous.

It seemed that most of the deaths on the Camino over the years had occurred on the part I had just completed. That another death occurred yesterday sent chills up my spine. *Am I biting off more than I can chew?* I wondered. Yet, intuitively I knew I was fine and, apart from sore muscles and toes, I was tough. I could manage this Camino no matter what was ahead . . . and would.

As I walked the slush got worse, as did the fog. My thoughts once again drifted to my marriage. Today I was more resigned. Maybe it is the best thing for both of us that we end now. Funny how we've been together for over 30 years, and at the end I wondered if our marriage had even mattered all that much to Patrick. How did that happen?

If I let myself think about it too much, I realized that I was getting angry all over again. "Really, Patrick?" I'd say, talking to his spirit. "Just like that, we are done?"

Not getting any answer from him, of course, I said, out loud, "Okay, I can accept what has happened. I can let our marriage go. In fact, I want to. Furthermore, I'm not going to hold on to anything. I'm not going to fight over anything. I'm not going to get into a battle of that nature. That is not me. I am just going to walk away, like I'm doing now."

Saying that, I felt some relief in my aching heart.

At one point an hour or so later, I came across a particular place, by a very large tree, where it seemed the entire web of mountain rivers converged, the water intensely rushing down, clearing away everything in its path. I sat down on a rock and watched it for a long while as I fished out and ate the second half of my PowerBar.

The river talked to me. *Let it all go, Sonia. Don't hold on to a thing. Not material things. Not feelings. Not the past. Not your judgments. Not even your identity. Let it all be swept away with the river.*

I must have sat there for half an hour, mesmerized by the river's conversation with me. Not a soul passed by. Then suddenly, as if waking me out of my reverie, a group of laughing Italians approached and wanted to take pictures at my spot, so I gracefully got up and started back on my way.

I had been walking for about three and a half hours when I turned and came upon a makeshift café in the middle of nowhere, where there were at least 20 pilgrims huddled together, all drinking hot coffee and eating snacks.

I was so glad to happen upon this oasis, as I was freezing and really hungry. I approached the counter and could see they were offering some wonderful things to eat, including an egg and potato frittata for only 1 euro. I opened my little trail purse, which carried my passport, one credit card, and my money, and pulled out a five-euro note, adding a fresh café con leche to my order.

As I waited, I looked around. Everyone was soaked and weary. My attention then drifted over to the corner of a small picnic table, where I overheard a middle-aged American woman, in a panic, just realizing that she had lost her wallet, with everything important in it, somewhere between Zubiri and this stop.

She was devastated, and I could understand why. She kept saying, "I have to go back. I have no passport or money or credit cards, so I can't go on." She apparently was traveling alone like I was, and was clearly distraught.

Several pilgrims gathered around her, showing concern, and one man seemed to have taken over the role of getting her out of that mess. He offered to give her enough money to get back to America, if she wanted to keep on walking to Pamplona with him.

She was grateful, but wanted to retrace her steps on the trail instead in case she could find the wallet. I understood. I would have wanted to do the same.

I watched this unfold as I ate my frittata. I wasn't sure if I should step in to help. So many people were rallying around her that she seemed overwhelmed. She just kept saying over and over, "I knew this was going to happen. I just knew it."

Then she suddenly got up and said, "I'm going back," without accepting a thing from anyone.

Before I could jump up and offer her money, not that I had much with me, she was gone.

Wow! That was upsetting to witness. I prayed for her and felt for her deeply, knowing how much effort I had put into getting here. It must have been awful to have to quit so soon after she began. Funny how she knew it was her destiny that this would occur.

Once she left, everyone looked at one another as if to say, "I hope you can stay in the game."

I smiled at a talkative fellow with an accent named Clint, from Kansas City. A tall fellow, wearing a snow-covered cowboy hat with a blue bandana underneath it covering his ears, and a bright red neck scarf, with a warm Midwest manner, he was quickly making friends with everyone. I have never been like that. I am shy and tend to watch and listen. Patrick was the one who talked with others and made friends easily. I admired him for that, although I am perfectly content to be the introvert that I am.

If I were talking all the time, how could I hear my inner voice or my guides? Quiet was so necessary for me. It was perhaps more necessary than eating.

Patrick and I were opposites in that way. He was far more social, and sometimes that would stress me out. He liked to be surrounded by people and I liked to be alone.

I know I confused him as well. After all, I could stand in front of 3,000 people and have a wonderfully fun time teaching them to listen to their spirit, and I loved every minute of that. It came easily to me. But when I wasn't teaching, I preferred to be quiet, the fewer people around me the better. Ever since I can remember I've always preferred to be with my family and a few close friends over a large crowd.

It's not that I don't like people. I love them. It's that I feel others' energy so deeply when I am with them that I get easily drained. I've always called myself a "deep-sea diver" as opposed to a "water-skier" when it comes to socializing with others. Conversations soon move to a very intimate and deep level with me and I invite that. I don't know how to chitchat. I connect heart-to-heart, soul-to-soul. It's the only way I know how to communicate. But connecting at that level is so intense that I need time to be alone after I share such deep connections with others.

Soon after the woman left, one by one, we all got up and started back on the trail, "Buen Caminos" shared all the way around. I made my way onward slowly. My toes and I were no longer friends. I honestly didn't know how I was going to get to Pamplona given the shape I was in.

Thirty minutes along the path, I saw a yellow arrow pointing upward and to the right, while there was a wide concrete sidewalk to the left. I hesitated.

Should I follow the arrows, or should I follow my intuition? My intuition said to go with the sidewalk, but the arrows clearly pointed in the other direction. The only guidance I received about the Camino was to follow the arrows, so I suspended my intuition and followed.

The path soon rose above the sidewalk and narrowed into a small, muddy trench that allowed for only one foot at a time, and sucked each foot into it up to the center of my calf, filling my shoes with thick mud.

I had to use my pole to free my foot with every step, swearing like a sailor the entire time. In the meantime, waves of pilgrims were cruising along the sidewalk down below, watching me and smiling as I fumbled along.

They'll see, I said to myself. *Who knows where they're going. At least I'm on the path.*

I continued my ridiculous struggle, soaked in mud, moving at a snail's pace, watching the people on the sidewalk stroll in the wrong direction with ease, satisfied that at least I was not wasting my time even if I was wading in mud.

Yet, a funny thing happened. My path never diverged from theirs. After 45 minutes of insane muddy struggle, my single-line gully spilled right out onto the beautifully paved sidewalk that the many misguided and very dry pilgrims who had been watching me struggle along had been walking.

Several even started laughing as I looked down at my legs, drenched from the knee down in mud. It was so absurd at that point that I had to start laughing as well.

"So much for following the rules," I said, shaking my head in a mix of disgust and incredulity. I was the only pilgrim who somehow missed the memo that walking along the sidewalk would take me where I wanted to go, and followed the arrows instead of taking the obviously easier way.

Well, that's certainly my Camino lesson for the day. Don't ignore the obvious!

That was such a perfect lesson for me. How many times had I ignored my intuition only to regret it? I knew better than that. Why did I ignore it now?

I knew in my heart when it came to all of my relationships that things were going terribly wrong, and instead of walking away earlier, I had just stayed in the game hoping that with enough loyalty and intention on my part, I could right what was wrong. I couldn't.

If anything, this internal conflict made me crazy. I still loved the people I was no longer connected to. I had loved believing in them. I trusted in the goodness of their spirits. I gave those relationships my all. Yet my intuition did tell me that giving my all was giving too much. That was my problem, and I intuitively knew it. Yet I ignored what I felt because I had been taught to stay in the game. Especially with my marriage. I said, "I do," and that meant don't quit, no matter what. Whose rules were those? Who said those were good rules? Yet I followed them even though I could have taken an easier path and wouldn't have suffered so much. No wonder everything blew up in my face.

This was the great dilemma of my life. Follow the rules, or follow my rules? As a good Catholic girl I was well trained in following *the* rules. Looking at the muck I was now soaked up to my knees in, I decided to follow *my* rules from now on. In fact, to heck with all the rules!

I walked with that decision all the way to Pamplona, which was, by the way, the longest walk ever. It was difficult enough to get there, but for Pete's sake, once I arrived I had to continue walking across the *entire* city to the old part of town to find my hotel. And after hours and hours of walking up and down, and up and down and up and down in the snow and rain, walking across Pamplona was mercilessly up again, and I had had it.

"Come on, Camino, give me a break! This is too Catholic! Enough suffering for one day," I cried as I miserably shuffled closer and closer to my destination.

I could already tell that this pilgrimage was getting to the core of some of my really ancient and limiting misery-making beliefs. As I pushed forward across the city, I began to notice how my beliefs layered one over the other. Some were creatively empowering, allowing me to directly access my Higher Self, and to work with my guides and the loving energies of the Universe at my side. Others were imprisoning, set in childhood, perhaps even carried over from past lives, put upon me like chains by the nuns, the Church, my parents, keeping me small, powerless, and fearful.

What a contradiction I am, I thought, sadly shaking my head at the conflicting jumble of thoughts and beliefs running my life. *I know better than to be in this mess. Why am I still so stuck and suffering like I am?*

> *Please God, please, strip away all the beliefs I hold on to that keep me from being happily and authentically me. I am so, so ready to be done with all this old crap!*

I pleaded with God to help me as I walked. I knew in my heart that what held me back were beliefs that had been hidden away in the core of my being for lifetimes, like mold in the basement or cobwebs in the attic, festering far beneath my conscious thoughts. It was time to clear the muck all the way back to the be

But not all of those beliefs were crystal clear or co be wiped away with mental Windex and—poof!—be a least not on an emotional level. I didn't want to feel bad. I didn't want to be angry. I didn't want to feel like a victim. I didn't want to be heartbroken. Yet I was. And I didn't want to be ashamed that I was.

And I was not only ashamed of my feelings; I was also shamed by others because of them. The nuns at school. My parents. Spiritual teachers that I had read and talked with. No one allowed feelings that weren't pretty. They all said or implied that having these dark feelings was not okay. It's not that I wallowed in them. If anything, I vehemently renounced, denounced, and denied them all my life as I was taught to do.

This Camino was now bringing up all these ancient and very deep wounds I had carried in my being to the surface. They were the wounds I had run away from. They were all haunting me, like ghosts. If I were to create what I truly yearned for, I would have to make peace with these ghosts. I knew it.

Looking up, I *finally* saw the stone gate leading into the old section of Pamplona.

Old Pamplona was exciting. It was medieval, with winding streets and open plazas that threw me back in time. The town was buzzing. Everyone was out on the street, even in the rain, drinking little coffees, eating tapas, sipping beer or wine. I hadn't expected such a vibrant and sophisticated crowd.

I actually found it confusing after the solitude of the day, so I asked a local, well-dressed elderly gentleman to help direct me to my hotel. Seeing I was a pilgrim, he decided that he would walk me there instead of pointing me in the right direction, for which I was immensely grateful, as I didn't understand Spanish and was too tired to wander around.

Five minutes later, I stood in front of a very cute little private hostel with the kind gentleman wishing me a "Buen Camino."

I could barely make it up the stairs with my bruised toes, but once I did, I was overjoyed to find Cheater sitting next to the receptionist's desk, and right next to it, an elevator!

Yea! Thank God for little miracles.

I had made it once again, and it was only 4:30. I had managed to get here in only eight hours, which seemed to be my pace.

My room was small but very comfortable. I was especially thrilled to see a large bathtub in which I could soak.

I wanted nothing more.

But first I had to spend a good deal of effort washing out my muddy pants, socks, and shoes, and blowing them dry at least a little.

Once that was accomplished, I took a very long bath.

It was 7 P.M. before I ventured out again to find some dinner. The bustling town I had entered was now completely deserted. I wondered if I had hallucinated the crowds I saw only hours earlier. Where was everybody? All the little cafés and bistros were closed up, and it was now a ghost town.

It was still raining, and it seemed like it was getting colder by the minute. I wandered into a small wine bar and asked what had happened to everybody.

The young man who worked there told me that after lunch everything closes until eight. Disappointed, as I knew I didn't have another hour in me, I asked for a glass of red wine and some french fries, which were delicious.

As I sat I thought of Hemingway's Pamplona and the famous running of the bulls. My Pamplona was a little different. I was running from the bullying of my own self-condemnation.

With that thought and now overcome with fatigue, I went back to my room to sleep.

I was getting into this.

Day 4

(23 km; 14 mi)

Pamplona to Puente la Reina

I shot straight up in my darkened room, gasping for air, as if someone were choking me. I was confused and disoriented, and for several minutes I didn't even know where I was. I sat breathing heavily, in the dark, trying to remember my dream. It was a variation on the recurring dreams I used to have as a child, where I was part of a secret religious order. In this dream a group of us was involved in a ritualistic ceremony. It was dark out, maybe even night, and I couldn't tell where we were. Suddenly I was being attacked from behind by people who had come to kill us. I woke up as I started to fight back.

I fumbled around for the light, my heart still pounding hard, slowly coming out of this nightmare and back to my body. When I turned the light on and my eyes focused on the room around me, I remembered, "Oh right, I'm in Pamplona."

I slowly began to move. Both my legs and toes were on fire they were in so much pain. Sighing, I got up anyway and looked at my watch. It was 6 A.M. I decided that I would take a shower to get my muscles warmed up, as it was once again freezing in the room.

"What's up with no heat around here?" I grumbled, feeling cranky because of the dream, my aching body, and the icy tile under my feet.

The shower washed away the hangover my dream had left me with, and I was soon feeling ready to tackle the day. Only my mood hadn't improved. I felt agitated and angry.

Even Gumby annoyed me, smiling stupidly on top of my backpack, as though without a care in the world. I promptly threw him into Cheater and zipped him away saying, "What are you so happy about?" I didn't wait for an answer.

Once again I had no window in my room, so I had no clue what the weather was like outside. Given that it was pouring rain and freezing cold when I went to bed last night, I decided to dress warmly. I put on my freshly washed and dry (yeah!) long underwear, my long-sleeve wool shirt, my clean (well, sort of) hiking pants, and two pairs of wool socks before I began to stuff my now completely trashed feet into my boots.

They rebelled. Under no circumstances were my toes going to be smashed in these boots for one more day. Screaming in pain, I backed out of them slowly and conceded defeat.

"Okay, okay, I hear you," I said to my angry feet. "I'll wear my other shoes and hope it isn't rainy like yesterday." Those barely felt any better on my toes, but they were soft and pliable, and once I had them on I was at least able to stand up and slowly move around.

"It'll get better, Sonia," I said, championing myself. "Just keep moving—one step at a time."

I managed to pack up my things and push Cheater into the elevator in ten minutes flat, and then I went to the lobby to get breakfast. I parked Cheater in the corner near the receptionist's desk where I had found him last night and wandered into the dining room. There I was greeted with a mouthwatering breakfast spread, which delighted me to no end, especially after having had only french fries for dinner.

There were croissants, cheeses, cereals, yogurts, fresh orange juice, and lots of fresh fruit, as well. *Feast or famine,* I thought. *I'm glad this morning is a feast.* I ate slowly as I noticed the other pilgrims sitting in the dining room with me. I had seen nearly all of them on the trail at one point or another over the last three days, so it felt natural to smile and say hello.

Two older Irish women, Margret and Val, who were eating breakfast together across from me asked if I was walking the Camino for the first time, to which I replied I was.

"And you?" I asked.

"We are here for the second time," they both answered, almost in unison in their lyrical Irish accents.

"We tried to do it about three years ago, but Val hurt her ankle after only five days, and we had to quit. So we are trying it again, only this time we are taking it in sections," replied Margret.

"What do you mean?" I asked.

"We are only going to walk for a week, then go home. We will come back next year, and do another week, and the year after another week until we are done. We pushed ourselves too hard the first time and so we decided to try this approach instead. And you? Are you walking the entire way?"

"I hope so," I said. "I'm not sure I can because I really hurt my toes, and it's painful to walk."

"I'm sorry," said Val. "Margret had the same problem the last time she was here. It's walking over the Pyrenees. You hit the front of your boots so hard as you descend."

"That's it," I cried, grateful for the sympathy and understanding. "I really bruised them and now they are so painful I can hardly stand up."

"Well, take it easy on yourself," said Margret, "so you don't end up like we did, and have to quit."

"I will," I assured her, not knowing how on earth I was going to be able to do that given that I had to walk at least 25 kilometers on average a day to keep up with my bag and my hostel bookings.

Oh well, if I can, I can. If I can't, I can't, I thought as I sipped my orange juice. *I'm not going to worry about it in advance.*

After breakfast, I got out my pilgrim's passport and had it stamped at the front desk before checking out and heading for the door.

I was greeted with a crisp morning and a bright sun, the first I had seen in several days. There was a light dusting of snow on the ground, apparently having followed me from Zubiri, and the sunlight dancing off it across the main square was breathtakingly beautiful. Suddenly I felt inspired.

Holy Mother-Father God, walk with me today, and help me make it to my next destination in one piece.

Just then I stopped praying to make sure I had remembered to put PowerBars in my jacket. I patted the pockets and yes, they were there.

I continued.

Please help me stay in good spirits as I walk, open and mindful of all the blessings the Camino has in store for me today.

Thank you and amen.

Taking a deep breath and setting my intention, I was off, my walking poles pushing me forward. Thank goodness for walking poles. They helped me so much. They guided me around obstacles, pulled me out of the muck, and kept me moving. I almost felt like a four-legged animal as I cruised along with them, and I liked the feeling.

As I walked, my thoughts drifted back to my dream, but the energy was no longer with me. It felt like a distant memory and was now out of my grasp.

I wondered why I dreamed that as I looked for the yellow arrows to guide me.

I intuitively felt that whatever I was revisiting in my dream had to do with the Camino itself and my own past lives on this path, perhaps as a pilgrim or a knight. But even the concept of past lives didn't seem quite right as I pondered this probability. It felt more like an alternate reality, one that I had reentered since starting the Camino, as opposed to a past one. But I couldn't say for sure, as these things are never crystal clear.

My mind couldn't stay focused on my dream for long, however. Once again, the path pulled me into the moment, and I had to concentrate fully on what I was doing. The arrows danced from here to there and if I didn't watch carefully, I could definitely wander off in the wrong direction. Also, to my utter dismay, the path was arduous and there were more steep, steep hills to climb along the way, which left both my feet and now my legs screaming in agony.

As I walked, the day began to reveal a theme, as it seemed to have done every day since I began. Today the theme that was emerging was *anger!*

I had woken up feeling scared and then angry, not unlike the way I had been feeling for the last few years. Of course, I wasn't angry all the time, but I realized that there were a few people in my life who left me feeling particularly irate. I also realized there were some recurring themes, or patterns, that I had in relationship to these people, which also left me feeling absolutely furious.

Apart from the people who made me so angry, the thing that really infuriated me was the long-standing message I had been given, ever since I was a child, that I wasn't allowed to be angry. Ever.

Whether it was my father or the nuns at school or people I had known along the way, I was told all my life that being angry was unacceptable. If I ever did get angry, I was told that I was out of line, dangerous, unacceptable, and deserved to be shunned or punished because of my fall from grace. And boy, was I punished.

It was as if being female and being "spiritual," or both, meant forever surrendering my anger and simply becoming some cooperative zombie who accepted whatever crap I was being dished.

"No fucking way!" I shouted to nobody.

Although I had received that message in one form or another my entire life, I never accepted it. I fought back. I rebelled. I refused to comply, to be meek, controlled, and submissive. Instead I was outraged. And if necessary, I attacked those who tried to force me to accept that message, yelling, screaming, raging my objections.

"Do not tell me what to do! Do not treat me that way! Do not act like such a jerk! Do not pretend you are not being a jerk when you are! Do not deny your passive-aggressive behaviors! Do not hit me! Do not ignore me! Do not call me crazy! Do not dismiss me! Do not manipulate me! Do not be a coward!"

And man, do I have a temper! I could become such a loose cannon that it was unbelievable. Maybe it was my Latin blood, but when provoked, I flipped.

I just had a fairly significant row with a male friend only weeks before I left. He had been drinking excessively over dinner and was getting more and more arrogant with each martini he downed. At one point I disagreed with him about something minor, and he jumped up and attacked me at full volume in the restaurant.

So I stood up and walked out. That wasn't the problem, though. Days passed before we spoke again, and once we did, he accused me of being too angry for him to be my friend.

It seemed it was okay that he let me have it with both barrels, but that I objected and gave it right back was too much for him. He said it made me "unsafe" to be around.

I seethed as I thought about this. Then I thought about my father. I was especially not allowed to get angry around him. If I got angry and talked back, I was silenced by a hard swat across the head, if not more, and sent to my room. He told me to "shut up and disappear." That thought made me boil inside.

Patrick also accused me of not having my anger under control. He was right. With him, I most certainly did not. He pushed every last button in me, and lately all I did was explode toward him. He was the single-most infuriating person I had ever known in my life, maybe with the exception of my mother. On second thought, he was definitely worse. Before he moved out, he only had to be near me, and I was angry that he was there.

The worst part, however, wasn't his or anyone else's judgment of my anger. The worst part was my own judgment and shame for feeling angry. I bought into the angry conspiracy hook, line, and sinker. I felt angry and ashamed of my anger at the same time. I couldn't win for losing. I was screwed all the way around.

I should have been able to control my anger. I should have been able to stay calm and centered. I shouldn't have gotten angry in the first place. I am spiritual. I am a teacher. I am guided. Why should I ever get angry? I had tools that showed me how not to get angry! I had gone to therapy and workshops to help me stop being angry. They all failed.

I was a failure and a spiritual fraud for being angry. All the judgment I received from others on top of my own far worse internal judgment buried me in more anger and more shame, creating a vicious cycle that sent me running. That was why I was here now, walking the Camino.

The more I walked, the more these angry feelings rose up in intensity and then subsided. After a long while, they rose up, but then slowly began not only to subside but actually to exit my body, leaving me with quiet in place of my inner rage. I didn't notice it at first. It happened at some point while I was engrossed in simply getting to the top of the next big hill, then the next, and then the next.

As my outer effort increased, my inner struggle abated. My sense of injustice began to ease up and my hidden shame began to lift a little as I breathed in and out, slowly putting one foot in front of the other, again and again, pushing my whole body upward. The muscles in my legs were on fire, melting into the extreme pain in my toes. I had no other option but to stay focused and keep moving, leaving my anger behind for now.

Eventually I started up a very long, steep climb known on the Camino as the Hill of Forgiveness. "What appropriate timing," I said to myself as I steadily made the ascent. I needed and welcomed this right now. The energy that came from millions of pilgrims over many centuries walking to this very point to be forgiven and to forgive was palpable. And now it was my turn to be here. But what exactly did I want to forgive today?

I couldn't answer that question because I couldn't stay focused on it long enough to find an answer. I had to use my full attention to simply get to the top, as it was the steepest climb of the day.

The wind was very strong, almost as if it were trying to push me back. I kept on. It was cold, but at least it was sunny and dry. Step-by-agonizing-step, I finally made it to the top.

Once I arrived, I looked around and caught my breath. I noticed that several other pilgrims were standing at the top with me, taking photos amidst a group of large metal pilgrim statues. Just beyond that others were looking out over the valley below.

Impressed with my accomplishment, I walked over and stood in front of the metal statues. "I made it, and I'm willing to forgive," I said to them, too happy at the moment to stay angry with anybody, including myself. "I don't want to be angry anymore. At least not now."

I stood at the summit, looking out to the valley below, and felt relieved. The view supported my decision, giving way to rolling hills and snowcapped mountains in the distance. Moving toward forgiveness by getting this far felt soothing to my aching heart. I felt how heavy pain and anger were to carry.

"Please, please forgive me," I prayed under my breath. "And please by the grace of this place help me fully, truly, deeply forgive the others." The wind blew directly in my face in response.

Soon my eye caught that of another pilgrim and I shyly asked him if he would mind taking a photo of me in front of the statues with my camera. He happily obliged, and by his accent I could tell he was Australian.

"Wow, you are a long way from Australia," I said, as he snapped away. I was impressed that he came all this way to walk the Camino.

"Yeea," he answered in his thick Ozzie accent. "That I am."

"Well, thank you for taking my photo. Would you like me to take one of you?"

"Sure, why not," he said, sounding neither here nor there about it as he handed me his phone.

Just after I handed back his phone, another man, who had just arrived at the summit, walked up to him and said, "I made it," while bending over to catch his breath from the effort. He was apparently his friend and a fellow Australian. They were funny and friendly, teasing one another and me, goofing off in the wind. It felt good to laugh.

Soon enough, we all had had enough of the Hill of Forgiveness and decided it was time to get moving again. It was freezing cold and too windy to stay any longer.

Even though the actual number of kilometers I was walking today was fewer than the previous days, due to the steep decline I was now on, it seemed like twice the distance. It took everything in me to remain grounded as I walked, as my lightweight shoes, unlike my boots, did not guard well against the rocks on the path. Without the strong soles of my hiking boots to protect me, the bottoms of my feet were becoming more and more bruised with each step. The round, smooth gravel that covered the path under my feet slid all over the place with each step I took, threatening to twist my ankle and sometimes succeeding.

"Great, this is all I need," I lamented, knowing this would only add to the challenges I had already had with my feet.

Thank goodness for my poles. They kept me from what could have been more serious injury. All I could do was take it very slowly, breathe, and concentrate as I made my way down.

Eventually I happened upon a café where the two Australians were casually seated outside, both drinking beers, looking as relaxed as if they were enjoying a day at the beach. It seemed as though they had bounded down the hill without the least bit of effort, like two mountain goats, which made me jealous and insecure. They both had on well-worn cowboy boots and no poles at all. *How on earth had they both managed to run down the hill so fast? And why did it take me so long? I'm not even carrying a heavy backpack, for Pete's sake. What's wrong with me? Why am I in so much pain? Am I really so lame that I can't take this without getting beaten up?*

A cascade of self-recriminating thoughts flowed through me as I made my way over to the table next to them. They didn't even have on warm coats, although it was bitterly cold out.

I shook my head at the injustice of it all as I set down Pilgrim and my poles. I looked at my watch. It was 10:30. I had been walking for a little over three hours. I entered the café and was greeted by a little old man who asked me, in broken English, if I wanted a "bocadillo," which meant a sandwich in Spanish.

"Por favor," I said, nodding my head enthusiastically, ready for some protein. One thing I'd noticed about the pilgrim's breakfast was that it was very shy on protein. Thank goodness for my PowerBars.

He pointed to the menu to ask which kind, and after looking it over I ordered an egg bocadillo and a café con leche. Suddenly, I was hungry.

He entered the kitchen and moments later emerged bearing a huge egg sandwich on a large crusty half loaf of bread, and a steaming latte.

"I'll never be able to finish this," I said as I took it from him. "And what a bargain." It was only 1 euro each for the sandwich and coffee.

I wandered back to the little table where I had left my things. The Australians were now gone, and I was left to enjoy my sandwich alone.

My first bite was hot and delicious and really hit the spot. Next thing I knew I had wolfed down the entire sandwich and was still left wanting more.

I finished off my meal with a protein bar and started to wash it down with the last of my coffee when all of a sudden I heard in the not-too-far distance several barking dogs. From the sound of it they seemed to be headed in my direction. I sat straight up and tilted my head to listen closely.

"Crap! I totally forgot to carry my pepper spray," I admonished myself. "Man, I hope I don't need it."

The dogs were getting closer, but at least I could run into the café if necessary, I calculated, shooting a look over to the door. I hadn't thought about demon dogs since I began the Camino.

I took the last sip of my coffee and held my breath, the barks getting closer and closer. I'd face them now and get it over with. I didn't want to run away.

Be calm, Sonia, I said to myself. *You are safe. Don't worry. Breathe and just don't look them in the eye.*

I reached for my poles.

"I guess it's just one of those kinds of days," I mused, remembering how I woke up feeling threatened in my dream.

Just then, the "wild pack" came running into view. They were two Chihuahuas and an old mangy mutt, no more than 18 inches high. I burst out laughing when I saw them.

My laughter scared one of the Chihuahuas so much that he nearly jumped a foot in the air when he heard me, and took off the other way. This only made me laugh all the harder.

Guess I passed the demon-dog test, I said to myself. *At least for today.*

Still laughing, I picked up Pilgrim and threw her on my back. I grabbed my poles and put on my sun hat. The wind had died down, and the sky was crystal clear. I did a quick calculation and figured I only had about ten or twelve more kilometers to go. I'd be there in no time.

The path evened out and my feet just whimpered instead of crying. One step at a time.

As had happened at the end of each day so far, a clarity set in that wasn't there only moments earlier.

As I walked I suddenly felt that I didn't want to be angry anymore, but that if I *chose* to be, or needed to be angry, I had every right to that feeling and would allow it without letting anyone guilt-trip me about it. Being denied the right to this feeling felt as though my power was being choked off. Anger signaled that my boundaries were being crossed. To be deprived of anger was to forfeit my right to my own identity.

I would never again feel shamed about being angry. Instead, I suddenly felt great protection of and compassion toward myself and my angry feelings. The angry "me" was the wounded "me." Underneath all that anger, the truth was that I was feeling extremely hurt. I used my anger to prevent myself from collapsing beneath the pain I was in. It distracted me so I could carry on. I wore my anger like armor, protecting the most vulnerable, needy parts of me. The parts I didn't like at all.

And I even felt some compassion for the vulnerable me under all the anger. I became fully aware of her. So much so that I felt like crying. Then I did.

And with that I became more calm and peaceful than I had been in my entire life.

I looked up. I could see the city sign for Puente la Reina. I had arrived.

Day 5
(21 km; 13 mi)

Puente la Reina
to Estella

My hostel should have been called "Hostile," I thought as I got ready to check out. From the moment I arrived yesterday afternoon, the staff who ran the hostel were, well, hostile.

When I first arrived, I limped in (of course) only to be greeted by a ten-minute wait as the two women at the receptionist's desk chatted away in Spanish to one another. Finally, one of the two turned to me and rudely said, "¿Sí?" as if I were interrupting her.

Once I managed to get across to her that I had a reservation, she looked at her book, found my name, reached over, grabbed a room key, and handed it to me without saying a word or once looking at me. Then she went right back to her animated conversation with the other woman. Looking around, I didn't see Cheater anywhere.

I waited for a pause in their conversation, then asked her about my bag, to which she only shrugged. I waited for a few more minutes, hoping their conversation would end, which it didn't, and then asked again. This time she rolled her eyes at me and pointed to a stairwell leading downstairs from the reception area, still saying nothing.

Guessing that she meant, "Look downstairs," I shuffled over and gingerly started down, suddenly aware that my knee was now aching like mad. Once at the bottom of what felt like a cave, there, in the dark, stood Cheater, among a group of many other bags. I picked him up and dragged him over to the stairs and lugged him back to the lobby with the last ounce of reserve in me. I then glanced at my key. Third floor again. UGGHH!

I started back toward the stairs, when the receptionist stopped me.

"No!" she said and nodded in the other direction.

An elevator. Hurray!

Smiling profusely as I pushed Cheater, Pilgrim, my poles, and myself into the small space that is a European elevator, I hastily pushed floor number 3 just to get away from them.

Once settled in, I went back out and had a small snack of some wonderful Spanish paella, the first I had seen on a menu since I started walking. I topped it off with a glass of delicious Spanish Rioja. The combination of fatigue, food, and wine knocked me out. It was five o'clock. Again, I skipped dinner and fell asleep by six.

I woke up to a beautiful day. I was especially happy because it was a short day ahead, with only 21 kilometers to my next town, Estella. While my body, and especially my feet, was still in agony, I was nevertheless looking forward to the adventure. The Camino was calling, and I could hardly wait to get going.

Breakfast was another buffet, this time a sad one. Dry pieces of bread, instant coffee, and canned orange juice. *What a loveless place,* I thought. I made up my mind that I wasn't going to eat any more than I had to because the food and the place had bad vibes, which I didn't want to absorb. I would rather stop somewhere else and pay for a better breakfast than punish my poor body with this substandard stuff.

I left Cheater at the front door with the other "Cheaters," clearly marking his next destination on a piece of paper and taping it with a Band-Aid again, in case the disinterested women who worked there weren't paying attention, and got under way. Still suffering aches and pains in all of my muscles from the strenuous physical effort I had put my body through, I had to go slowly. I had no other choice.

Just moments after I left the hostile hostel, I noticed a cheerful café down the street, filled to the brim with other lively pilgrims, and was drawn in for a more substantial breakfast than the one I had just turned down.

Settling into a steaming Spanish omelet, a freshly squeezed orange juice, and a freshly ground hot café con leche, I began to notice that whatever was going on inside me was immediately reflected in my experience on the outside.

Yesterday I was filled with anger, and that is exactly what I was greeted with when I entered the last hostel. I also noticed what it felt like to be in angry energy. And it didn't feel good at all. Today I was tired of it.

Drinking up the last sip of juice, I looked at my watch. It was nearly 9:30 in the morning. I had not started walking the Camino this late since I began, but suddenly I realized that there was no rule that said I had to start out early. Unlike the other pilgrims, who were in a rush to get a bed at a pilgrims' albergue in the next town before they were all occupied, I realized I could actually take my time.

In fact, leaving a little later allowed me to avoid the Camino "rush hour." In the early morning, droves of pilgrims fell into unison along the path, spilling out from the various hostels, pilgrims' albergues, and hotels to get their day under way. At times there were 20 or more pilgrims walking alongside me for the first hour or so. I was glad that I might miss all of that traffic today.

I didn't like the feeling of being crowded each morning, as the path was often so narrow that crowding was inevitable. It made it difficult to dial in on my own thoughts when a fellow pilgrim was so close to me I could hear his breathing. Because I wanted to avoid all of that, I ordered another cup of coffee and sat back a little longer.

It was nice not to rush, given that my feet were so sore. In truth, I was not exactly moving at much of a clip, but there was still the internal tendency to rush myself. I had been aware of this habit for some time.

Patrick had a much faster pace than I did, and from the time I met him I was often rushing just to keep up with him. He would often say, "Let's go! Let's go!" urging me to go faster still when I was going fast already. After living with that urging and pushing for 30 years, like being in a chronic state of emergency, I had internalized it as my own pace, although it really wasn't natural to me.

This internal pushing left me feeling me agitated and anxious. I decided with this new awareness to dedicate my day to moving at my own natural, calm pace, and not pressuring myself to get going, get moving, or hurry up at all, something quite different from what I otherwise did.

I slowly paid the bill, gathered my things, and then set off. Looking for the yellow arrows, I starting singing, "Follow the Yellow Brick Road."

On my way out of town, I had one last chance to admire the beautiful architecture. Puente la Reina was a major crossroads for several pilgrimage routes to Santiago. A magnificent Romanesque bridge with six spectacular arches was built specifically for the pilgrims to safely cross the rushing river at this point. In fact, the town itself came into existence just to accommodate the flow of pilgrims on the way to Santiago. I energetically fell into the flow with these past compatriots and felt personally strengthened by their numbers. As soon as I got a little way out of town and into the countryside, I stopped and said my prayer.

> *Holy Mother God, help me walk this day at my own pace and free me of the fear that I must go faster or get to the next town faster than is natural and comfortable for me. Keep me present to the gifts of the Camino today, and please help me ignore the pain in my toes, because it scares me.*
> *Amen, and thank you.*

Once that was said and my intention was set, I started off again, free of yesterday's angry energy, and now contemplating how to feel anger and express anger appropriately. Only I couldn't think of this for very long. The path itself once again demanded my full attention, and my thoughts gave way to silent focus as I concentrated on putting one foot in front of the other, looking for arrows and Camino shells to guide me along the way.

The good news was that aside from my toes, my muscles didn't feel as sore today as they had in the past few days. My body was starting to acclimate to the walking, and I felt stronger than any day up until now.

Walking along the path, I was taken by how peaceful it was. My soul actually felt nourished by the beauty, especially the parts of my soul that were so injured. I saw a falcon hovering over me in the air, not actually moving. As I looked up, a Swiss woman approached me and spontaneously shared with me that whenever a falcon is hovering like that, it is the Holy Spirit. I had never heard that before; nor had I ever seen a hovering falcon before. I took that as my inspiration for the day and felt energized and watched over.

It was still quite cold outside, but the sun was shining and the colors all around were gorgeous. The grass was standing tall and endlessly green, and the flowers were spectacular. I once saw a sign that read, "Flowers are God's way of laughing," and I thought that today was a laugh riot with all the bright reds and blues and yellows lining the way. I could not remember a time when I had ever been bathed in such natural beauty for so long.

Waking the Camino each day, I began to see the same people over and over as we made our way from town to town. When we passed each other, we wished each other "Buen Camino." I loved this tradition, as it was such a succinct way to say so many things at once. It literally meant, "Have a good way." It also meant, "Hello," "Carry on," "Good luck," and "Good-bye," or "I don't want to talk to you any longer, as I now wish to get back to my own thoughts."

It said all of this without ever leaving anyone feeling bad or confused. It was all just understood.

Today, for the first time since I started on the Camino, I felt like talking a little bit more to other pilgrims. Perhaps it was because my body was getting stronger and today's path was easier, so I had more available energy to converse. In any case, I was feeling social.

I stopped for a café con leche around one, and when I did I started to speak with the same Swiss woman, whose name I learned was Inga. She had been walking for almost two months and had started in Switzerland. I was so impressed my jaw dropped and I told her so. She had to walk through the Alps, and here I was barely able to hobble through the Pyrenees.

I told her how difficult it had been for me the past four days, and she said not to judge myself so harshly. It had been equally difficult for her at the beginning. She then said, "You know, it isn't the Camino that is difficult. It is carrying all your mental and emotional baggage that is so difficult. The Camino doesn't like this negative energy, and invites you to let it go. It's holding on to your misery that makes it feel so impossible to keep going. At least that is what I found."

I knew what she was saying was true. I had felt that myself. But it wasn't as though I could simply decide to stop thinking and feeling what I was thinking and feeling.

I had to let it travel into my consciousness, accept it, then allow it to leave when it was ready. I shared this with her.

"You are right," she said, nodding solemnly.

We finished our coffee and she set off for the restroom, and I set out on the path, as I have the bladder of a camel and didn't want to wait in the ten-person-deep line.

Once I started walking again, I came upon two other pilgrims who were standing by the side of the road. One seemed to be having great difficulty breathing.

I stopped and asked if I could help.

The one struggling, a man from Ireland, said he had asthma and all the fresh green grass and flowers were strangling him. He was really struggling to take a breath.

I showed him a few breathing techniques to help his breathing become less labored because I could see he was in trouble. One of those techniques actually seemed to calm his breathing down a bit. I was as relieved as he was.

After he thanked me, he assured me that he was used to this struggle, and that he would get through it as he always did.

"I just pray through it," he said, between gasps. "Seems to work, as I'm still here."

After sharing a "Buen Camino" with both him and the pilgrim he was traveling with, I set back on my way. Soon my thoughts began to return to my anger and what caused it. I wanted to get to the bottom of it so I could let it go.

As I walked it suddenly occurred to me that while I felt I was really generous with friends, exceedingly so at times, if they didn't return the generosity, or more exactly, the same spirit of generosity with me when I needed it, I would get really angry. And it was an anger that wouldn't let go.

That was not an easy revelation to have. If others didn't share the same values or have the same priorities, or more specifically, give my needs the same priority I had given theirs, I became deeply wounded and felt ripped off and exploited. This was at the root of a great deal of my anger.

Wow, I have never realized the depth to which I felt this before, I thought. Until I had this much time to be with myself, to walk alone in nature, and to examine what made me tick, I had never been able to identify this unconscious trap.

When I came to this realization, I knew that, once again, the culprit behind my misery was not other people but was me. As if a giant lightbulb had been switched on in a dark room, I finally understood what I was doing to cause myself so much pain, so now I could stop it.

I walked with this insight for a long time. The more I did, the greater the clarity about my anger descended upon me. My generosity toward others showed up at first in the form of enthusiastic championing, but eventually and sadly, caretaking and rescuing, taking responsibility for people who acted so irresponsibly they got into all kinds of trouble, usually financial. Time and again I volunteered to come to their rescue, until it wore me out. Always the classic hero saving the day—no wonder I was so angry. I was tired of this "Dudley Do-Right" act of mine. Those whom I rescued and supported came to expect it of me because I did it so freely, and after a time they didn't even try to meet their needs or responsibilities on their own because they didn't have to. It was a good thing I had severed these relationships—for everyone's sake.

Maybe I was unconsciously acting out my father's grand rescue mission with my mom, and attracted needy people in order to do that. While hers was a real need when she was a young, newly released prisoner of war with no family or means of support whatsoever, my so-called victims needed no rescuing at all. They just needed to grow up and take responsibility for their lives, and I needed to get out of the way so they could. If anything, they were enabling my unhealthy pattern, and I owed them an apology.

I also saw how playing the hero gave me a sense of control. Clearly, that was the payoff for me. It wasn't like I was consciously doing any of this, however. It was automatic. When anyone close to me seemed to be out of control, it stressed me out and I felt compelled to rescue him or her in order to restore a sense of normalcy. That, too, was a hangover from childhood, as there were many out-of-control and scary moments growing up in my family.

The Camino and I continued our deep conversation about this pattern when out of nowhere I stepped on a rock that suddenly rolled and threw me forward so quickly I fell and hit my head. It was as if the Camino were trying to knock some sense into me. Humbled but not really hurt, I couldn't help but get the message.

"Ow!" I said out loud, rubbing my bump. "Okay, I get it. I didn't realize any of this before," I said to the Universe, in my defense. "Now I do. Thank you."

I started to relax. Like uncovering a giant clue to solving a really old, frustrating, and painful problem, I was overjoyed. I understood. I could see how my own pattern caused me so much pain and rejection. Therefore I could find my way out.

"I'm going to adopt the attitude of 'Every man for himself,'" I announced to the Universe. Then I started laughing. "I'm just kidding."

But I did decide that I would not compulsively take responsibility for others anymore. It would take awareness and practice, but I was motivated. Anything else would only cause me and others more pain.

I felt a wave of relief wash over me, in spite of a simultaneous wave of physical pain and exhaustion shooting through my toes and body. I decided to rest.

I was tired of asking so much of myself and of others. I needed a break.

I reached into my pocket and pulled out my PowerBar. Like a gift from the Universe, there was a large rock on which I could sit and watch the pilgrims go by.

Drinking water from my water bottle, and then my water pack, I ate slowly and relaxed.

This was actually the first time I had allowed myself to relax since I had set out on the Camino. Up until now, each day had been fraught with low-level anxiety as I navigated my aching body along the path, fearful that I wouldn't make it to the next destination.

The weight of seeing how I set myself up to suffer and get so hurt and angry had been lifted. Now, seeing a way out of this pattern, my body began to let go of my sadness, leaving me feeling more spacious inside.

I also suddenly had faith that I would manage to get to Santiago, no matter what lay ahead. My body would make it. Somehow.

And with that awareness, a huge wave of relief washed over me.

I stood up. I still had quite a few kilometers to walk before Estella, the town I was headed for, and if today were anything like the days past, the last few kilometers would be the most difficult.

My mind was quiet for the rest of the way. I walked in silence and felt the spirit of the Camino as I did. This was a powerful path. I could feel the spirits of all who had gone before me, and it was humbling. I felt their souls accompanying me and cheering me on, their energy overlapping my own. I was alone but walking with millions.

As I walked I let go of expectation after expectation. It felt so freeing to have no expectations of a change. Not of others. Not of myself. What a great gift the Camino offered me today.

Day 6
(20 km; 12 mi)

Estella to
Los Arcos

I woke up before the sun and lay very still in my very small bed, in my very cold room, in the dark. I was stiff and in pain all over. Nothing in me wanted to walk anywhere today. I didn't even want to be here. I didn't care about the Camino. I didn't like Spain. I was tired of this entire effort and was ready to go home.

I couldn't remember why, for the life of me, I felt the need to do this. Walk across an entire country? What on earth was I thinking? My toes felt like they were ready to fall off, and my butt muscles ached like mad. What was the point?

I had gotten what I needed. I didn't need to suffer like this for one more day. And I wouldn't.

I chased around my mind for an escape route. I could take a bus to Burgos, which was the next big city, and from there I could take a train to Madrid and then fly home. I didn't care what it cost. I was over the Camino, big-time.

"That's what I'm going to do," I decided. "I can be home by tomorrow afternoon." The thought was liberating.

I turned on the light. Right next to it sat Gumby, looking at me as if to say, "You are kidding, right? Since when do you quit at the first twitch of discomfort?"

"Twitch of discomfort? I am about ready to lose my toes. This is more than a twitch—this is torture!" I argued back. He just smiled at me.

Ignoring him, I headed for the shower. I was freezing and needed to warm up. I could tell from the small window in my room that it was once again raining outside, which only added to my now substantial resentment toward all things "Camino." Groaning, I turned on the nozzle in the shower and "spritzed" myself with the trickle of barely warm water that came dribbling out for about five minutes. Then I gave up because this sorry experience wasn't at all doing the trick in helping me warm up.

Sighing, I stepped out and dabbed myself with the thin, miniature towel hanging up next to the shower. A Kleenex would have worked just as well. Then I sat down on top of the toilet and examined my toes.

Barely touching them left me shrieking in pain. Each toe was bright red around the toenail, and the nails themselves were nearly black. I had really bruised them, and the daily pounding that they took, going up and down the hills, didn't help. I had hoped to find a shop along the way that would sell some type of open-toed hiking shoe, but so far I hadn't come across a single one. I was still wearing my lightweight shoes, but the bottoms of my feet were getting almost as bruised as my toes were.

Getting dressed, I layered on more clothing than usual to fight the shivers. On top of the usual gear, I also donned a down vest I happened to bring along (thank God) and topped it off with my heavy windbreaker and cashmere hat. Then I headed down to breakfast.

The dining room was crowded with pilgrims, all happily chatting with one another. As soon as I walked in, several familiar faces cheerfully greeted me with bright smiles and warm "Good morning's." A fellow pilgrim named Joseph, from Canada, walked up behind me at the buffet and started up a conversation.

"How are you today?" he asked, with a cheery look on his face.

Not wanting to ruin his good mood with my surly one, I rallied and lied, "Great. And you?"

"I'm fantastic!" he said. "Do you mind if I join you for breakfast?"

"Not at all," I answered, not sure I'd be good company.

Yet, as soon as we sat down, I was glad he did. He laughed so easily and was so overjoyed to be doing this pilgrimage that his positive energy was contagious.

"This has been a lifelong dream for me," he said, wolfing down his toast, "and now that I am retired and in good health, I am so happy to have finally begun. It is a privilege to be here on this sacred road, with other pilgrims such as yourself."

I began to feel ashamed that I had been thinking of quitting only moments earlier. He was so enthusiastic that I started once again to reconnect with the spirit of the journey that had somehow slipped away in the night.

"You inspire me, Joseph," I confessed. "When I woke up I was not at all in the mood to walk anywhere today, let alone 20 kilometers. In fact, I was planning on quitting and going home early."

"Oh no, you weren't," he responded, brushing off my confession as if were nothing more than an insignificant passing thought. "You are just about to enter a new level of experience, that's all. It always happens like this. You've peeled away the first layer of your mind, and are about to start unraveling the second one. Don't worry about it. Just put one foot in front of the other and keep walking, no matter how you feel, and it will pass."

"Have you ever felt like quitting, Joseph?" I asked, just wondering if he were always this cheerful.

He laughed hard. "Every morning. I just don't pay attention to those thoughts. I just keep moving."

Then he turned to me and asked in earnest, "You don't really want to quit, do you? You've come so far. Over 110 kilometers by now from St. Jean to here."

"No, I don't. I'm just frustrated because my toes hurt so much, and it is so hard to walk in this much pain."

"Let me see them," he said.

"I'm too embarrassed to show you," I shot back, shocked that he asked. "They aren't pretty."

"Aw, come on. Since when are pilgrims' feet pretty? You should see mine."

That made me laugh.

"Okay, if you're sure."

I slipped off my shoes and pulled off my socks and pointed to the damage.

Taking out his glasses from his front pocket to get a closer look, he turned to me and said, "No wonder you're in so much pain. There's a lot of pressure under your nails because there is so much blood accumulated under there."

I nodded in agreement, glad to have some sort of explanation for the immense agony I was in.

"I used to be a nurse in the Army a long time ago," he said. "I'm going to tell you how to make your toes feel better. You must get a needle and gently, slowly go under each toenail and lift it off the bed just enough to release the blood. It will be painful at first, but once you do this, the pressure will be relieved. You'll feel much better, I promise. Do you have any alcohol pads?"

"I do."

"Perfect. And antibiotic cream?"

"Yes, I have that, too."

"Then you are ready for surgery," he said, laughing. "Just be certain to wipe off the needle with the alcohol pad before you begin so your toes don't become infected, and then put on some antibiotic cream after you've finished."

"Okay. I'll do it right after breakfast," I said, laughing with him. "Anything has got to be better than this pain I'm in. Thank you, Joseph. You are my first Camino angel on this pilgrimage"

"I am honored!" he said. "Good luck."

Finishing up our breakfast, we wished each other a "Buen Camino," and he headed out while I headed back to my room. Once inside, I grabbed my first-aid bag and fished out a needle, the alcohol pad, as well as the antibiotic ointment, and whipped off my socks. I was ready to do this.

Slowly, I worked the needle under my first nail. "Ow! Ow! Ow!" I said as I maneuvered the needle as far down as I could stand it. Then just as Joseph had promised, the nail released a lot of blood. I was surprised just how much, in fact. Fascinated, I then squeezed it to release more blood and instantly felt much better. How I wished I had known about this days ago!

Oh well, no use lamenting the past, I thought as I began to work on the second, then the third, and then the fourth toe, each one as relieved as the last to be freed of its misery.

I flopped back on the bed, taking in a deep breath of relief, before I began working on the second foot. Then I was at it again.

I proceeded a little too fast this time, and jabbed my toe with the needle, sending myself into more pain. *Learn from this, Sonia,* I said, talking to myself, Gumby closely watching me from the nightstand. *Go slow. Everything works out better for you if you go slow.*

Once I had finished the grand operation on both feet, I slathered antibiotic cream all over my toes, and then added some more for good measure, before putting on my socks. I was amazed at how much relief I felt as I eased my shoes back on. My toes were still sore, for sure, but not like they were only moments ago.

Suddenly I knew I could walk again and was even eager to get going.

"See, Gumby," I said, feeling more cheerful as I packed up Cheater and got ready to go. "We never know what good things are coming our way. I didn't expect a Camino angel today, but I got one anyway. And now, I can continue on without being in agony. Isn't that great?"

And because I was so happy to feel so much better so quickly, rather than stuff Gumby into my bag, I decided he could ride up front with me today, and placed him just under my backpack strap across my chest, looking out.

"Let's go," I said, not exactly running out the door, but certainly moving a whole lot faster than I had been the last few days.

After dropping off Cheater, checking out at the front desk, and getting my pilgrim's passport stamped, I walked outside into the heavy rain and started looking for the yellow arrows.

I saw one straightaway and followed it to a roundabout, but from there I simply could not locate the next arrow for the life of me. A man working in a garage not far from where I was standing was watching me walk around and around the roundabout. On the third round, he mercifully came out and pointed to the arrow I kept missing, and set me on my way.

"Apparently, it's my day for Camino angels," I said, grateful to be relieved of the frustration of going in circles. "Thank God."

I stopped to say my prayer for the day.

Holy Mother God, thank you for bringing me a Camino angel named Joseph this morning. I am so grateful for his help in relieving the pain in my toes. I especially appreciate the gift of his laughter and enthusiasm when I was sadly out of both. I ask for help on the path today, especially in finding the arrows and shells and not getting lost. Please make me aware of all the gifts the Camino will bring to me this day.

Thank you, and amen.

That said, I was finally on my way and looking forward to the 20-kilometer walk ahead of me. The first two kilometers led me through a suburb of Estella, an uninteresting walk winding toward a steep, rising hill. For the first time I was actually glad to see the climb ahead, as it promised to rescue me from the concrete dullness that I found myself passing through.

With my toes still tender but far better able to manage each step, I started uphill with less pain than I'd had in the first few days. The more I walked, the more beautiful the route became. The fog clung close to the ground as I strolled through vineyards with tall pines all around. I felt as though I were being bathed in clouds.

My spirits lifted more and more with each step, and soon I was singing at the top of my lungs as I ambled along. Nothing about this day felt strenuous, and I loved traveling all alone through such a magical reality.

The pines smelled wonderful and reminded me of the Sunday car trips our family took to the Colorado mountains every summer to picnic and play in the mountain streams. Suddenly I found myself feeling the same vitality and joy I'd felt as a kid.

The colors all around me seemed to pop with a brighter-than-normal hue, the sky a charcoal gray, the deep green pines dancing against waves of various other shades of green grass, with lots of tiny red budding flowers paving the route as if rolling out the red carpet for me as I walked.

Several times the route was so spectacular all I wanted to do was sit and take it in, and did. Just being in these glorious surroundings was pulling sadness and grief out of my bones. I could actually feel the energy of the ground underneath my feet, with a pulse and a force of its own. It was so strong that at one point I was compelled to slide off the tree stump I was resting on and sit directly on the ground instead. I didn't care that it was wet—my rain poncho kept me from getting entirely soaked. I even allowed myself to lie on the ground, wanting the earth to work even more magic on my heavy heart.

The path curved and wound through gentle pastures and eventually tumbled into a place called Irache, where there was a private family-owned vineyard, and just next to it, a fountain where pilgrims could fill up their flasks with free wine for their journey.

Not surprisingly, there were quite a few pilgrims waiting to fill up their flasks and water bottles to the brim. Not wanting to miss this free nectar, I took my place in line.

The young Frenchman in front of me was having a fit. Apparently, he didn't have a water bottle or flask in which to collect his wine. So I offered to give him the water pack around my waist. He was completely taken aback and asked me several times if I were sure, as he could tell that it was expensive.

I told him I was absolutely sure and, in fact, would welcome the opportunity to be rid of the extra weight. Besides, I had a water bottle with me, as well.

He took the flask and hustled up to the front of the line, where he filled it to the brim, laughing with glee at it spilled all over him. His friend stepped in front of me to take a photo of him, and then asked if I minded taking one of both of them as he, too, filled his flask. I gladly obliged, charmed by their boyish joy in getting free booze.

As soon as I handed back the camera, the two of them were off, and I stepped up to fill my bottle with a little wine as well, not wanting to miss my share of "the blood of Christ." The minute I turned on the spigot, a few drops spilled out and then nothing. The fountain had apparently run dry for the day. I couldn't believe it! I was so surprised that I had to laugh.

No good deed goes unpunished, I said to myself, half-kidding.

Oh well, I certainly didn't need to have wine so early in the morning. It was only 9:30. I'd wanted to partake of the ritual more than anything else, and that I did. Shortly after, two women approached the wine fountain, eager to get their free spirits for the day, and were as disappointed as I was to find it dried up.

We all shrugged in acceptance and decided to take a few photos of each other, if for nothing else than to remember the free wine fountain in the middle of nowhere.

The drizzle continued, as did the fog, as I once again set out on the path. Just a little past the wine fountain there was a monastery that had served pilgrims since the 10th century and had only closed in the last 30 years. It was locked up, as were all the churches and monasteries I had passed since starting out in St. Jean.

What is up with that? I wondered, frustrated at finding yet another locked door. I sat down for a minute just outside and pulled out my PowerBar, as I contemplated pilgrims walking by this very spot for over 1,000 years. It must have been brutal for the pilgrims back then. They did not have transporters carrying their Cheater bags, and they probably didn't have very good shoes either. I could only imagine what sort of devotion and faith must have powered them forward.

Although I was still moving very slowly today, I felt no desire to hurry up. I sat by the side of the road and watched as other pilgrims passed me by. I saw German, Japanese, Australian, Spanish, Italian, Thai, and Polish pilgrims; and that was in only 20 minutes. I marveled at how many cultures, races, and ages were still walking along this ancient route toward Santiago. Soon a chill spread over me, and I knew it was time to go. The only way to warm up was to start walking fast. I walked in silence and listened to the sounds of nature all around.

There were so many little birds singing to one another, and to me, at one point it felt as though I were listening to a choir. Their songs were soothing and made the kilometers go by quickly. Before I knew it, I had arrived at a small café, where I was greeted by even more pilgrims, most notably a group of Italians who were so animated and welcoming I felt as though I were stepping into a private party thrown just for me. I shuffled over to the one open seat at their table and decided it was time for a Coke.

Giuseppe, the self-appointed leader of the group, an exuberant and extremely handsome man, with thick dark hair, bright eyes, and a contagious smile, jumped up and introduced himself to me the minute I sat down. When I said my name was Sonia, he threw his arms up in the air and declared that he considered me an honorary Italian. "Ciao, Sonia!" he said, pronouncing each syllable the way it's supposed to be pronounced and never is. "So-knee-a, So-knee-a." He must have said my name five more times. It made me laugh.

I also met Cristiana and Augustina. Cristiana eerily resembled a woman who had caused me a considerable amount of pain in the past year. When I had first seen her on the Camino a few days earlier, I freaked out, thinking, *You've got to be kidding. She followed me here!* Soon enough I realized she was not my nemesis back home, but still I had a "yuck" reaction to her and had kept my distance.

So of course, being the Camino, here we were face-to-face. And, not surprisingly, this quiet woman sitting before me was perhaps one of the kindest and gentlest souls I could possibly encounter.

I listened to Cristiana as she tried to "show-and-tell" me, her Italian hands waving like crazy as she talked, that walking the Camino was her lifelong dream. She was a devout Catholic and had prayed to be able to do this for years and years, but never thought it would be possible. Then, out of nowhere, her boss at the hospital where she worked quite unexpectedly gave her the time off and the means to come this year, saying she was too old to make the journey herself so she wanted Cristiana to make it for both of them. And so, here she was. Cristiana cried when telling me her story, and I was so moved that I cried with her.

All of this unfolded while huddled under the one umbrella covering the table, trying to protect ourselves from the now heavy rain once again pouring down on us. We quickly finished our Cokes and agreed that it was time to get moving again. I pulled my rain-poncho hood over my head before I set out. Happily, the combination of rain poncho over windbreaker was like being wrapped up in a big plastic bag and took the sting out of the cold air. I looked at my watch. It was one o'clock.

I had another eight or nine kilometers to go before I arrived in Los Arcos, and with my feet still tender I hoped I would make it by four. Considering I was on an all-out "Camino strike" this morning, I was happy with my progress. *Who knows? I might even get there in time to take a nap and then actually show up for a real dinner for a change.* And with that I grabbed my poles and set off. I had a goal, and I wanted to accomplish it.

Once I started walking, I found my toes hurt a little less, mostly because I was so intent on following the arrows and not losing my way that I had little time to think about them. As much as the morning seemed to fly by, the afternoon dragged on and on. Never had it seemed as though I were going as slow as I was now. I felt like I was treading water and making no progress whatsoever.

"Help me!" I prayed when I thought I had no more gas to go on in me. "I have to get to Los Arcos today. I have no choice—Cheater is waiting for me."

Just then, a man walked up beside me, as if out of nowhere, and said, "Buen Camino." He was a cute guy, 6'2", thick head of white hair, friendly face, big smile, nice energy, and seemed to want to talk. Normally I preferred not talking on the Camino, as I talk all the time at home. I wanted to listen, to meditate, to pray, and to walk in silence.

Yet he seemed so kind, and I was really struggling to keep going, so I started talking to him as a way to distract myself, hoping that as we walked together I might make more progress than I had been crawling along in my own thoughts.

We exchanged a few pleasantries and the next thing I knew, I was pouring my heart out to him. With only the slightest urging on his part, I told him I was nursing a broken heart and was trying to heal from a lot of very old grief and pain that I had ignored my entire life. I shared with him how ashamed I felt over my marriage ending, how angry I was with my soon-to-be ex-husband, and how miserable I was with all the changes I was facing. I was making this pilgrimage to heal my heart and leave the past behind.

It was as if I were talking to a long-lost friend. I marveled at how much I just dumped on him, but he didn't seem to mind. If anything, he encouraged me to talk.

Eventually he asked me what my name was and I said, "Sonia."

I asked what his name was, happy to make such a wonderful acquaintance.

He said, "Patrick."

I was silent. I silently asked the Universe, "You are kidding, right?"

The first person I'd had a meaningful conversation with and openly shared my pain and grief with and his name was Patrick! I couldn't help but laugh out loud as I shook my head in disbelief.

Then I said to myself, *Of course it is. And of course I would meet him now, an hour after I just realized, with Cristiana, how important it is not to project my feelings from the past onto someone innocent in the moment. What a divine joke!*

Patrick asked me why I was laughing.

I told him my husband's name was Patrick.

He paused, and I could see that he was disappointed to hear that.

Then he said, "Let me guess. Irish, charming, good-looking, dark, argumentative, holds a grudge for years, moody, messed-up family, unable to get along ever?"

"Do you know him?" I answered, laughing even more.

"Well, I know the type. I was born and raised in the U.S., but I'm as Irish as they come, and those are my people. But, I hope that you don't hold that against me," he said, smiling but in earnest.

"Of course not, Patrick. Not at all."

In a few hours we were in Los Arcos. He was so light on his feet he was almost dancing, even with a huge pack on his back.

I shuffled in as though I were 95 years old, feeling as if I could barely take another step.

As we walked into the center of town, he asked where I was staying. I told him and asked him the same.

"I'm staying at a pilgrims' albergue if I can find one that still has beds," he said. "But I'll walk you to your hostel first if you'd like me to."

I told him that wasn't necessary, but was taken by his good manners and generous spirit. He walked me there anyway.

I urged him to get going, as it was late and the pilgrims' albergues might all be full.

Then he said, "You're right. I do need to find a bed. I tell you what. I'll meet you back here at 7:30. We can have dinner together."

I looked at my watch. It was four thirty.

"Oh, and by the way," he continued, "I promise I won't hit on you, so you can relax and enjoy my company."

That made me laugh all over again, and relieved me at the same time, as it had crossed my mind.

"I appreciate that," I answered. "I'll see you in a while."

He was my first dinner companion since I began this pilgrimage. I promised myself that I wouldn't talk about my pain with him anymore. I didn't want to.

At dinner we ran into other pilgrims we had separately met along the way and ended up having a fun time together, with lots of red wine flowing, although I couldn't keep up with the rest, and especially with Patrick.

Having been mostly antisocial up until now, I really enjoyed being with others and sharing our stories. The night flew by and before I knew it, it was almost ten, far later than I had managed to stay up since the day I began the Camino.

After dinner, Patrick asked me if he could walk with me tomorrow. I said no, but told him it wasn't personal. I liked his company a lot. I just needed to be with my own thoughts for now and found walking alone to be very healing, bringing with it tremendously valuable personal insights. He was gracious and said he understood. We then said good night, wished each other a "Buen Camino," and went our separate ways.

Before going to sleep, I wondered if I should have said yes to Patrick. But my heart and intuition were adamant. I needed to walk alone and in silence as much as I could. That was how I would heal. So I sent him good vibes and let it go. He was my last Camino angel of the day. There was no need to give it any more thought.

Drifting off to sleep my last thought was, *Patrick. Really, Camino?! Patrick?*

Then I was out.

Day 7
(26 km; 16 mi)

Los Arcos
to Logroño

I woke up at six the next morning to a crowing rooster, coming out of dream in which I was engaged in a deep conversation with a medieval scholar, maybe a monk, about entering the Order of the Knights Templar. In my dream I was asking what I had to do to become one of them. He took me to a library and was showing me old books I had to read to prepare for my "tests" when my natural alarm clock sounded.

I lay there thinking about my dream and wondering what my soul connection to the Knights Templar actually was. I'd had strong feelings, from a very young age, that I was somehow connected to the Knights Templar, but no matter how much I tried to remember just exactly what this connection was, the door to the part of me that might shed some light on this question remained mostly shut, allowing in only small snippets of remembrance that were hard to piece together. The feelings I carried in my heart around the Knights were heavy and oppressive.

I got up and turned on the light. I felt surprisingly refreshed and very hungry. I waddled over to the heater to check on my clothes. They were toasty warm. I opened the shutters covering my window hoping to see sun, yet was once again met with gray sky and heavy rain. Disappointed, I decided to be grateful for the rain. *At least it makes it easier to walk the Camino,* I thought. If it were really hot outside, it would be far more difficult.

Once I got dressed, I packed up Cheater and headed downstairs for breakfast. I had an extra-long day ahead of me—26 kilometers—and I'd heard other pilgrims last night saying that there were a lot of steep hills, so I was eager to get on my way. I was also starting to love the long contemplative walks and the insights that came with them, and looked forward to what the Camino would reveal today.

Breakfast was wonderful. The croissants were freshly baked; and there were Spanish omelets, bowls of fresh fruit, and juices available. And the best part was the delicious coffee. I had two cups because it had been days since I'd had coffee that tasted this wonderful. I was happy to start my day with such a great breakfast, as it meant I could eat one less PowerBar on the trail. My supplies were starting to dwindle and I still had three and a half weeks of walking ahead of me. Just to be sure I didn't eat them too fast, I had been putting only one bar a day in my pocket to eat on the trail, which was risky because some days there was nothing to eat or drink for long periods of time. I filled up my water bottle, made sure Cheater was clearly marked with the next destination, checked out of the hotel, got my pilgrim's passport stamped, and was on my way. It was 7 A.M.

The rain died down about an hour after I started out, and the sun began to peek through the clouds. The first few kilometers were easy and the route was mostly on a natural path, which was great, because on some stretches of the Camino I had to walk on concrete roads, or even along the side of the highway, and that was not easy on the feet and not a pleasant experience. But soon the route began to ascend, and I found myself climbing a gravel and rock path up a steep hill, which challenged my knee a lot. I used my poles to keep from sliding around too much, but I unwittingly had such a death grip on them as I sought to steady myself that soon my hands ached like mad. At least I had new pain to deal with, which distracted me from the chronic pain in my toes. For some reason, all these aches and pains, old and new, made me laugh. "I am hopeless," I said to myself. "Why didn't I read the memo that said it's better to get in shape for this thing?"

Eventually I fell into a rhythm and was able to ease my intense focus off of the changing terrain and drift back to my thoughts. Still thinking about the Knights Templar, I wondered why aspects or remnants of that past soul imprint remained so strong in me.

As I wandered over the first hill, I descended into a small village named Torres del Río. It was only 9:15. Soon I happened upon a small 12th-century octagonal church called Iglesia del Santo Sepulcro. To my delight it was open, the first since I had started the Camino. (I later figured out that all the churches are open every morning, but closed for lunch hours.) Upon entering, I discovered that this church was linked to the Knights Templar and to a similar octagonal church in Jerusalem, also called the Church of the Holy Sepulcher. The simple interior contained a rather scary-looking 13th-century crucifix, a vaulted ceiling forming an eight-pointed star, and not much more. Yet the energy was palpable and intense. I sat quietly and prayed for a while, remembering that I had forgotten to pray before I set out this morning.

> *Holy Mother-Father God,*
>
> *No matter what my past was or how it might be connected to the Knights Templar, I ask that this deep-seated heaviness and oppression that I feel is connected to it and that I've carried in my heart for so long—lifetimes, maybe—start to lift and be released as I continue to walk the Camino. If I have unfinished business or karmic lessons I've yet to learn related to this, please bring them to mind so that I might grow and complete this past. If it is no more than a hangover of another time past and does not serve my heart and your plan for me today, please help lift this energy and allow it to move on, and replace it with peace in my heart. I know this is a big request, but I hope you grant it.*
>
> *Amen, and thank you.*

I sat in silence and took in the grace of the church for a little longer. A moment later, a very old Frenchwoman, who had quietly entered while I sat, started singing a hymn in the most beautiful, strong voice, the acoustics of the church amplifying and filling the air with her song clear up to the ceiling. I closed my eyes and took it in. When the music stopped, I opened my eyes and turned around to thank her, but she had already gone. I felt grateful for this unexpected gift from the Camino. I remained a minute longer and then, like a flash, I could sense the spirits of the thousands of pilgrims gone before who had passed through these doors. After that, all was still.

As I continued walking, I thought about releasing the past. There was so much that I wanted to release. I wanted to release myself from the pain of all the relationships in my life that had fallen down like a house of cards in the past year. I especially wanted to release my guilt over my failed marriage. I wanted to release myself from the fear of my impending divorce. But the more I walked, the more I wondered why it was so difficult.

I certainly didn't want to hold on to these painful feelings. And yet, a mere mental decision on my part to release them hadn't worked. Goodness knows, I tried that, almost daily. So why was I still holding on to these feelings? Or were these feelings holding on to me?

It wasn't something that I could answer. I had an especially difficult time releasing Patrick. It was as if he and I were somehow connected in a way that didn't want to be released even though we both believed that we did.

I walked with this awareness for some time, simply noticing the energetic cord between us. It was a strong one. I couldn't shake it free. Since I didn't want to struggle with it today, as I was so used to struggling with it, I began to direct my attention back to the surroundings and feel the spirit of the Camino once again.

I walked for a long time, my mind now silent. Then I began thinking again.

Is there something I am hiding from? Is that why I can't release myself from what I want to be released from? I know I've hidden my real needs for a long time. Not just from others, but from myself as well. Maybe I want and need a lot of support, and I have been in complete

denial of this truth all of my life. Maybe I want to relax and stop prov-
ing to others that I am so spiritual by taking so much responsibility for
everything, and asking for so little, and then being angry because what I
was asking for wasn't really true. Maybe I am tired of asking so much of
myself, and I am angry that others don't feel the need to do this like I do.
Maybe I don't know how I feel and I am not as clear about how others
feel. Maybe I am completely confused. Maybe if I accept all of this I can
release the past more easily.

Those thoughts shot though me like a cannon. They were jumbled and confused and jumped all over the place and exploded to the surface of my awareness all at once, like popcorn kernels in hot oil. And they all felt so true.

"Fuck everything!" I suddenly screamed out in full volume. "I'm sick of all of this impossible expectation!"

That surprised me so much I had to sit down. The earth was so welcoming. So soothing. It didn't expect a thing of me. It felt kind to my soul. The truth was I only wanted to rest my soul, and my feet, without feeling guilty. And so I did.

Day 8

(30 km; 19 mi)

Logroño to Nájera

I had to pay close attention today. Yesterday, just before the turn toward Logroño, I missed the yellow Camino arrow and wandered three kilometers in the wrong direction. That meant walking an extra three kilometers back to get on track. Fortunately, a farmer saw me and told me to turn around as I wandered through his field. Had that not happened, who knows where I might have ended up. And, of course, this took place just when I was almost at the end of the day. AARRGGHH! It was torture. By the time I arrived at the hostel, I was nearly in tears from exhaustion and pain.

Today I faced another 30 kilometers. I couldn't allow myself to think about it too much because it caused me to worry before I even began. The only saving grace was that I hadn't had a single blister since I started. Thank goodness for the protection of double socks. A pilgrim I met at the hostel restaurant last night had to quit the Camino because he had developed such huge blisters that he couldn't walk at all. Suddenly my trashed toes seemed minor. At least I kept on moving ahead. The only other problem I was experiencing was with my ankles, as I had not been able to put my hiking boots back on because they were far too painful to walk in for long distances. Even with my "surgery," my toes still hurt to the touch and didn't like to be smashed into my boots. My other shoes offered no ankle support whatsoever.

The hostel in Logroño was basic. My bed was not much more than a simple cot, and once again heat was not available, not even in the shower. I didn't mind. I passed up the shower and curled up in my sleeping bag, wearing my long underwear and hat, and passed out.

The next morning I woke up starving, and couldn't wait to get to breakfast. Pilgrims' breakfasts varied quite a bit on the Camino. They were either extremely delicious and satisfying, or ran from various degrees of bleak to bleaker. This morning was the bleakest. One dried-out piece of bread, instant coffee, and butter if you asked for it three times. That was it.

At least I had the pleasure of commiserating with several other pilgrims instead of suffering alone. They were Anya and Martin from Germany, as well as Thomas from South Africa and Juan from Argentina. Both Juan and Thomas were biking the Camino rather than walking it. I asked them if they found it difficult. There were times when the path was so steep and slick from the wet rocks and gravel that I couldn't imagine biking on those trails. The thought itself made me weak.

They said no, but they didn't bike the trails. They mostly biked along the national highway and covered up to 65 kilometers a day, easily. They planned to complete the entire 840 kilometers from St. Jean to Santiago in less than two weeks. Wow! They were having an entirely different Camino experience than the one I was having. I asked them if they had time to contemplate the Camino and tune inward. They both said not really, but that wasn't why they were doing it. For them it was purely sport.

Interesting. The entire world is here and yet we are we all in our own world, I thought. They were off in a flash, with me wishing them a "Buen Camino" as they hurried out the door. Anya and Martin were exactly the opposite. They chose to walk half the distance at most that I was covering each day, and only planned to walk for two weeks before they would take the train to Madrid and go home. They said they would return next year and do two more weeks. With their pace and plan, they thought they would finish the Camino in six years. We all laughed about that.

Giving up on the breakfast, I dropped off Cheater, checked out, and decided to stop at the next real café and order an egg bocadillo, or sandwich, like the one I had a few days ago. My second breakfast was far more satisfying than the first, and I ate slowly and enjoyed it, taking my cue from Anya and Martin. While I had managed to slow down at times on the Camino, I still was intensely aware of how much I pushed myself onward all the time, so it felt good to sit back and decide not do that today.

Besides, even though I had an extra-long walk ahead of me, I had been arriving in the towns each day around 4 (with the exception of yesterday, of course, because I got lost), so another hour or two more wouldn't make much of a difference. The sun was still up and dinner wasn't served until 8 anyway, so what was the rush?

When I paid my bill, I also got my pilgrim's passport stamped, as I had forgotten to get it stamped at the hostel. I was so happy that I remembered; I loved my daily pilgrim's stamps. They were victory badges, each one saying, "Yes! I made it!" Each stamp reminded me of where I had just been and what it took to get there. I didn't want to miss any of them. Some were intricate. Some were religious. Some were nondescript. But having them in my passport recognized me as a true pilgrim. And I liked that.

Once on my way, I inched out of town, following the yellow arrows through what seemed like the longest, dullest, grayest, endless concrete suburb for hours.

Perhaps the only good thing about winding through this concrete misery was that I became acutely aware of just how important and healing it is to be in nature. Living in Chicago, I so easily got disconnected from nature. Now, I not only wanted to get away from the cement and back to nature, I realized how much I needed it. In spite of all the workshops and trainings I had attended, and the fantastic teachers I had studied with, nothing calmed my spirit more than walking alone for eight to nine hours a day in nature, with no distraction, no technology, no telephone, and listening only to my inner voice as I had been doing this past week.

By the time I finally managed to get back to a natural path, it felt so good that I was willing to walk it for as long as it would take me to arrive at the next town without a word of complaint.

My enthusiasm for the trail was short-lived, however. The rain from yesterday had turned the path into an ankle-deep swamp of sticky muck that threatened to suction my shoes right off my feet with every step.

"Aw, come on!" I complained to the Camino. "I was so happy to see you, and you treat me like this? No fair!" Each step took a considerable effort, as the ground was like glue, and I had to stop and retie my shoes again and again before I admitted defeat and just allowed them to be sucked off of my feet. This was ridiculous!

Eventually I found a dry spot in which to sit down and change back into my hiking boots, which I had tied to the outside of my backpack, as my lightweight trail shoes were no match for the muck.

When I slipped back into my boots, I nearly passed out in pain. But I had to wear them. They allowed me to be more sure-footed. The sticky mud didn't have the same suction-cup effect on my boots that it had on my shoes. I took three ibuprofen and wore only one pair of socks to ease the pain. It helped. While I still had to stomp as I walked, at least I didn't have to fight every step of the way.

"What the muck!" I swore to myself, not knowing whether to laugh or be incredibly annoyed at this new challenge. "Just when I think I'm prepared for what's next, I'm thrown another curveball. What a metaphor for my life right now."

Stay focused, Sonia. Just kept putting one foot in front of the other, and keep on walking, I urged myself, gently. At least the sun was out and it was warming up a little. The path was still fairly hilly, but it wasn't nearly as challenging as it had been yesterday.

As I walked, I began to notice mounds of stacked rocks, mini shrines created by pilgrims gone before, marking their prayers, their intentions, and the sacred nature of this pilgrimage. All of a sudden it occurred to me that I had forgotten to pray before I set out this morning, and I felt the need to do that right away, so I began to collect small gray stones to create a shrine of my own. Eventually I found myself by a lake and sat on the ground to set up my shrine and pray.

> *Holy Mother God,*
> *I am so grateful for this journey and those who have gone before me, marking the path and guiding me along the way. Thank you, guardians in the spirit world. Thank you for guiding my thoughts as well as my feet so that where I have been lost, I return, and where I might become lost, I catch myself. I feel your presence and again, I am grateful.*
> *Amen.*

I sat for a long while and listened to the birds singing in full force, thinking about my intentions for this pilgrimage. My prayer said it all. I wanted to return to my spirit and no longer be lost in the pain of my past mistakes. I wanted to be present and let the past go. I took a breath and looked at the beauty around me as I ate my PowerBar. Maybe because I had been unplugged from any technological distraction for over ten days, I found listening to nature deeply soothing to my heart. I didn't move for over 30 minutes. Then I remembered it was a long trek to the next stop, so I got up.

Every time I stopped to rest it took a few minutes to get going once again, as my feet and muscles still ached so much that with even a short rest, they stiffened up and didn't want to move. That's where my poles came in handy. I used them to pull me forward when my mind and body tried to hold me back.

As I walked I thought about praying. "God knows, there is always a prayer in my heart," I said out loud, again talking to myself. "It's not like I ever stop praying. So I wonder why, when I actually pray with intention, like when I set up that shrine, or an altar, it feels so powerful? I know God doesn't need my prayer. I guess that I'm the one who needs it.

"Isn't this pilgrimage a continuous walking prayer?" I asked, still talking to myself. "Aren't I praying just by being here?"

True, I thought. *But when I add my voice to that walking prayer, I feel even more available to God's grace.* I listened to the birds. *I see you pray by singing, so today I'll continue praying by singing, too.*

And with that I started singing one song after another, sloshing along in the muck. I sang songs I knew. I made up songs. I sang melodies I knew and made up the words. I sang hymns like "Amazing Grace" and "Hallelujah," and Rolling Stones songs like "Jumpin' Jack Flash" and "Angie." I sang Christmas carols and nursery rhymes. I used the rhythm of my boots, one foot in front other, as my percussion, and kept time with each step. The path had very few pilgrims on it today, so I was free to sing my heart out, and for that I was grateful. I am much too shy to sing in front of others. Before I knew it, I had sung all the way to Nájera. And then, like an oasis in the desert, right before entering the town square, I saw a store filled with all kinds of hiking gear, including shoes that would give my toes a break.

I was so grateful I almost fell down on my knees in gratitude. "Yes! My prayers have been answered. Hallelujah! Thank you, Jesus!"

I walked into heaven's door, sat down, and nearly begged to the guy behind the counter to please help me.

He looked at me with pity. I was clearly another tortured ill-prepared pilgrim looking for relief. I pulled off my muddy boots, and socks, and showed him my toes, no longer concerned in the least with how ugly they looked.

He approached, and then, with only one glance, cringed, stepped back, and in broken English said, "Oh!" and then, "I am so sorry."

An hour and $250 later, I exited with not one but two pairs of brand-new hiking shoes to replace the miserable ones that trashed my feet. One was a pair of Keen's, a shoe with such a wide toe box that they looked oddly similar to clown shoes. Mine were bright orange to add to the circus effect. The other was a pair of Teva sandals, complete with two more pairs of gray wool hiking socks to cushion against the Velcro straps. My prayers had been answered.

I shook my head as I continued to walk down the main street, marveling at my good fortune. Then I had to laugh. Here I was, me, prima donna, Prada-wearing, city-slicker Sonia, wearing ugly rubber sandals, with even uglier socks, looking as though I just escaped from an Oregon crunchy-granola hippie farm. Even better, I was delighted with my Tevas and new socks! Overjoyed, in fact. Yes, a true spiritual transformation was taking place in me. I now even looked like a true pilgrim. And felt like one.

I hobbled onward with my now four pairs of shoes—one inside my backpack, two tied to it, one on my feet—and found my way to the hostel, which thankfully was not far away. What a day!

Day 9
(21 km; 13 mi)

Nájera to Santo Domingo de la Calzada

I woke up to a beautiful day. So beautiful, in fact, that I was eager to get on my way in case it started raining again. It was a shorter day today, only 21 kilometers, although a big section of it was straight uphill. No problem. I was getting used to that, and now that I had my new clown shoes on, I was ready to roll.

I wolfed down yet another unmemorable "pilgrim's breakfast," wondering if they got bleaker on purpose the further I got into the Camino. Two slices of toast and a small, but not bad, café con leche were all they had to offer, and I had to ask for the second piece of toast while facing down a hostile stare in response. That experience behind me, I put Gumby in my pocket, then packed up Cheater, which by now was far heavier than when I started out, and grabbed three PowerBars in spite of my dwindling supply, as I heard from another pilgrim that there might not be a place to stop and get a snack along the way. I wanted backup in case this was true.

I left Cheater in the lobby, got my pilgrim's passport stamped, and skipped out the door. I had on my heavy windbreaker because it was cool and quite windy when I left, but shortly into my walk I was dripping in sweat and had to take it off. It seemed like such a nuisance right then, and far more than I wanted to carry all day, so I stuffed it into Pilgrim and continued.

> *Holy Mother God,*
> *Please keep my emotions steady and my heart open so that*
> *I can learn what I need to learn today. And please keep me cool.*
> *Amen.*

The path was wide and lined with flowers of all colors, but mainly bright red poppies. That, of course, led me to start singing "I'm Off to See the Wizard" once again. With my clown shoes on, I felt like the Scarecrow, as opposed to the Tin Man I was feeling like yesterday.

Walking for so many hours in silence was the best meditation of my life. There were long passages where I found I wasn't thinking at all. I was simply present to the experience at hand. In many ways I had to be. Like following *Blue's Clues,* the detective show my kids watched when they were young, the Camino demanded my full attention. If I didn't give it, I might miss a pilgrim scallop sign or yellow arrow pointing the way, and wander off in the wrong direction. Fortunately, I was now developing a sixth sense about the path, so I caught myself earlier and earlier when I drifted, with only minor backtracking necessary to correct my course. Yet, every step counted.

As a result of not thinking, my heart was becoming lighter. So many of the things that I came to the Camino burdened with were slowly starting to shake free as either I dropped them or my perspective changed. The most significant change I experienced so far was how my anger and pain over my relationship with my father had given way to nothing but pure neutrality. I felt his spirit traveling with me and talked to him as I walked.

"Dad, I know you are with me," I said. "I can feel your spirit and, if anything, it is what I learned from you about going after things rather than shrinking away from them that gave me the courage and incentive to make this pilgrimage in the first place."

I thought of my father's faith. He was a man of few words, but he had a deep faith in God, and he instilled that faith in me. One thing my father never did was complain. He met whatever came his way with quiet resolve. He steadily did what he had to do. With seven kids, and all the trouble we brought to him (and it was a lot), he still got up every day, got dressed in his best clothes, always looked and acted the part of a gentleman with others, and worked hard.

He had strong values, and working was one of them. He had no illusions that life was supposed to take care of you. It was what you made of it, according to him. I never gave it much thought when he was alive, but my dad never went to college, and didn't read much because he was working all the time. And yet, people respected him. They treated him well and held him in high regard.

He sold tractors and farm equipment for a living and, as low-key as he was, his steady way with customers won him the salesman of the year award year after year, clear up to the point of his retirement. He was consistent and thorough and took care of his clients with the same devotion he took care of his family. If anyone had a problem, he worked tirelessly to fix it. His customers loved him for that and were loyal to him year after year.

The more I walked, the more I realized just what a good man my father was and how much like him I was, in both the good ways and a few of the stubborn ones. I rarely complained, and I didn't like to show weakness. Maybe that is why I never felt supported, whether in my marriage or with friends. Maybe I wasn't open to much support.

"Dad," I said aloud. "I am not sure doing it all by myself works for me. I think it's time I change that." A cool wind blew by in answer, as if to say, "Good idea."

As I walked, I noticed the birds were not singing today. All was quiet. The sun was getting hotter and brighter, so I pulled out my Foreign Legion–looking sun hat and put it on, happy for the chance to wear it.

Today was making up for the lack of sun over the past week. Eventually I sat down by the side of the road to cool off. Shortly after I did, a young man from Austria came down the path and said, "Buen Camino," and then asked if he could sit with me. I was surprised by his outgoing and forward nature, but welcomed him immediately. "Of course. Please do."

We talked for a moment, and he asked me how it was going so far. I told him I was, surprisingly, moving along and still in the game, although a little worse for wear because of my toes. He nodded in sympathy. Then I asked him the same question. He said it was okay so far, but he hadn't expected such cold weather and said it was a bit difficult, as he didn't have a coat. Without so much as a second thought, I asked him if he wanted mine.

He looked at me as if he misheard me. "Excuse me?"

I asked again if he wanted my coat. "I have a coat I don't want to wear anymore. You can have it."

"It's warm today," he said, "but that may change."

"No, I don't think so. It's almost June," I answered as I reached into Pilgrim, pulled it out, and handed it to him.

Surprised, he said, "This is a very nice coat. Are you sure you want to give it away?"

"I'm sure," I said. "And if you don't need it, give it to someone else."

He was delighted and stuffed it into his backpack.

I then asked if he needed any shoes, looking at the high-top Converse sneakers he was wearing.

"What do you mean?" he asked, laughing.

"I have many pairs of shoes as well. Do you want one?"

He laughed even more, pointing to his very large feet. "You Americans are so kind," he said, "but I doubt your shoes are big enough for my feet."

I had to agree. "Too bad," I said. "I would have gladly given you a pair."

"You are so generous."

"Well, I could say that I am, but I really don't want to carry extra things. If you take it, it's one less thing for me to carry."

"I see your point. Well, in that case, I am happy to accept the coat in order to lessen your load." Then after another moment, he stood up, lit a cigarette, and said, "Buen Camino, and gracias," and started walking again.

"Keep moving forward," the Camino urged me on. Even when I wanted to sit for a while, it wouldn't let me.

Soon I was getting a bit frustrated with my new shoes. They allowed small pebbles on the path to get inside the shoe and lodge under my socks. I was in denial that this was happening for a few hours, as I was so happy that I had relief for my toes, but eventually denial wasn't working. I had socks full of rocks, and it was as annoying as hell.

Every 15 minutes or so, I had to stop, take off my shoes, and shake them out.

"Why didn't that salesman tell me this was a possibility?" I grumbled. "He knew this would happen. I can't believe he didn't warn me."

Then, "If I create my own experience, what on earth do I hope to gain by all this constant aggravation? It is not like I didn't put effort into getting the proper footwear!"

I kept walking.

"Okay, fine. I should have broken in my boots, but still . . . this is too much!" I complained.

"So much for your belief that you don't complain much," I could feel the Camino respond to all my whining.

That silenced me for the time being.

I walked for almost four more hours in my clown shoes before I pulled them off for good.

"You guys are worthless!" I cursed at them. "You are fired!"

I shook out the countless small pebbles inside and stuck my shoes in my backpack, considering throwing them away on the spot instead. I put on my old boots once again. "Good thing I had the intuition to bring these along. Another four hours of tiptoeing through the pebbles is enough to drive me crazy!"

"Ow!" My boots hurt my toes. But I had no choice. At this rate, stopping every few minutes to shake out my shoes, I would not arrive before dark.

I grabbed my poles, pulled myself back onto the path, and kept moving forward.

Soon the path led me into what looked like a modern-day ghost town. There were many new houses dotting the landscape, and eventually, a brand-new golf course, but they all looked abandoned. It was weird—there were no people in sight. "How did this get here, in the middle of my medieval journey?" I wondered.

I imagined it was the tragic economy crippling Spain that had buried this town. But even such a logical explanation did not make the place any less strange. Walking the Camino takes you far out of this world and pulls you into another, far more mystical, more mysterious reality. To walk out of this mystical frequency and into a ghost town such as this felt like a time warp commercial break in the middle of my alternate reality, life-changing spiritual movie.

Escaping the ghost town, I entered the last stretch of the day, which took me along the highway. I had to play a bit of dodge ball with the trucks and cars whizzing down the road at European-driver speed. Once free of that craziness, I turned back onto a natural path, and soon started winding my way into Santo Domingo.

The closer I got to the center, the more charming I could see this medieval town was. Linked to this town was also one of the more romantic legends about the Camino. Apparently, a couple and their son entered this town on their pilgrimage and stayed at an inn. The daughter of the innkeeper made advances to the son, who rebuked her. She was so incensed by this that she hid a silver goblet in the young man's backpack and told her father he'd stolen it. The father had him caught and hanged. His parents, oblivious to his fate, continued on to Santiago and on their return found their son hanging on the gallows, but still alive. They ran and told the town sheriff, who was just sitting down to dinner, that their son was not dead, to which the sheriff replied that their son was about as alive as the chicken he was about to eat. Just then the cock stood up from his dinner plate and crowed. This miracle was not lost on the sheriff, who rushed to the gallows and freed the son and gave him a full pardon. This miracle was attributed to Santo Domingo, the tireless saint who worked his entire life to improve the route for all pilgrims, as well as build hospitals to care for them. This fable seems a bit far-fetched, given the amount of time it would take to get to Santiago and back, meaning two months or more, but I liked it anyway.

I felt my desire to heal my heart by walking across an entire country asking for forgiveness for my past karma was a bit far-fetched as well. But I believed in the power of my journey. Maybe that is what this chicken fable was really all about. That things can heal in what seem to be utterly impossible ways to the logical mind. That's what miracles are. There was chicken memorabilia in the windows of the little shops all over town. I bought a chicken postcard to help me keep the faith in experiencing a miracle of my own.

I walked a little farther and saw the magnificent Santo Domingo Cathedral, which I went directly to before even looking for my hostel. Walking inside took my breath away. I was especially moved by the complexity and beauty of the altar at the front of the church. It reflected both the power of the medieval church and the power of the Camino. I could hardly fathom how it was built so long ago, and what it took to build it in terms of manpower and money. The first version was completed in the 12th century, the last in the 18th.

The cathedral awakened in me the incredible depth of history the Camino contained. I felt the energy of the Knights Templar once again, and of the secret societies in the Church that oversaw the building of this edifice. The Camino was not only the path of forgiveness: it was also a path of great intention. To make this pilgrimage, one had to have great faith, as the challenges medieval pilgrims met along the route were often life threatening. I'm not sure why, but it felt in that brief moment as though this was not my first time here. Like a wave of energy descending over me, somehow I knew in my soul I had experienced this all before.

I sat for a while and then felt called outside. For the first time since I started the Camino, I didn't feel like rushing to my hostel, and instead went and joined a few other pilgrims I had met along the way to share a glass of white wine in the sun in the town square. The atmosphere was lively, everyone happy that the sun had shone all day and that it was warm outside, not to mention, of course, the feeling of accomplishment that comes with once again making it to our day's destination.

I relaxed and listened to the conversations swirling around me. At my table were two nuns from Mexico and one from Canada, as well as a Jewish man from New York who showed up to see what all the fuss was about. I also saw my young Austrian friend, whose name I learned was Eric, and a woman from Holland named Petra whom I had seen off and on since I began in St. Jean. We were all in a festive mood and drank wine and ate olives for about an hour. And then suddenly, the wine hit us all en masse and everyone started to leave, headed to their night's resting spot until dinner, including me. I was actually impressed that I had the energy to sit and enjoy everyone as I had. Usually I am so eager to rest that I just go straight in and take a nap. Today I wasn't tired at all.

My hostel seemed about as loveless as the town square was lovely. It had a small shower and a single bed, but I didn't need anything more than that. I took off my boots, took a shower, and then took a nap, knowing dinner was still hours away from being served anywhere in town. After eating all those olives, I wasn't even hungry. In fact, I decided that I just wanted to sleep until morning. So I ate a PowerBar and was out like a light.

Day 10
(22 km; 14 mi)

Santo Domingo
to Belorado

Breakfast at the hostel was all wrapped in plastic. The croissants were wrapped in plastic. The fruit was wrapped in plastic. The coffee was a small packet of instant coffee and small packets of powered nondairy creamer, wrapped again, in plastic. I graciously declined these offerings, saying my stomach didn't feel good today, so I wouldn't hurt the feelings of the kind woman who was pushing all these plastic things on me. I ran upstairs, packed up Cheater, grabbed Gumby from the nightstand, put him on the front of my backpack, got a stamp in my passport, and checked out, in search of a good place to eat.

> *Holy Mother God,*
> *Please help me get to Belorado. My feet hurt, and I need*
> *your help.*
> *Thank you, and amen.*

Not far down the road I saw an appealing café next to the cathedral. When I walked in, I saw two familiar fellow pilgrims, Alice and her sister, Kate, from Seattle, both in their early 20s, sitting in a booth. Kate's leg was propped up on a chair, and she looking as if she were in a fair amount if pain.

Once I greeted them I asked Kate what happened to her foot. She said she had severe tendonitis and couldn't walk, and was probably going to quit and take a flight to Germany to meet friends instead.

"Oh no. And what about you, Alice? What are you going to do?" I asked.

She said she would carry on. Today Kate would take a bus to the next town, and they would decide from there if Kate would stay on, but Alice was going to finish no matter what. Sitting with them was a young guy from Amsterdam, who seemed committed to carrying on with Alice. She wanted to walk by herself, though, and told him right then and there, just as I had told Camino Patrick two days ago.

It was good to see that I wasn't the only one who seemed to treasure my alone time on the Camino. Alice turned to me and said as much. I understood. Coming all this way and being in the sacred energy of the Camino was something to protect and savor. It was so easy to get dragged down with inane conversation that took one far away from its power if you allowed it. I still regretted having spent so much time dumping my emotional baggage on Camino Patrick the other day, even though he did not seem to mind at all.

It bothered me, though. I didn't want to squander my time or focus on my wounded ego. I wanted to heal my soul and get free of the wounded, selfish parts of me that kept me feeling like a victim.

After wishing everyone a "Buen Camino," I sat at the counter and ordered an egg bocadillo, noticing what a creature of habit I was. There were so many delicious things being served there, and I could have tried any number of them, but the egg bocadillo was now my go-to meal, as I knew I couldn't go wrong with it.

Once I was properly fueled, I resumed the walk. The day was sunny but cold, and I wished I had not given away my coat so soon. Still, I was bundled in layers and knew that as I soon as I was under way I would warm up. I was glad that Eric had the coat. He needed it more than I did.

The path out of town crossed a river, and as I looked down I wondered how on earth the ancient pilgrims crossed these rivers. This one was long and wide, and due to the rain, the waters ran fairly high. It must have been treacherous back then. I wondered if there were snakes in the water.

The path soon took me along the highway. Lots of people complained about walking along the highway, but I didn't mind it today. It could get a little scary at times, as the cars and trucks seemed to ignore that there were streams of people with backpacks walking along the edges.

In a way, I actually appreciated the break from walking over the round rocks and gravel that came with the dirt path. My feet, thanks to the stupid clown shoes I had worn, had quite a few big blisters now, and my Tevas with socks created the same problem as the clown shoes, with tiny rocks and pebbles getting stuck under my socks as I walked.

I was doomed to have sore feet the entire time. I had resigned myself to this fact, and now just made the best of it. At least walking along the highway, fewer little rocks could get stuck. I appreciated that small benefit.

The state of my feet was a disaster. I had purple toes, some blisters, and was now developing a strange burning sensation along the sides of my feet that grew hotter and hotter as I walked. I thought it might be a nerve running along the sides of my feet and wondered how on earth I would be able to doctor this.

Eventually the path vectored off the highway and back to the hills, and I found myself hiking up and down rolling hills under a now warm sun.

I had forgotten to take a PowerBar with me today, and the longer I walked, the hungrier I became. I kept hoping to happen upon a café along the path, as there were often a few, but today I just kept walking and walking and saw nothing in sight.

My blood sugar was beginning to drop and I started getting desperate. I needed food in order to keep going. I was at least 15 kilometers away from Belorado. I had to sit down frequently to keep from passing out, and even found myself wanting to fall asleep, as often happens to me when my blood sugar suddenly drops.

156

I pushed on for a while, but soon my body was on empty. *Crap.* I'd already drunk up all the water in my water bottle and didn't have anything at all to eat or drink. Why was I in such a hurry that I forgot to grab a PowerBar? This was serious. It's not like I could stop a passing pilgrim and ask if he or she had any food. At least that was the last thing I wanted to do.

I sat down and started to pray for help. *Maybe if I pass out, someone will find me and call an ambulance to come and get me. That would be wonderful.* I lay down on the ground and stared at the sky for about a half hour, when suddenly, out of desperation, I thought I would check in Pilgrim to see if there might be a PowerBar inside even though I did not put one there this morning. It was wishful thinking, really, but since I had no energy to keep going, I had nothing else to do.

I emptied the entire backpack right there on the ground and, to my amazement, out came a thin, unopened package of turkey jerky that my friend Debra had given me right before I left. I had stuffed it into Pilgrim in Chicago and completely forgot I had it.

I ripped that vacuum-sealed bag open as fast as I could and tore into the turkey jerky like a wild animal. I shoved strips of it into my mouth faster than I could chew and had to force myself to slow down and swallow.

"Hallelujah, another Camino miracle!" I was not to be left to rot by the side of the path today after all.

The protein fortified me and in about 20 minutes, the time it took for this stuff to hit my bloodstream, I was back up and once again on my way. I had eaten almost the entire pack, but kept some for later in case there wasn't a café until I came to Belorado.

I was so grateful for my find that I started singing once again.

"Amen! Amen! A-a-men. A-a-men, A-ay-men, ay-men ay-men, Sing it over."

I was now channeling Harry Belafonte from the movie *Lilies of the Field*, so happy to be back in the game.

The path twisted, turned, rose, and fell—and it was all very calming to my spirit.

I walked at a leisurely pace, not wanting to burn off my reserves in case I had to walk on the little I had for the rest of the day.

As I walked, for the first time in a long, long time, I suddenly missed Patrick. Not Camino Patrick from two days ago, but Patrick, my husband. At least I missed what I called "good Patrick."

We had traveled quite a bit together over the years, and had a great many wild adventures together. There were times when we had to scramble to find food, and it was always Patrick who succeeded. He watched over the food supplies for us and made sure I always ate well.

He was a wonderful cook, and when we were home, his dinners were legendary among all of our friends. *What I would give for one of his famous dinners right now*, I thought.

We also traveled many years ago across Spain and on to Morocco. It was early in our marriage, when we were so in love. I had fun with Patrick on that trip.

I began to wonder what had gone so terribly wrong between us. After all, I had married for life, and yet it was me who finally said, "I quit."

Being intuitive makes me highly sensitive to energy. Patrick's energy stressed me out. Maybe it was unfair that I felt that way. Maybe I should have been able to meditate more or be more detached and not so reactive toward him.

Maybe he was just nervous, and it wasn't fair of me to have a problem with it. All of these thoughts left me confused. He was who he was. And I was who I was. What would have been the solution? I so wished I could have come up with it because I missed him at the moment.

Maybe I am too high maintenance? I wondered. *Maybe I am so sensitive to energy that it's best if I live all alone and not be around anyone.* I was such an introvert that I ran for cover a lot of the time. I never minded being alone. Except I minded it right now, as I walked along this beautiful, wide-open path, flanked by thick forest on either side of me, with birds flitting to and fro in play. I thought of how much Patrick, who loved long walks in nature more than perhaps any other thing, would love walking the Camino.

I wished I could somehow share it with him right now.

"What a shame we screwed up," I said out loud.

Maybe we were both just too different and too wounded to be able to live together. I knew I had been carrying some wounds in my heart for a long time. Patrick had felt wounded, as well. He wasn't a bad guy at heart. He was as wounded as I was.

We hurt each other. And boy was Camino Patrick right about an Irishman's grudge. I have never met anyone who could hold a grudge as long as Patrick. I'd get over something pretty fast, but he could stew for days, months, years. I couldn't stand that about him. "Come on," I'd say. "Are you still upset? Let it go."

Maybe it's the difference between being Latin and being Irish. As a French-Romanian Latin woman, I can be hotheaded and have a temper, but I move on just as quickly. I blow up at times, but I don't hold on to things. Or at least I try not to.

In the end I was holding on to a lot of things, though, and I had a huge grudge against Patrick. So maybe it wasn't just him with this problem.

As I walked I was slowly beginning to realize that holding on to anything negative was truly harmful to me. The more I could work it through, then let it go, which is what I suppose forgiveness means, the better for my spirit.

So much was starting to shake loose and I could feel myself letting things go, bit by tiny bit, as I walked. But I wasn't fully there yet, as evidenced by the flood I'd spilled onto Camino Patrick once he asked about my life.

I needed help in letting go.

I often accused Patrick of having too much pride and not enough heart, and yet here I was, guilty of the same. I actually began to realize how much more "spiritual" I thought I was than Patrick. I felt he was not spiritual because he was more likely to be negative and pass judgment on things, and yet was I really any better?

While I don't generally pass a lot of judgments on those other than Patrick, I judged him mercilessly. So I wasn't really any better at all.

Just then a hawk dived-bombed and landed right in front of me. He looked straight at me and didn't move. I didn't move either, both of us only a few feet apart from one another. He stared right at me and I felt his spirit. The minute I breathed he took off, almost in slow motion. He was huge and graceful. In a moment he was gone.

That hawk was Patrick's spirit. I knew it. His totem was a hawk and he had many hawk visitations over the years. I knew his spirit had come to let me know that on a soul level he heard what I had just been saying. He was present to this awakening in me.

I wondered if my spirit ever came to him.

I walked in silence for another two hours, and once again, as usual, crawled into town, found my hostel, and shortly after dinner, passed out.

Day 11
(24 km; 15 mi)

Belorado to San Juan de Ortega

My hostel was brand-new and so comfortable that I nearly cried with relief and appreciation. Before I even checked in, I was offered a glass of red wine and some olives, and welcomed warmly by the owner, which was a first for me on the Camino. I noticed a sign that said they offered laundry service, which I was in desperate need of, as my little sinks were not doing the trick when it came to getting the mud and sweat off of my clothes. No doubt about it, I was starting to smell like a medieval pilgrim, and it wasn't nice. So as soon as I got to my room, I bagged up everything that I needed to wash and handed it to the lovely British receptionist. She told me she'd done the Camino five years earlier and had such a life-changing experience that she'd moved back just to help other pilgrims. I could understand. I, too, was having a life-changing experience already, and I had only walked 231 kilometers. I still had more than 600 to go.

Once I handed the laundry over, I took a very long, hot shower, and then fell asleep on my brand-new bed. I set the alarm for 8 P.M. and went down to dinner. It was wonderful. I had a steaming bean and pork stew, a fresh green salad, and a thick, creamy rice pudding for dessert. While at dinner, I met several other pilgrims who were equally enamored of the meal, because so far, most of them had been pretty bad.

Two American men, Charles and Lawrence, friends who now lived in two different parts of the world, Paris and South Africa, had arrived yesterday to begin their pilgrimage the next day. They both worked for the State Department and had decided to meet every year for one week to walk a part of the Camino. This was their second year. John and his wife, Frances, from Cleveland, were also here to walk a section of the Camino. They had already completed four days, and John was having a very difficult time of it. Apparently, he'd slipped on the wet rocks on the path two days ago and threw first his back out, then his knee, and he was in a fair amount of pain.

I felt better than usual and was happy that other than my really sore feet, I was in pretty good shape. After walking for the past ten days, I was definitely getting stronger and had no major complaints. We all enjoyed a nice chat as we drank wine, but soon enough we were all off to bed, ready for sleep.

The next day was clear, and the sun was out again. Hurray! I was eager to get going. I dressed in my freshly laundered (and now strange new shade of green-gray) clothing, loaded up Cheater, and put Gumby in my pocket.

"Ready, Gumby?" I asked just before I stuffed him in. "I wonder what unexpected new experience we will have today."

Breakfast was fantastic. I had three delicious homemade croissants, an egg bocadillo, two glasses of freshly squeezed orange juice, and two large, steaming hot, freshly ground cafés con leche. I was so stuffed I wanted to go back to bed. That meant it was time to start walking. Moments earlier John, Frances, Lawrence, and Charles had set out for the day, having gotten up a lot earlier than I had. I decided to take my time, sipping the last bit of my delicious coffee, before getting my passport stamped, and was headed for the door when John and Frances walked back in.

"Did you forget something?" I asked, surprised to see them again.

"No," said John. "We decided to quit. I am in too much pain to go on." His face was gray, and he could barely stand up. Frances had her game face on, saying it was a good idea and that she supported his decision completely, but she was clearly disappointed. She sat down across from me as I put on my hiking gloves, while he hobbled over to the computer in the corner to see if he could get their travel plans changed so they could go home.

"Are you okay with this sudden ending, Frances?" I asked.

She shrugged. "I have to be," she said, then added, "I should have trusted my original impulse and come alone. John insisted he join me, but he has had nothing but difficulty since the moment we began. I think his mind was not really here from the start, and it certainly has affected our journey."

"That's too bad, Frances. I'm so sorry to hear that. Can you send him home and carry on by yourself?" I asked. "Is there a reason why you should quit, too, other than the solidarity of being a team?"

"Oh, he'd never go for that," she sighed. "It's a nice idea, but it's not going to happen."

"Well, I hope he gets better and that it all works out for both of you. I'm so sorry you had to quit before you were ready."

"Me too," she said. "Buen Camino."

I put my small purse on, threw on Pilgrim, put Gumby in my pocket, got my beloved walking poles, and headed out.

Wow. I didn't know how I'd feel if I were with someone who needed me to be by their side every step of the way. It would drive me nuts to have to adjust to someone else's experience and not be able to fully focus on my own here on the Camino.

At that moment, I felt so grateful for my total freedom. It was a gift.

The first long stretch of the Camino was along the N-120 highway, but there was little traffic, so I didn't mind. Then the path meandered through a wonderful section of sweet-smelling pine trees.

Shortly into the walk another pilgrim who was walking fast and on his phone passed by me. That was a first. I couldn't imagine even getting service out here in the middle of nowhere, let alone talking to someone. Right behind him was a second pilgrim, trying to keep up, and given their body language it seemed as if the first was trying to get away from the second, and they were arguing about it. At any rate, it was clear they were unhappy with one another. Then he hung up and looked over at me.

My presence seemed like a welcome distraction for the first one, and he greeted me with a shy, but clear "Buen Camino." I felt his frustration as I returned the greeting, but kept walking. He slowed down and kept pace with me, hovering only two feet away as we walked for a full 15 minutes. Tall, around 6 feet, dark skin, and unruly hair, wearing a heavy windbreaker with many pockets, into one of which he shoved his phone into, he stuck to my side. He continually glanced over at me, ignoring the concept of personal space, so it was quite awkward. If I quickened my step, so did he. If I slowed down, he did as well. Finally I stopped in the hope of distancing myself from him and returning to my own thoughts and prayers, but he stopped, too, and sat down right next to me.

Okay, I said to myself. *Clearly this is a person I am supposed to meet.*

He was Greek and spoke very little English. I don't know Greek, but I do speak French, so we garbled together a conversation in a Greco-French mishmash but it worked. He was also walking for just two weeks, and today was his second-to-last day. The man walking with him was not his friend but wouldn't leave him alone. I nodded in sympathy. Camino time is special, and I understood not wanting to waste it in bad company. Or in any company if not wanted, as I felt I was doing as we sat.

We smiled and struggled to communicate. He seemed fragile somehow, and like me, was trying to find his lost pieces. I wondered if that was the reason most of us arrive here. His energy was also a little clingy, and I didn't like that feeling. After five minutes of chatting and smiling, I jumped up and said, "Buen Camino," and got going once again. I think he got the message, as I noticed he held back and waited for his "not-friend" to catch up.

Once I started up the path, I was relieved to be free of him. As nice as he was, I could feel how much he wanted to attach to me.

I wondered why. He had just met me. Maybe he just does that in life. I am so the opposite. I am a free bird; I don't want anything or anyone to glom on to me. I never have.

In many ways Patrick and I were well suited that way. He didn't mind the times we were apart, and neither did I. That is, until the end when I was away almost all of the time, but that was intentional so I could escape him. He minded that.

I quickened my step just in case the fragile Greek pilgrim caught up with me once again. As I did, the path began to gently rise. It was wide and wandered through majestic oak trees. Sunlight danced through the leaves and as I walked, I felt as though my soul were being bathed in pure love. I stopped several times and simply enjoyed being there. I got a PowerBar out of Pilgrim, rolled up my hiking pants for the first time since I started out because it was now so warm, and rested my spirit.

I could feel myself unwinding at the core, something I have rarely been able to fully do my entire life. My life was too crazy to let my sensors down. I was constantly on duty. I used my intuition to scan the borders, look for trouble, for openings, opposition, and opportunity. I did this for myself and for others. Because this was also my work, my inner self was on high alert almost all of the time, a state I was used to but which left me exhausted. Resting and relaxing my intuitive sensors for a minute felt so good.

I got up after I finished my PowerBar, as I still had a long way to go. Soon the path changed and I began a very steep uphill climb that seemed to go on forever. I had learned by now to take small steps and go slowly when going uphill, remembering to breathe as I went. I thought about the steep climb over the Pyrenees. "You've come a long way, baby," I said to myself as I took the next step. That seemed like a century ago. Thank God I'd gotten stronger since then. All I remembered was how emotionally scared I'd been and how physically threatening it felt at the beginning.

As I walked, I thought of all of the times fear makes something seem far worse than it actually is. It reminded me of my favorite quote from Mark Twain: "I've had a lot of worries in my life, most of which never happened." I laughed at that as I inched uphill, thinking about all the drama I'd put myself through just getting ready for the Camino. In retrospect, I could see how it was all such a waste of energy.

As I walked I noticed a group of French pilgrims, just off to the side of the road, sitting down to share a picnic in a group of trees.

I had been crossing paths with this group since I started out in St. Jean and I had to admire their style. Every day, one of the men dragged a fairly large wagon behind him, strapped to his waist, and in it were food, a picnic blanket, folding chairs, and several little tables. Every time I ran across them they were stopped by the wayside, sharing a "grande bouffe," as the French called a good meal, complete with wine, cheese, bread, and chocolate. I knew this because on several occasions I sat close enough to see what they were eating. It seemed like quite a commitment to drag a wagon of food along on the Camino, especially in the mud and rain, and over the impossible grooves and stones that lined the path, but then again, knowing the French, it might have seemed far more impossible to attempt the Camino without eating good food along the way.

I overheard them discussing the "sad American" who didn't have any sense but to eat a PowerBar instead of delicious food, not realizing I spoke French. It wasn't true. I did have the sense to eat well, just not the interest to go to the lengths they did to make it happen.

As I sat I realized I had forgotten to pray once again before I set out this morning. I felt badly about this, but then thought, *Maybe I am beginning to feel supported in the core of my being, so praying out loud is not something I now feel the need to do compared to when I started.* For the moment, I was at ease. I didn't feel disconnected from God's grace. I was sitting in the middle of it.

But that brought me to the next thought. I shouldn't think of prayer as only asking for something. I should be praying with absolute gratitude for all that I was experiencing, for each and every moment of this extraordinary pilgrimage.

Holy Mother God,

I feel so blessed by this mystical path and your love and guidance every step of the way. Thank you for allowing my mind and heart the courage to say yes to this pilgrimage, and for allowing me to receive all the blessings and healing I am experiencing on this journey.

Amen.

I stood up and said "Salut" to the French contingency, meaning, "Bye." They smiled, happy to hear their native language. Then I added, "Buen Camino," for good measure, to which they all answered the same back to me, in unison.

I continued on to the summit, which was over 1,000 meters high (or 3,280 feet), and once again sat down for breather. Looking around at all the beauty, I shook my head in amazement.

I marveled for a moment at the strangeness of where I was in comparison to my daily life back home and how very far away from it I felt, as if I were on another planet, in another world. I was. Perhaps it was the ley lines that the Camino follows, or the energy of the Milky Way overhead, but I genuinely felt as though I were not on planet Earth. This path was something different. Something extraordinary.

Eventually I started down the hill. This time I had to be more careful, as it began to really strain my knee. I traversed downhill as if I were skiing down a mountain, going from side to side at a gradual pace. It seemed to work. My knee felt better.

Thank goodness for Patrick, I thought. He was a professional ski instructor, and many years ago he taught me how to ski properly. Before I knew him, I just bombed straight down the mountain, getting really hurt many times.

He showed me how to gently traverse, back and forth, all the way down the hill and that made all the difference in the world. Skiing went from a weekly life-and-death experience in my native Colorado backyard, after which I profusely thanked the powers that be for saving my neck, to a truly pleasurable experience that left me uplifted and not at all injured.

Maybe I owed Patrick my life. Had it not been for him, I might be dead, or a paraplegic. I certainly was on that trajectory, the way I skied back then.

That brought me back to thinking about Patrick. I knew he would have liked this walk today. I wondered what in the world would have happened if we had taken this journey together.

We probably would have fought, I decided. We did things so differently. He would have walked so fast that I would have been annoyed and stressed out chasing after him. It would have ruined it for me. Or would it have? I wasn't sure.

Not long into the descent, the path rose again, at an even steeper incline than before.

I decided to take the same approach upward as I did downward. I crossed side to side as I ascended, my poles pulling me along as I did. I honestly don't think I could have made it without my poles. They pushed me along, pulled me up, coaxed me down, and kept me cruising.

After nearly eight and a half hours of walking, I finally arrived in San Juan. It was a small medieval village, and an important stopping place for the ancient pilgrims. I liked the feeling here. I crossed a small river and wound my way through old streets. Just as I passed the only pilgrims' albergue in town, two women came running out the front door almost gagging as they did. One caught my eye and said, "I seriously do not recommend that you stay here. It is disgustingly filthy and stinky inside."

My eyebrows rose in alarm. "Okay," I said, "I won't," knowing I was never going to stay there in the first place and decidedly grateful for that given their reaction to the place.

I looked for the name of my hostel as I walked along the path, and soon was right in front of it. It was a charming little place behind a small gated entrance and looked rather sophisticated, like a lovely boutique hotel. I was excited. What a treat.

I went to the front door and saw a sign that said no one was there and to report to the San Juan Café just ahead to get a key.

Five minutes further down the path I happened upon a lovely long terrace with pilgrims sitting all around, relaxing, drinking cold beers and small glasses of wine, and enjoying the warm sun. I looked around and right in the center was the San Juan Café. I took off my hiking gloves, placed my poles against the wall, and went inside.

The guy working the café was very busy and ignored me for over ten minutes while I stood at the counter. He was single-handedly manning the show, drawing cold beers from the tap, brewing cups of coffee, and uncorking bottles and pouring red wine.

Finally, he looked up at me and said, "¿Sí?"

I was a little intimidated, as it seemed as if I'd better spit out what I had to say and fast as I was intruding on his world.

"Yes," I said. "I have a reservation at the hostel down the road."

Before I could finish he shook his head. "It's full."

"No," I argued. "I have a reservation there. They expect me."

"No, it's full," he repeated.

I started to get nervous. This had never happened before. I reached into my tiny little purse, which carried my passport, my one credit card, my debit card, and my reservation list. I showed him.

"See," I said, almost sounding (and feeling) like a scared child, pointing to the paper. "Here it is. Here is the name of the hostel and my reservation number."

"Ah, no!"

He threw his hands up in the air with an over-the-top dramatic flair, and said, "I do not have this reservation!" clearly annoyed with me for bothering him.

He then grabbed a book from the shelf behind him and leafed through it in case he missed something. My heart was pounding.

"No, not anything for you," he said, triumphant.

"But here is my confirmation from Camino Ways," I argued.

"Ah, Camino Ways. They make a mistake. No Camino Ways."

I was so upset and tired I almost started to cry.

"Yes. It is here," I said, pointing to the sad crumpled-up piece of paper I carried with me, almost shaking with worry, fearing

I'd have to go to the dreaded pilgrims' albergue I had just passed, besides having no idea where Cheater might be.

At that point he said, "Calm down, peregrina. I check." He then pointed to a chair, poured me a large glass of red wine, and said, "Sit down."

I hope I don't need this, I thought, grateful to have it anyway.

He got on the phone and screamed at someone in Spanish for ten minutes, then he looked at me and shook his head. "I know," he said.

I breathed and gulped the wine down. I seriously hoped that meant, "I know where you are staying, and where your bag is, and that it is nearby."

He hung up and then said, "You are staying five kilometers from here."

"What? No!" I cried, far too tired to face the prospect of continuing on for that far. "What about my bag?"

"We have your bag, but your reservation is not here," he said, now reassuring me, as he clearly did not savor the sight of a crying pilgrim collapsed on his floor, and he knew I was going down fast.

"No worried," he said in bad English. "The man is coming for you. He will take you and your bag to the hotel."

"Okay," I breathed a sigh of relief.

I wondered who "the man" was, but I didn't care. As long as he wasn't going to make me walk another five kilometers today and he had my bag, the man was clearly my friend.

But a ride—was I cheating? I wondered.

No! I reassured myself. *I made it this far. If I got tossed a curveball and am offered a ride I'm going with it,* I shot right back, immediately shutting down that guilt trip.

"Where is the hotel where I am staying?" I asked the bartender once I regained my composure.

"By the highway," he answered.

"Will he bring me back here tomorrow, so I can continue on?"

"Sí, is okay. If you want," he said, getting back to the now piling-up orders being placed in front of him. He then poured me another big glass of red wine.

Funny how well this is going down right now, I thought. *It's been an up-and-down kind of day all the way around.*

Fifteen minutes later, a ramshackle old car drove up with Cheater in the backseat, as if to say, "Hiya! I missed you. Hop in."

The next thing I knew, I was checking in to the equivalent of a Spanish Motel 6, right next to the national highway.

This was not nearly as charming as the boutique hotel I had seen in San Juan. I wouldn't have minded it so much had I not seen the other one, but since I had, this felt like a big step down.

I judged too soon. It was a relatively new hotel, and my room was very nice, with twin beds, a very large shower, and a deep bathtub, in which I luxuriated as soon as I could fill it. It felt so good to have a bath to soothe my aching calf muscles.

It's good to be flexible and unattached, I thought. That had been the recurring lesson of the day. *Go with the flow. Trust the Camino. It all works out.*

"Thank you, Jesus!" I shouted out loud as I soaked.

Once I settled down for nap, I looked at Cheater and then re-membered, "Oh no—I forgot my poles!"

How could I continue? I needed them. I ran to the front desk and asked the guy who drove me over here if he could call the café and see if they were still there. He did, but soon shook his head. They were long gone.

Rats, I thought. Suddenly the walk ahead looked as if it were going to be a lot harder than today.

"Don't worry," I reassured myself. "I'll make it. I'll get some new poles once I get to Burgos. It's only one day."

That calmed me down, only leaving me to worry about the 24 kilometers between here and Burgos.

Just then I turned around, and there stood the Greek from earlier in the day.

"Sonia," he beamed, and glommed on to me like glue. "I am so happy to see you. We have dinner tonight, no?"

I wanted to say, "No!" but seeing that there was only one din-ing room and we were in the middle of nowhere, I could hardly do that. We would be having dinner together no matter what. I smiled and said, "Sí. Of course."

I met the Greek for dinner at 7. I was surprised that there were no other pilgrims, or people for that matter, staying in the hotel. It was only him and me, and the receptionist/waiter/cook. He was convinced that meeting me again, here in this unlikely outpost, meant we were supposed to spend time together, alone.

Maybe he was right, as this was the Camino after all, and nothing happened by chance. He asked me why I was on the Camino and I just pointed to my heart and demonstrated that it was broken. He shook his head, and then pointed to his own heart and said, "Me too."

Then, bit-by-bit, he proceeded to pour his heart and soul out to me. Through broken language, the use of his translation book, and sign language, he told me all about his childhood without a father and about his mother and the endless stream of men she had invited into their home, who abused him in every way. He winced when he said this. He then began to cry and told me he has been filled with shame and self-loathing his entire life, as well as so much anger that he thought he could actually kill someone. I could tell that he was in extreme pain, and I felt a great deal of compassion for him.

He talked more freely as the wine poured, and with every glass more details came forth. He confessed to his many deep dark secrets, including his sexual problems, his addictions, his financial problems, as well as his depression and suicide attempts. He then said that he had had a dream that told him to walk the Camino when he was in such deep despair that he thought he couldn't go on, and in that dream he saw my face, which is why he had looked at me so intensely that morning.

It took him by such surprise that he couldn't take his eyes off of me. He was scared to approach me when I sat down to rest because he knew I didn't want to talk to him, but he felt that he had to try anyway, so he took the chance, although he was very embarrassed to do so.

He felt that he'd lost me forever once I got too far ahead (ran away) and was out of his sight, and he was sad for the rest of the day, thinking he blew whatever the dream was trying to tell him. When he saw me again in the hotel tonight, he knew I was his angel and he had to tell me everything.

The Camino is a mysterious place, and I believed that what he was saying might be true. I, too, thought it was no accident that we had run into each other again in such an unlikely place, especially since he said he had only decided at the last minute to keep going because the pilgrims' albergue was so filthy that he couldn't bring himself to stay there for the night.

We spent the next four hours talking. I mostly listened. Then I told him he was a beautiful spirit. He cried some more and said that no one had ever said that to him in his entire life and that he didn't feel beautiful. I assured him he was.

As the Camino is the Way of Forgiveness, I asked him if he had found, as he walked, that he could release some of the pain from the past, and begin to forgive, sharing that this was what was starting to happen with me. He shook his head, and said, "A little. More now that we've talked." He then said he had to finish the Camino for all to be forgiven, but he couldn't do that at this time. He had to get back to work after tomorrow.

He said he was actually feeling disappointed with how little he had shifted since he began the Camino in St. Jean 12 days ago, although he didn't know what he had expected. Then he saw me this morning, on his second-to-last day, and his faith in God was restored. He said I was his soul mate and angel.

Maybe it was true. I don't know. I believe soul mates help each other grow on a soul level. They are not necessarily romantic partners, as so many people believe. In fact, I think they seldom are. They come together by divine appointment to help each other stay true to themselves and their authentic nature and soul plan.

In that regard we could have been soul mates of some sort. While sharing this time together did allow us to help each other, I have to admit I did not feel the same connection to him as he did to me. It felt almost as though he were trying to attach to me, which caused me to energetically put up my boundaries, although he seemed not to notice. He kept reaching for my hands and wanted to hold on to them and wouldn't let go. I let him until it became uncomfortable for me.

In spite of his needy energy, I knew he was extremely fragile, and I was grateful that I could be his sounding board and confessional, and help him see his spirit as separate from his experiences. I could tell that it lightened his load. I did my very best to help him see himself in a different light, the way I saw him, as a beautiful man with a beautiful spirit that he was now in the process of recovering.

I told him I trusted he would heal completely and encouraged him to believe it as well. He was quiet for a while and then said, "I do believe it. Now that I hear it from you, I do."

Sometimes experiencing a person who sees us in the light of our true spirit and helps us remember who we really are is all we need to recover ourselves. I had that in my teacher Charlie Goodman, whom I met when I was just a teenager. I also experienced this in my sister Cuky and both of my daughters. I've also always been able to be that for people, a clear mirror who reflected their light and authentic spirit back to them. I was grateful to be able to serve in that way for him. In doing so, my own spirit was uplifted.

I sat with him for as long as I could, but the wine and the extremely long day, as well as the intense concentration it took for me to communicate with him, were taking their toll on me, and I was starting to fall asleep. I didn't want to cut him short, but I needed to go to bed. I yawned and told him I would see him in the morning and wished him a good night.

We both got up and looked around. The place was desolate. The waiter had long since disappeared, and it was dark everywhere. I started heading back to my room when he asked where it was. I told him and he said, "I am just across the hall." I smiled and turned to open my door when he grabbed me from behind and tried to kiss me.

I fended him off, which wasn't easy because he was more than a little drunk by now, having finished off almost two bottles of wine. It was very awkward and he almost fell down, causing him to grab on to me once more and then try to kiss me again. I grabbed his hands, which were now groping me, and firmly pulled them down to his side as I helped him regain his balance and said, with a warm smile, "Good night. I hope you sleep well."

He looked as though he were going to cry, but I felt at this point it was more the wine causing this than his soul. I then turned as casually as I could so as not to embarrass him, and opened my door, saying, "Buen Camino."

He started to lurch toward me again, but I was too quick for him. I was in my room before he could take a second step.

"Whew! I said out loud, once inside the door. Then to my angels, "I'm all for being in service to someone's healing, but please, let it happen when more people are around. That was stressful."

Not knowing whether to laugh or be freaked out, I decided to laugh. We humans get so confused so much of the time, not knowing how to be intimate with one another. So many of us think intimacy should lead to sex, when in fact that is not the kind of connection we crave or need. I'm all for sex, but sometimes the connection we yearn for is one with ourselves, with our true nature and spirit. We can't get that from hooking up with others, especially strangers, although that is what so many of us do. At least I knew that this was true for me. I prayed for the Greek and thanked my angels for allowing me to be here for him tonight. I genuinely hoped I was able to do my part in our soul meeting. Two minutes later I was sound asleep.

Day 12

(22 km; 14 mi)

San Juan to Burgos

I got up at the crack of dawn, in order to leave before I saw the Greek again. On a soul level, I felt our Camino appointment was complete. There was no point in having to go through a long good-bye all the way to Burgos. Besides, I wanted to be alone and with my spirit and thoughts as I walked.

Before I left, I put Cheater in the lobby and marked the hostel in Burgos so we would meet up later with no problem. I nodded to the waiter/receptionist that my bag was here, and he nodded back, as if to say, "Got it." Then I grabbed a coffee and toast, but I ate fast because I was afraid if I stayed too long, my plan of escape would be foiled.

I asked the waiter for a pilgrim's stamp for my passport and with indifference he nodded to the left, where there was a stamp and ink pad sitting on the counter. I expected him to come over and do it as the others before him had done; but soon enough I realized that I would be the one to place the stamp in my book if I wanted one. I felt a little disappointed by the lack of ceremony over my hard-earned walk, but then again, my Camino matters only to me, so it was fitting that I put the stamp in the passport.

Right before I was to leave, I asked if the driver from yesterday was around to take me back to the original path as he had promised. The waiter said, "No, not working today." That meant either I had to walk the extra five kilometers back on foot or follow the national highway just out in front of the hotel all the way to Burgos. I decided to follow the highway since I had 22 kilometers to go, and today I was really physically tired. Exhausted, in fact. I didn't think I could manage an extra five kilometers.

Holy Mother God,
Help me remember that everything that happens on the Camino happens for a reason, and then help me to discover that reason.
Thank you, and amen.

The moment I stepped outside, I was slapped in the face with freezing-cold rain, and a lot of it. It seemed to be following me across Spain. I pulled the hood of my rain poncho tightly around my face and set off, this time without my poles. It is funny how attached to things we become. Walking in the windy rain without poles was torture. I could barely move. Maybe it was the fact that I had walked over 150 miles in the past two weeks and was fatigued. Maybe it was the cold rain. Maybe it was that the poles really did help push me along, and without them walking was a lot more difficult. In any case, I felt as though I were trudging through cement, and I could barely move ahead.

Holy Mother God,
I need your help. Walking seems so difficult today, and I'm afraid I'll end up stuck on this highway, out of gas and stranded. Give me the energy I need to keep going. Thank you.

I prayed as I walked, fearing I would never, ever make it to Burgos, and then what? It wasn't as if I could call a taxi, and there were no buses or other means to get there. After I prayed, I had the idea to listen to my iPod, and let the music help push me along, something I had not yet done on the Camino. It was the perfect idea. The minute the music started flowing through me, my mind quieted and my spirit came alive. I walked to the rhythm of disco, rock and roll, Indian chants, ballads, and Bible belting blues. I soared through the rain, singing along with the music as though on a magic carpet ride.

This worked until my iPod ran out of juice, and once again I was left in the silence of myself, with another 12 kilometers to go. I ate my second PowerBar of the day and looked around. Since I was on the highway, there were no rest stops in which to find respite from the cold, driving rain. I just had to keep putting one foot in front of the other.

I wonder how I can make this easier? I thought.

Then I began to think of all the things that dragged me down and sent my spirit running. Surprisingly what surfaced were things that had happened all the way back in my childhood and teenage years, long ago forgotten and dismissed.

Maybe it was because of the sexual abuse the Greek described suffering as a child, but I suddenly remembered several extremely traumatizing assaults I had experienced when I was a teenager, none of which I ever told anyone about because I, too, was ashamed to share them. Crazier yet, I even felt guilty over what had happened, as though it were my fault.

The worst was when I was around 16. I was called to do an intuitive reading for a man at his house in the mountains, about an hour from my home in Denver. (Yes, I can see in retrospect that this was an extremely dumb thing to accept, but then again, I was a dumb teenager.) He said someone I had previously worked with referred me to him, so I trusted that it would be okay if I went. It never occurred to me not to.

When I arrived he was a little drunk. That scared me, but I tried to pretend I didn't notice as I began the reading. Suddenly he said he preferred that I do the reading for him while naked, and pulled a gun out from under his jacket and put it against my forehead and ordered me to undress. I freaked out and pushed him back as far as I could. Then I turned to the right and ran for the door, going 100 miles an hour. Only the door was not on the right. It was on the left, so instead I ran straight into the wall at full speed, shattering my eyeglasses and leaving me dazed. Still, I managed to fumble toward the door and got out before he could stop me. Panicked, I made it back to my car and drove all the way home on the dark mountain roads, barely able see a thing without my glasses. I am sure the only reason I made it in one piece was because my angels drove the car home.

I didn't tell my parents because I was scared I would get in trouble for putting myself in that situation. I blamed myself for what had just happened and felt very guilty and ashamed about it. I didn't realize at the time just how much it traumatized me. I only came to realize it much later, as I had recurring dreams where I was back at his house, replaying the same scenario all over again, ending up in the same panic before waking up.

Eventually I just pushed the entire thing to the furthest recesses of my mind and forgot about it. Until today, that is. As I walked, it was as if I were right back at the scene of the crime. Only this time I got really angry over what happened. I started telling the guy off, as if I were talking directly to him.

"How dare you?"

"Who the hell were you to threaten a young girl like that?"

"A coward and a jerk, that's who."

"What a sick person you were!"

I screamed at him until I was hoarse, for the first time in my life giving voice to the part of me that went through this experience.

I was now grateful that I was alone on the highway with no one else around so I could yell as freely as I wanted. I wouldn't have had the same freedom on the trail, as there were other pilgrims sharing the path. How perfect was that?

As I yelled, the rain seemed to wash away the pain and terror connected to that event that had been lodged inside of me for all these years. I was being washed clean.

The more I expressed my anger, the more I began to feel exactly as if I were that 16-year-old girl once again. I felt my optimism, my enthusiasm, and my trusting spirit in full force. I felt my humor and joy and my intensely good intentions and desire to serve, and was amazed that those aspects of me had not been lost in spite of this experience. I had managed to keep these qualities alive in me even in the face of this threat to my life. I didn't shut down or become cynical. I hadn't internalized the belief that life was unsafe. I loved the strong and resilient spirit that I was then and still am.

It felt so good to let the part of me that had been so frightened so long ago have a voice and roar.

I appreciated the genius of the Camino. Yesterday I helped the Greek. Today, because of his story, it helped me. Before I knew it, I had walked another seven kilometers, my anger now quiet, replaced by a calm energy deep in my bones. I had unearthed and then let go of the self-indictments of shame and guilt I had buried inside of me over that episode.

I let go of blaming myself for someone else's behavior.

I let go of feeling as though I asked for the assault and therefore had it coming.

I let go of feeling I had to hide and pretend it didn't happen.

I let go of the need to beat myself up about it.

The combination of walking and letting my anger fly into the wind and rain freed me of this ancient experience. And with that, suddenly and surprisingly I was able to forgive the man who caused me this pain. What a troubled soul he must have been to go to that extreme in his own life. How sad and shameful for him.

I was left with only neutrality and compassion for him and deep self-love and appreciation for the vulnerable and naïve young girl in me. I could also see how that experience had set up a pattern of subsequent traumas and threats, all following the same basic story. And as soon as I recognized it, like a house of cards, all of the other similar old traumas came tumbling down as well.

For the first time in my life I was genuinely over them. That was true forgiveness, and it felt exhilarating.

I breathed in deeply as I found myself approaching the edges of Burgos. The rain had stopped as I ambled through a long stretch of industrial buildings on the outskirts of the city and ultimately found my way to the heart of town, and the towering cathedral standing right there in the center.

Before looking for my hostel, I walked into the cathedral to light a candle of gratitude for the healing I had experienced on my walk today. A dark place in my soul had just been returned to the light and I was feeling so much more peaceful for it. I was amazed by how the Camino was working its magic on me. I could never have planned this, or even known it was something I needed to heal.

The cathedral was an astounding masterpiece of Gothic architecture. It had an incredible vaulted ceiling and stained-glass dome, which were breathtaking. I was awestruck by their perfect proportions and grandeur, especially given they were created so long ago, sometime between the 12th century and 15th century when the cathedral was built.

I wandered some more and found a statue of Madonna and child, which touched my heart. Unlike much of the Gothic era, this statue evoked a warm, loving feeling and comforted me to look at it. There I sat and prayed for a very long time. Then I lit candles for my daughters and family, and one for the Greek. He helped me so much—more than I could have ever realized last night.

After touring the church, I left to find my hostel. I was relieved to discover it was only five minutes away. Cheater was there to greet me along with an elegant male receptionist who checked me in. Again finding a simple but adequate accommodation, with a single bed, thin pillow, and slightly larger bathroom, the heat not yet turned on for the day, I left my bags and set off to find better than a "pilgrim's" lunch, and then buy new poles. I succeeded in accomplishing both in a little more than an hour, which delighted me to no end. I then returned to the hostel. I was spent and needed to read, relax, and rest, which I did.

Day 13
(20 km; 12 mi)

Burgos to Hornillos del Camino

I woke up once again to gray skies and rain, so I layered up for warmth. I had washed my clothes in the bathtub and placed them on the heater (yes, there was one), so I felt refreshed and ready to go. Since the strange burning sensation across the entire side of each foot was getting worse, walking was getting more difficult. I rubbed arnica cream on each foot and wrapped my arches in some medical tape. That helped a little. Since my toes were starting to recover, I put my original boots back on. Thank God they felt okay, as I had a 20-kilometer walk ahead of me today. I wished I had another day to rest before carrying on, but my schedule didn't permit it, so I put that thought out of my mind.

Gumby was watching me from the nightstand, smiling away as usual. "Okay, Gumby, you get to ride in front again today," I said, putting him in Pilgrim instead of in Cheater.

As a precaution, I also decided to bring along my detested orange clown shoes in case my boots started to hurt my feet. I tied them to Pilgrim and threw in extra arnica pills so I could keep taking them along the way. My feet were on fire, so I added ibuprofen to Pilgrim as well. I was going to attack this pain head-on.

Once downstairs, I handed Cheater to the receptionist in the lobby; got my passport stamped; had an unremarkable pilgrim's breakfast of toast, yogurt, and lousy café con leche; and was on my way.

Before I set out on the path, I decided to visit the cathedral once again. There was a magnificent stained-glass window inside the church, which was mesmerizing. I'm not an expert in sacred geometry, but I knew enough to tell that this stained-glass window had a sacred geometric energy that I could feel. I basked in its mystical rose-colored hue as I said a rosary, asking for a miracle in my marriage. I wasn't sure what that miracle looked like, as I didn't want to go back to the awful relationship Patrick and I had been in. I couldn't. But I couldn't see the future either. Or feel it. All I could feel was my pain and the pain my daughters were in, as well. I had no idea if Patrick was in pain. If he was, he hid it well.

Once I finished my rosary, I decided to get another stamp for my passport at the cathedral, so I went to the back of the church to look for someone to do that. I was met by a kind man who asked me to follow him, which I did. He led me to the sacristy of the church, put on priest's garments, and then said a special blessing over me and kissed my forehead, saying, "Buen Camino, good pilgrim. You are a beautiful sister in Christ." Then he placed his hand on my back, near my heart, and said, "Have faith, peregrina. All is well."

This unexpected blessing let me know my prayers had been heard today. I felt encouraged as I left the church. Following the scallop shells marking the way around the back, I saw a young man sound asleep, or passed out, on the ground in a small doorway just behind the church. He had a scallop shell on his Pilgrim, which was lying on the ground next to him, and his feet were bare, his torn canvas shoes lying next to him. I stopped and looked at him for a moment. Then spontaneously I quietly bent down, picked up one of his shoes, and compared it to one of my clown shoes for size. Since I have fairly big feet, I was not at all surprised to see they were about the same size. I then untied my shoes from Pilgrim and placed them next to him, hoping they might give him more support than the tattered shoes sitting there. I don't know. He might have loved his shoes, but just in case he didn't, he might like these better. He didn't move a muscle the entire time I was near him. He was out.

Once I did that, I was ready to get under way.

Holy Mother God,
Help me enjoy every step of the way today, and not com-
plain.
Thank you, and amen.

I was happy to be leaving the intensity of the big city. It was surprising because I am a big-city person. I love cities, especially my own. And yet, having been away from all the craziness of a city for the past few weeks, leaving Burgos behind was a relief. I yearned for the calm and quiet of nature and looked forward to returning to it as quickly as possible. That took a little while, as I had to wind my way out of Burgos before I returned to more pastoral surroundings.

The rain had stopped and the sun was beginning to peek out, which I welcomed. Still, it was cold. My new poles were proving to be annoying. I had to twist them open to adjust them to my height, and yet, with each step I took they collapsed into themselves just a little. Every half hour or so, I found myself hunched over like Quasimodo, so I had to stop and re-extend them back to the original height in order to stand up straight. I lost patience with this constant interruption after a few hours, so I collapsed them altogether and hooked them onto my Pilgrim. It was going to be another pole-less day after all. At least the path was relatively flat.

I had now entered a part of the Camino known as the Mesata, which was a high plateau of mostly rolling hills, and large expanses of farmland and open fields. A friend of mine who had walked the Camino three years earlier told me that you really don't begin to enter the deeper contemplative spirit of the Camino until you start to walk across the Mesata. I wondered what he meant and if that would prove to be true for me as well.

The first thing I noticed was that there were few trees; there were wide-open spaces all around. It definitely affected my thoughts. I found myself less focused on my physical aches and pains and far more tuned in to my emotional ones today.

I began to wonder how I had contributed to my own unhappiness. How much was due to present-life mistakes, and how much was the result of past-life karma? I truly felt the answer was it was a bit of both. I knew I had karma of some sort stemming from past lives here on the Camino, and that perhaps part of my pilgrimage now was to seek forgiveness for those mistakes and sins committed a time long ago. I even felt that I had karma with Patrick and that perhaps he, too, had been involved in some way with the Camino of long ago. I wondered if I were a knight who had killed him. He certainly was metaphorically killing me this time around. Maybe he was someone royal and I was Knight Templar who was sponsored by him. Maybe I was corrupted. Maybe he was corrupted. Maybe we were both bad guys, and this now had to be worked out. It was entertaining to energetically try on various scenarios in my mind to see if any of them fit.

Not surprisingly, I once again closed in on the Knight Templar scenario. I no longer questioned that it was part of my past. But I did wonder about Patrick. Who was he in this past-life drama? Maybe he had been a poor pilgrim, and as a Knight Templar, I had failed to save him from attack on the Camino, which is why I felt so driven to try in this lifetime. Maybe I carried some ancient guilt over this that was asking to be released.

Maybe it was more sinister. Maybe he borrowed money and couldn't repay it, and I showed no mercy. Or maybe as a Knight Templar, I showed little mercy in asking for the poor (Patrick) to build our castle and made him work to death. Now I was getting carried away with my imaginings and guilt-tripping myself.

The Catholic Church was clearly a highly wealthy entity in medieval times, as evidenced by the incredible churches that dotted the entire length of the Camino. Building them took vast amounts of wealth, and while much of it came from kings and queens, some came from the people themselves, who were often poor beyond belief. I wondered where Patrick and I fit in with all that.

Maybe Patrick was a poor peasant and I was a wealthy Knight Templar, and that is why we needed to come back together again, to work out our past karmic differences of power. Maybe I abused my power and used it against him once upon a time and now owed him some form of karmic retribution to wipe the slate clean. I felt it was something like that, but it wasn't fully clear. But then again, maybe he was the bad guy and I was the "poor one." Maybe I was to forgive him so we could both be free.

That was why I was here. Upon finishing the Camino I hoped to have cleared any negative karma I had with Patrick so I could move on in peace.

Maybe going our separate ways was the miracle I had been praying for.

Still, no matter how I reasoned it out, it felt lousy. I didn't want to be divorced. I didn't want to go through that process. I didn't want to have a broken family. I didn't know what I did want, except for maybe, peace. Everything else, at this point in my life, seemed unimportant. I just wanted to be peaceful and accept what had happened between us and move on.

I came out of my thoughts because it started raining again and was getting windy. I tightened my rain poncho and huddled underneath it, hoping to block both the harsh wind and the harsh thoughts toward myself that I began to unearth as I walked.

I vacillated between extreme guilt and remorse, and intense anger. This lasted for quite a while. I tried to pray, and even sing, but my mind would not relax. I had worked myself into a fit of anxiety and tension, the walking doing nothing to release it.

I tried everything to calm down and come back to my spirit. I talked to my Higher Self. I talked to Patrick's Higher Self. I gave myself pep talks. I swore and told everyone I could think of in my head just exactly what I thought of him or her.

I yelled at God for a while, and even told Mother Mary and all the other heavenly helpers that they had failed me and I was very angry about it. Then I was done. I saw a café just ahead and was thrilled at the prospect of a rest, a Coke, and a snack.

When I arrived, I ran into my friend Camino Patrick from days earlier. I was certain that I had lost him to the Camino abyss, so I was happy to see him once again. He had the happiest Irish smiling eyes, which made me laugh and smile as well.

"Patrick!" I yelled, swooping in to hug him. "I thought I'd lost you forever!"

He seemed happy to see me, too. We sat and swapped stories of what we had each experienced since we had seen each other last. He was starting to develop a deep cough and wasn't feeling very well, and said everyone in the pilgrims' albergues was coughing and complaining of chest colds, bronchitis, headaches, and more . and it seemed to be spreading fast.

He looked weary and said today's walk was difficult because last night he coughed so much he couldn't sleep at all. Fortunately, the walk was shorter today than some and we only had five more kilometers to go. He asked if I minded if we walked together, and I said, "Not at all."

I know what it's like to walk when you are feeling crappy. Distraction helps. Besides, I was sick of my own thoughts today. As I stood up, one of my poles completely collapsed and I nearly threw it in the garbage.

"These stupid things," I said, telling Patrick how I left my poles and how useless these new and expensive ones were.

"Here," he said. "You can have mine."

"Really, you don't mind?" I said, grabbing for them before he changed his mind.

"No, I don't mind at all. I haven't used them once on the Camino. I prefer not to use poles. I don't like them."

Looking them over and seeing that they were exactly the same as the ones I left in San Juan, I was thrilled.

"Oh my gosh, Patrick, thank you so much! Now I can go on."

He laughed.

We started walking and I checked in on how he was feeling physically. He didn't want to focus on it for too long. He asked me how I was feeling instead. I shared with him that I had had an emotionally turbulent day and was swimming in conflicted thoughts about my Patrick, and my marriage.

The more we walked, the more he encouraged me to express my real feelings about Patrick, saying he could tell I was holding back. By the third or fourth time he pushed me to open up, I exploded. I ranted about Patrick for over 30 minutes, swearing like a drunken sailor the entire time.

While I had been aware of my frustrations for years, I don't think I had ever once allowed myself to cuss and curse about Patrick to anyone as freely as I just had. By the time I was finished, Camino Patrick seemed shell-shocked. All I could do was laugh. And laugh some more. I felt liberated from all that had possessed me all day long. Camino Patrick laughed with me. He seemed to feel just as good about it as I did. The next thing I knew, we were in Hornillos.

Day one: Starting out in Saint-Jean-Pied-de-Port, France, and walking into Roncesvalles, Spain.

START

My first pilgrim's dinner.

SANTIAGO DE COMPOSTELA 790

Day two: Wow! A long way to go!

Woke up to snow in Zubiri on day three.

Finally arrived in Pamplona.

This is where the wine ran out.

Cold and windy, but the first section is over!

Well under way, but
still a long way to go.

Arrived at the cathedral in Burgos. I look a little crazy here.

It's a long way ahead today.

Meet Camino Patrick.

Gumby and I are enjoying a proper pilgrim's breakfast.

This about sums up
how I felt walking
today.

Cussed all the way into Hornillos.

A real pilgrim's cloak from the Middle Ages hanging in a museum.

The inside of a small church in the middle of nowhere.

My wonderful hosts at the B and B.

Colum and me.

The knight's bridge.

Gumby and I are finding our rhythm.

A pilgrim totem cheering us on.

Running ahead of the storm in Astorga.

Just left my big rock on the pile of burdens at Cruz de Ferro.

The Knights Templar castle in Ponferrada.

Gumby sitting among the totems left behind at Cruz de Ferro.

Deciding to ride a horse along the Camino.

The penny I found on my glove

left to me by my father.

The path to O Cebreiro was gorgeous.

A guardian angel in yet another small but gorgeous church along the way.

The wise tree at
Triacastela.

"Scary" dog along the way.

The passage from the Bible that was highlighted for me to read.

The beautiful
sanctuary with
no one inside.

My friend, the mud.

Counting down to the last 100 kilometers!

along The Way.

Thank God for the signs

A makeshift shrine honoring prior pilgrims.

One of the Camino signs I followed.

Celebrating my arrival at the end of a *very* long day.

I've grown on the Camino!

I can hardly believe I am
so close to the end.

Hanging in there!

I'm feeling so proud of myself as I approach the end.

An egg bocadillo.

I could feel the spirits all around on this morning.

Made it! Standing in front of the cathedral in Santiago.

The pilgrims' mass in the cathedral in Santiago.

The tomb of St. James in the cathedral.

My pilgrim's compostela or certificate.

*

Day 14
(18 km; 11 mi)

Hornillos del Camino to Castrojeriz

After I had my "exorcist" moment of cursing like a mad person when I walked into Hornillos, 1 began slowly lightening up and letting go of some of the dark feelings that had had a hold on me for such a long time.

It started to rain hard as we ambled into the center of this tiny village and searched for our respective places to stay. Camino Patrick soon learned from other pilgrims that the only pilgrims' albergue in town was full and that the next one was at least ten kilometers away. At the same time, I found out that my hostel was not located in this town at all, and that I had to walk another five kilometers in the opposite direction to get there. Either that or I could wait and get picked up in an hour, said the Spanish pilgrim who called the hostel for me on his cell phone after I had walked from one end of town to the other three times and still hadn't found it.

Since Camino Patrick's chest cold and cough were worse than ever, we inquired if there were another room at the hostel where I was staying so he could stop and rest, but were told, "Sorry, but no." So, before he wasted too much time and fell behind the other pilgrims in racing to the next pilgrims' albergue, he decided to keep going. Sad to separate since we had just reconnected, we wished each other a "Buen Camino" with the hope we would meet up again along the way.

Since I had an hour to kill, I entered the local (and only) café and decided to order lunch. The place was jam-packed with pilgrims, so I had to wait a little while before a table opened up. Once it did, I immediately jumped on it, as I was cold, wet, and starving. Mine was a table for four, and since I had three extra seats, I motioned to three other pilgrims who were also waiting for a table to share mine, which they gladly did.

After we ordered our meal of pork, potatoes, and salad (the only dishes they served), we started talking to one another. All three spoke very little English. Two were Austrian and one was German. They had met on the Camino several days earlier and were now traveling together. The three of them then fell into an animated conversation in German, leaving me out, but I didn't mind, as I was too tired to make small talk in any language. I just wanted to eat and go to my hostel and take a nap.

Before I had a chance to finish even half of my meal, eat my dessert, or drink my full bottle of red wine (yes, there was always plenty of wine), my ride showed up to take me to the hostel. I turned to the guys and asked if they wanted to finish what I had left over, and before I even stood up, the wine was pouring and my food was on their plates.

When I got into the car, I asked my driver if Cheater had shown up at the hostel.

"Sí. Is there. No problem," she assured me, smiling.

I then asked her if she would bring me back to the Camino tomorrow morning.

"Of course," she answered. "What time you like?"

Hmmm. I had to think about it. "Is eight okay?"

"Is perfect," she said, smiling. This time I trusted I would get the promised ride back to the Camino, so I relaxed.

"Thank you. By the way, what time is dinner?"

"When you want," she answered, in an easygoing manner.

"How about 6:30?"

"Okay. No problem," she said, eager to please.

I was happy it would be early. I didn't think I would last much past that.

"Can I wash my laundry?" I asked.

"Sí. I will wash it for you."

"Oh, that's not necessary," I argued. "I can do it myself."

"No, you are peregrina. I wash for you," she insisted.

I was happy for the help. Once again, the dirt and mud and sweat from the road had settled into my clothes, and they really needed to visit a washing machine. Bathtubs and sinks just weren't doing the job, and I was embarrassed by how badly I stank.

My driver told me that the hostel was new, and that she and her daughter lived there and ran it. She treated me as if I were a guest in her home and I was grateful for her kindness. It felt good to be so warmly welcomed.

After a sound night's sleep, I woke up the next morning to a hazy day, but there was no rain in sight. The caretaker had breakfast ready: three hard-boiled eggs, fresh orange juice, and toast. She then asked to stamp my passport. As I took my last sip of café con leche, she motioned to the door and told me that Cheater was already sitting in the backseat of her car and she would drive it to the next hostel. That, too, was a relief. Some days I worried that he would get lost because other pilgrims had told me their transported bags were lost for almost two days. I hopped in her old dusty car and settled in. Fifteen minutes later I was back on the Camino, Gumby riding up front with me.

As I took my first steps, the sun was starting to come out, but there was a stiff, freezing-cold wind blowing directly into my face. It got stronger as the day unfolded, and soon I was barreling into such strong headwinds I felt as though I would be blown away.

This was a first. I had been met with snow, rain, freezing cold, and now an arctic gale. Lucky me.

"Okay, Camino," I said, shaking my head, "bring it on."

It was time to pray.

> *Holy Mother-Father God,*
>
> *Help me face this cold wind with strength and keep me moving forward. I am open to all the gifts the Camino brings to me today.*
>
> *With gratitude,*
> *Amen.*

191

While I knew I had no choice but to put one foot in front of the other and just keep following the yellow arrows and blue Camino shells on the path, it was not easy. The wind was so intense I had to fight it each step of the way. It did, however, silence my thoughts, and I welcomed that. It felt good to focus only on the moment and be free of all thinking. I felt weightless and peaceful when I fell into those spells while walking.

Eventually, though, my mind became accustomed to the wind, so my thoughts drifted back to the circumstances of my life, and suddenly I was overcome with deep sadness. Up until now I was too angry to feel my sadness, or even allow it. Today it took me by storm. My defenses were dropping away, and my vulnerability was coming through. I also felt ashamed for feeling vulnerable, because I was taught by my father that being weak was not acceptable. Still, I couldn't stop. I started to cry.

As I did, I realized how defended my anger had kept me and how it actually blocked my deeper feelings of sadness and grief. I always considered Patrick to be the defended one. Now I realized I was just as defended as he was. I had wanted him to drop his defenses while I kept my own in place. That's unfair—like asking a knight to shed his armor while his opponent keeps his on.

I was afraid of Patrick's moods and how they controlled things. I was so sensitive that I absorbed his feelings like a sponge, and that brought me down and left me feeling as though I would suffocate. In response, I tried to fend them off so I wouldn't have to experience that energy. My efforts to please him were self-serving. I wanted him to feel better so I could feel better. It didn't work. And that left me feeling frustrated and angry. That is why I traveled so often. I never admitted it to him, but I did feel better when I was away.

The longer I trudged into the cold winds, the more confused I became. I felt a complete sense of failure. I have always carried high ideals throughout my life. I was in love with developing people's inner gifts, and had devoted my life to bringing their potentials to fruition. Seeing clients' lives transformed for the better was the joy of my existence. In my personal relationship, however, these very same high ideals created unrealistic expectations that left me feeling disappointed and rejected.

My mind drifted back to my recurring dream: the rituals, the heaviness, and now the despair and grieving feelings related to the Knights Templar. Could the demise of my very existence in this other life have occurred because, then too, I adhered to high ideals that were not shared by those I loved or served? As I walked, reflecting on how I had just ended so many relationships all at once, it felt as though I had re-created this entire story all over again.

I had to clear and release this energy. I had to let go of every-thing with love and forgiveness and compassion in order to be truly free. I had to stop believing that my noble ideals were the "right" way to live and allow everyone their own best way. That is exactly what "Buen Camino" means: Have a "good way," each one finding what that means for them.

I had to let go of the rigid standards I had not only set for myself but expected others to uphold, as well. Not consciously, of course. I had thought I was being loving and giving, when in fact I was imposing my version of noble living onto others. It was too much maybe—for them and for me. It was time to let these high ideals and dreams die. I needed to find a more compassionate, more allowing, gentler, and more accepting way.

Maybe I was tuning in to my soul history, maybe I was making it all up. It didn't matter. The message was still the same. Let the past go. Ease up. Relax. Allow. Forgive. Move on.

My mind traveled back to the natural surroundings. The path was captivating today, with bright green fields as far as I could see in every direction. I saw signs that said that before the Camino, this was an ancient and well-traveled Roman road. I wondered just how many people had walked it before me. Hundreds? Thou-sands? Millions?

I could feel the energy of pure love coming from nature as I walked. I did not feel as if I were observing nature from the out-side, as I so often had. I felt, instead, as though I were a part of the beautiful energy surrounding me. I was nature, too. With the next breath, everything came alive. The few trees were alive and watching me. The tall green grasses were alive and watching me. The birds flying overhead were watching me. I wondered, did they enjoy me as much as I enjoyed them?

The sun cast long shadows across the path, and for some reason when I saw this I suddenly felt my entire ancestral lineage on both sides of my family walking with me. I also felt the spirits of endless streams of ancient pilgrims walking alongside me. I could almost hear their footsteps and sense their breathing. I had entered some sort of alternate state where I was no longer bound by present time and space, even though I was still aware of it. I wasn't looking down on myself from above, but it also didn't feel as if I were in my "Sonia" body. Then, as if waking from a dream, I was back in the third dimension, back in the moment, back to me.

The Mesata was definitely having an effect on me. A previously darkened space within me was now filling up with light. It was remarkable to feel the ancient pain shaking loose and then falling away. I was almost afraid to notice or acknowledge what was happening, for fear it might stop. I was starting to feel the first rays of compassion for myself.

I recognized how all that striving served the development of my soul; it also caused me to disparage my natural human vulnerability. Keeping up my rigidly high expectations had worn me down.

I also knew in my heart that the reason why Patrick and I came together in this life was to find unconditional love and compassion, for ourselves and for one another. There was no alternative for either of us, and no escape. This joint destiny was the only real thing between us that mattered. Only I hadn't found it yet.

Eventually I entered the tiny village of Castrojeriz, realizing that the wind had all but disappeared.

Day 15
(25 km; 16 mi)

Castrojeriz to Frómista

I woke up early and was ready to leave by 7 A.M. It was to be a long day and I had been told there was a long, steep climb ahead of me, once again, with few rest stops along the way. So I packed three PowerBars in Pilgrim for added fuel, even though I was now down to only 12 bars. I didn't know what was going on with my feet, but unless I wrapped medical tape around my arches, I couldn't even take a step anymore, as they were on fire with pain. I was only halfway to Santiago, so I hoped the tape and my feet would last. Once I got going, the pain subsided somewhat, but if I stopped for even a few minutes, my feet went into flames of pain all over again. "Penance," I told myself. "This is penance for all my past sins. I am being forgiven bit by bit as I walk, but I clearly have to earn it."

Gumby looked at me from the nightstand, as if to ask if he could ride up front on Pilgrim today. I looked at him and said, "No problem. You're in." He made me smile. He made others smile, too, when they saw him. He was definitely earning his passage. He was a good little totem, and I was glad I'd brought him along for company.

Stuffing the rest of my belongings into Cheater, I headed downstairs for breakfast. When I got there, I met a young woman from Canada named Rita who was suffering with the same cough and congestion as Camino Patrick had. She was miserable because she wasn't at all dressed for the weather and couldn't seem to get warm, which is why she'd spent the money to stay in the hostel instead of the pilgrims' albergue.

I understood how she had come to be so underdressed. Who would have thought we would have needed to layer up like we did? After all, it was nearly June and yet it was still so cold it felt like it was no later than March (in Canada). As she shared her misery with me, the waiter piped up, telling us it was the coldest spring since 1816, and all of northern Spain was just as upset over it as she was.

I couldn't bear to see her so miserable, so I ran back upstairs, opened up Cheater, and grabbed one of my long-sleeve wool shirts, some thick wool socks, and an extra jacket I had with me, and gave them to her, hoping to bring some relief. At first she hesitated to accept them, but I insisted, so she gave in, putting everything on right away, as she was only wearing a light skirt and a thin top, a thin jacket, and sandals without socks!

Her cough sounded serious and her eyes were bloodshot, so I asked if she wouldn't rather take a day of rest and walk tomorrow, as it looked as though she might have a fever. She shook her head and said she was meeting her boyfriend in Frómista and there was no way to contact him, so she had to go on. I shook my head. The things women do for love.

I wished her a "Buen Camino."

I took a few more minutes to finish my breakfast and then went back to my room. I closed up Cheater, took him to the front desk, and got a stamp for my passport before I set out.

Once under way, I found the sky was clear and the sun was shining, but it was still freezing cold and windy. Ugh! Oh well, the only thing I could do was put one foot in front of the other and follow the yellow arrows.

In spite of the cold, my spirit felt calm today. The heaviness I had carried into the Camino was starting to lift a bit, and with it, I started returning to a happier state.

Holy Mother God,
Thank you for helping me clear the past.
Amen.

As I followed the Camino shells and arrows to the edge of town, I started singing, "I'm Off to See the Wizard," making up words to match the moment, laughing at my own silliness as I did. I even managed a skip or two, although it hurt my feet.

A little way out of town, I noticed an old man who was running, rather than walking, the Camino. He had on nothing more than runner's shorts and a tank top in spite of the brisk cold, looking as though he weighed no more than 75 pounds at most.

A Dutch couple walking near me noticed my reaction to seeing him and volunteered that he had been running on the Camino since France. They said he'd made a bargain with God when his 28-year-old son was diagnosed with cancer. He promised God that if his son lived, he would run the Camino 100 times. His son lived, so he was keeping his part of the bargain. This was his ninth time.

I had never seen such a skinny man in all my life, but I did notice that as he ran he had a huge smile on his face, as though he were in some sort of meditative bliss. The Camino does pull you into an alternative Universe filled with grace and magic if you are open to it. I'm sure that once he committed to his pilgrimage, he left planet Earth and was in another realm entirely.

Seeing him gallop along like a skinny racehorse was humbling to my aching bones. I wished him a "Buen Camino" when he passed by, but he was long gone before he could respond. Impressed as I was with him, I was fine with walking the Camino at my own slow pace. I've been pressured to rush ever since I was six years old and started school. Every morning was like fire drill at my house, as I rushed to get up, get dressed, eat breakfast, clean up my dish, grab my book bag, find my shoes and coat, and pile into the car, fighting my brothers for who got the window seat, all in the space of 20 minutes.

And if that weren't bad enough, when I dashed from the car and into school before the bell rang, I was met with fearsome, scowling nuns who rushed me through the rest of the day, with the threat of eternal damnation over my head if I fell behind.

The ability to go slowly was healing for me right now. Rushing around the way I often did at home didn't allow me to acknowledge my feelings. As a result, so many had been shoved aside and archived for another time, hidden beneath my conscious awareness.

Like things thrown into the basement that are not wanted or don't seem useful, my discarded, wounded feelings mounted until I reached a point where there was no more room to stuff them away. Now I had to clear out this old stuff in order to fully heal and grow as a soul.

As I walked, I remembered as a teenager watching a horror movie called *Don't Look in the Basement*. It was quite possibly one of the bloodiest, goriest, most god-awful movies I have ever seen in my life. Laughingly, I said, "This is my real-life encounter with 'don't look in the basement.'" I had to look in the basement, as the ghosts of my wounded emotions were now creeping into my conscious life and were not to be denied. I had to address these ancient feelings so they could heal. I couldn't hide them away anymore.

Maybe that is what transformation is all about. Feeling one's feelings then allowing them to naturally move on, rather than covering them up or pushing them away. It certainly was transforming me.

My mind drifted back to the moment, and the path.

It was demanding, as usual. I first walked across a plain and then up the promised long climb. It seemed as though I would never arrive at the summit. But by the grace of God, and having no other choice but to keep going, I finally made it. As I crested the peak, I saw a local man to the side of the road sitting by a little makeshift stand, selling coffee, water, and bananas. Since there had been no cafés along the way, he was a welcome sight. I ordered a bottle of water and a banana, both for only 1 euro, then sat down and looked around. Spring was bursting forth in a bountiful array of colorful flowers as far as the eye could see.

When I finished eating my banana, I stood up again. "OUCH!"

My feet were screaming. I caught my breath and sucked up the pain before starting to move again, gently easing forward with my poles. After a few minutes I was moving along, the pain subsiding into a dull ache. The path led downhill, and as I said before, that wasn't necessarily good news for my knee.

I started traversing the path from side to side as opposed to going straight down. The sun was getter hotter as it got closer to noon, and I starting peeling off layers of clothing, as I was now in a full sweat. I was grateful for my silly sun hat, which covered my entire face in the front, and for my sun gloves, which I picked up at the last minute before I left because someone told me you can get a sunburn on your hands when walking with poles all day long.

As I walked down, I eventually came to a village called Itero de la Vega, where I entered a 16th-century church just off the plaza. It never ceased to amaze me how beautiful these little medieval churches in the middle of nowhere were. What impressed me most was that in almost every church I entered I didn't find the traditional "Jesus on the cross" on the altar, which I was so accustomed to seeing in other Catholic churches around the world. Instead, a statue of Mother Mary stood there, emanating a much warmer presence. I found this both surprising and a paradox, as the medieval Church was anything but loving and warm.

Once I learned to time my days so that I could enter the churches during open hours, it was becoming a big part of my daily Camino ritual to go into at least one church a day and say a rosary, which, for me, was form of meditation. As I prayed today I noticed my heart was beginning to soften and calm down. I found my anger had subsided somewhat, giving way to a quieter energy. Perhaps after having the chance to be heard, a lifetime's worth of rage had now run out of fury. I was walking through it and was seeing the other side.

The journey itself was long today, and because my feet were on fire it seemed endless. Yet, though long, it wasn't difficult once over the hill, and there were parts that were so peaceful that I actually didn't want them to end.

I especially loved walking along the canal leading into Frómista at the end of the day. It was such a calm, peaceful path, and the weather had settled into one of the first nice days since I had begun nearly two and a half weeks earlier.

As I walked, I thought about the two men I met last night at dinner in the hotel. One was a 72-year-old man named Colum, from Vancouver, and the other was named Alan, from Rhodesia. Colum had a dignified look about him, almost as though he were a retired actor of some sort. He wore a pressed white shirt, a neat ascot around his neck, and polished boots. Alan was robust, tall, muscular, and casual, wearing a T-shirt, baring his muscled arms, and leather sandals. Both were extremely friendly.

I soon learned both were Irish born. Alan was walking the Camino for the first time, and Colum was doubling back, as he had walked the last two weeks of the Camino to Santiago a few years earlier. Now he wanted to walk the part he had skipped over to complete the full journey.

I also thought about the group of women who were at the hostel last night, all of whom decided to stay at the hostel because so many people in the pilgrims' albergue were getting sick. Everyone was coughing all night long.

One of the women I met, Charlene, had started out in Arles, France, another of the many different starting points for the Camino and had already walked almost 1,100 kilometers in a little over two months. She was having the best time of her life and after a lifetime of service to others, she was now enjoying the peace and quiet of her journey more than she could possibly explain.

I asked her if she had ever gotten lonely on the Camino, and she said, with great vehemence, "No, never! I wish I could make this last forever! I am alone. I am free."

She made it clear that she had spent most of her life taking care of and suffering the abuses of alcoholic men, beginning with her father, then her husband, even her male boss, and on to her sons. Now, she said, she was done with all of them. This was her emancipation journey. She honestly didn't even know if she would ever return to France once she completed the Camino.

"I have my pension now," she said. "I don't have to go back. I may stay and live in Spain. I am liking it very much, so far."

She sounded as if she had just escaped from prison, and I could appreciate her sense of liberation in getting away from her miserable circumstances at home. I listened carefully, as I felt certain that this, too, was part of what I was to complete in my own soul's journey as I made my pilgrimage to Santiago. I didn't want to take care of any more adults who failed to take care of themselves either.

In spite of the lovely path, the last few kilometers into Frómista seriously challenged me. I had to sit down every 15 minutes because my feet were throbbing. I got out my iPod and started singing along with it in order to make it through the last three kilometers. Kundalini yoga chants had the most "oomph" to them and were the easiest to sing along to.

With that extra help I shuffled into Frómista around five o'clock and headed straight to the center of town, looking for my hostel. As the town was so small, there was no missing it, right across from the church on the main square.

As I found my way across the plaza, I noticed a group of pilgrims sitting in the warm sun having a beer, and among them was Camino Patrick!

I shuffled up and gave him a big hug and asked where he was staying. He indicated the pilgrims' albergue, which was right next door to my hostel. He had a few beers under his belt, as did the others at his table. Up until then I had been drinking copious amounts of red wine at the end of my days, but today, in the delicious and welcome sun, a cold beer sounded fantastic.

I quickly registered for the night and got a key to my room, happy to hear that the caretaker had already taken Cheater upstairs. On the Camino you are on your own with the bag, so extra assistance like this was rare.

Then I went directly back outside, plopped myself at the table with the others, and ordered a large, cold beer. That first sip tasted so good! What a thirst quencher. No wonder everyone was drinking with such gusto.

I asked Camino Patrick how he felt today and he said "somewhat better," but he was still coughing and fighting a chest funk that was threatening to take him out. He had also developed some sort of extreme pain running along the nerves in his legs. They felt as if they were on fire. He said it was almost impossible to sleep it was so painful and even a sheet over him was too much to bear. For just a moment, he with his legs on fire, me with my feet on fire, I wondered why we were doing this. Were we crazy?

Sitting with him were two young Americans, John and Alexia, both from Cleveland. They were friends on a post–college graduation trip across Europe, and this seemed like the most affordable way to do it. John had arrived in Frómista by bus today, as he had pulled a tendon and injured his knee two days earlier, so he was unable to walk at all. This was his second day taking the bus from town to town, and he said he might do it again tomorrow depending how much pain he was in.

Shortly after I arrived, Colum came strolling up to the table and, like me, was truly spent and ready for a beer. He checked into the hostel, while Alan went to the pilgrims' albergue next door and joined us ten minutes later.

Pain aside, we were all in good spirits. It was an instant "Camino party."

I sat with everyone for a while, watching beers disappear as fast as they were served. Everyone got drunk under the table, as stories flew around at an ever-increasing volume, only to be drowned out by gales of laughter.

Eventually it started cooling off a bit, so I decided to go to my room to take a hot shower and a short nap before dinner. Since the only restaurant in town was at the hostel, I agreed to meet Camino Patrick and the others in the dining room at eight. That gave me an hour and a half to rest.

I went to lie down but found I didn't need a nap today, unlike the past two weeks when, at the end of the day, I all but passed out. I was definitely getting stronger and, apart from my crazy sore feet, I felt pretty good. I was especially grateful not to have the "Camino funk," as the coughing, chest-cold thing was being called among the pilgrims. More than half of those staying at the pilgrims' albergues and many of those staying in the hostels had some version of it. In fact, it was the main talk of the Camino.

I relished the hot shower in my room and the nice warm blankets on my bed that made up for the absence of heat. I also cherished my privacy. At least I wasn't sick.

I decided to close my eyes after all, and the next thing I knew it was morning.

Day 16

(19 km; 12 mi)

Frómista to Carrión de los Condes

I woke up to another freezing-cold but sunny day, and looking out my window, I could tell the wind was blowing, but not as intensely as it had been the past two days. I was tired today and didn't feel like walking at all. "I wish I could take a taxi to Carrión," I said out loud. But Gumby was staring me down, as if to say, "You wouldn't."

"Fine," I snapped back at him as I threw off my sleeping bag. "Don't guilt-trip me!"

I stood up and tested my feet. They hurt all along my arches. The hostel I was staying in was fairly modern and for some reason I had been checked into a handicapped-equipped room (Camino humor, no doubt). So I shuffled to the shower, where I was able to sit down on a chair placed in there and relax under a stream of hot water until I woke up.

I dried off, still feeling tired, but resigned to keep moving. I then peeled my socks, underwear, and wool shirt from the luxurious towel heater on the wall where I had placed them after I rinsed them out last night. They were toasty warm and felt wonderful, helping me shake off the final remnants of resistance I had been feeling.

Before my socks went on, I doctored my feet with medical tape and downed extra arnica pills to ease my pain. That did help some. I put some ibuprofen into my pocket to take with my breakfast for added relief. I threw everything into Cheater; grabbed my little purse, which held my passport, credit cards, my pilgrim's passport, my list of hostels and phone numbers, and some euros; threw it into Pilgrim; and took everything to the front desk.

While I'd had a great time at the party last night, I looked forward to my solitude and silence once again today. I wanted to listen to my heart and to God instead.

Holy Mother God,
I am listening. Please guide me this day.
Amen.

Over the past few days, I'd begun noticing a significant difference in vibration between my ego mind and my spirit. Whenever my ego was reflecting on my life, I felt like such a victim, so isolated, rejected, alone, and unloved. It roared with indignation, taking offense at so much and so many, some of whom I had not even seen for years. It found fault with everyone and blamed all who were in my path for my unhappiness. It was amazing, actually, to observe my ego in action.

I knew my ego was not my true spirit, but never before had I recognized how destructive it was. It didn't want resolution. It didn't want to be peaceful and filled with compassion. It certainly was not forgiving. Quite the opposite. My ego wanted to feel hurt, to suffer, to see others as enemies, and to retaliate.

Fortunately, the more I walked, the less interested I was in my ego. In fact, I was getting to the point where I could only listen to it for a short while before I got bored with it, noticing it sounded more like a broken record than anything else.

I saw how it prevented me from moving forward and tried to suck me back into drama and suffering. I saw how it sabotaged my effort to reach more peaceful ground. As I walked I also observed my ego trying to regain control, as it knew it was losing its influence on me fast.

It was trying to do everything in its power to seduce me back down the rabbit hole of pain. It threw negative thoughts, like poison darts, into my head, telling me that Patrick wanted to hurt me, that my divorce was going to be awful, that I had better watch my back, that I would be the laughingstock of so many people who would call me a failure. It wouldn't give up in its desperate attempts to have me in its fearful grips once again. But unlike when I first began walking the Camino, these thoughts simply didn't stick anymore. They rose and fell away, at first like exploding fireworks in my brain, but now more like weak fireflies at dusk. They were there, but they had no power over me anymore.

I breathed deeper and felt more alive than ever. The air was cold earlier this morning, but now it had warmed up quite a bit and I had to take off my jacket, then my wool shirt. I ended up walking in only a T-shirt, as I was in a full sweat.

The path was gentle and flat. I thought about my brother Bruce for the first time in a while. I felt his presence all morning long. He wasn't a traveler like I was. He often thought I was crazy for traveling so much and told me so. I almost bought him a T-shirt from a shop a few towns back because that was my tradition with him. He liked the T-shirts I brought him and he looked forward to getting them from me. I was already at the checkout counter when I remembered that he was dead. I couldn't believe that I had totally forgotten. I missed him and was sad that I couldn't give him that T-shirt.

I enjoyed the walk and sang hymns and songs, and talked to my Higher Self and my ancestors, as I felt they were close to me. I knew I was being escorted on this pilgrimage, and I was grateful for their unseen support. I was recovering my spirit. I was releasing what was not serving me and felt my difficult karma with relationships was coming to an end. I wasn't there yet. But I knew I was well on my way.

Eventually I entered a town known for its Templar cathedral. I could see it in the distance. It was a massive structure, and I could feel the power that built it. I paused and looked at it for a few moments. I remembered this place somehow. Not as a place where I had lived. But as place I nevertheless knew well.

As I got closer, I noticed a plaza directly in front of the cathedral filled with pilgrims eating lunch and drinking coffee. I walked over to the wall surrounding the cathedral, set down Pilgrim and my walking poles, and began to ascend the stairs.

It was an eerie feeling, a complete déjà vu experience. I was overwhelmed with a strange sense of nostalgia as I looked at the carvings all around the entrance. My heart was pounding. I walked in and looked around. It was an immense structure but not necessarily an impressive or beautiful one. There were not many adornments; it felt cold and severe inside.

It was not a place that felt alive. I took a seat and closed my eyes. I wanted to feel it rather than see it. Instead of opening the door to the past, as I had expected it would, I suddenly felt the door was closing. I shook my head to check and see if I was registering the energy correctly.

I was. I prayed, under my breath, to be free of the karma associated with this place and with the Knights Templar. It was all just so heavy. I prayed for all the souls in my life who were connected to this history, and for their freedom and peace. I prayed for my parents, my brothers and sisters, those relationships I had just ended, and for Patrick. I also especially prayed for my daughters that they would forever be free of this soul story or the family patterns that both Patrick and I had brought to them. I prayed for forgiveness from everyone, as well. I yearned with all my heart and soul to be forgiven for any pain I had caused anyone, but especially my precious daughters, whom I knew I had hurt with the ugly drama between Patrick and me. I was so sorry and told them so.

The cords were breaking. I was slowly freeing myself. Something big inside me was shifting. I felt less caught up in the past. I was feeling freer to go forward in peace.

I sat for a while and said a rosary. Then I got up and walked around. In the back of the cathedral was a place in which to put my own stamp in my pilgrim's passport book.

I walked outside into the blinding sun. I reached over to pick up my poles and Pilgrim, then turned around and saw Camino

Patrick sitting at a table at the café, in the sun, smiling brightly at me.

"Hi, Patrick. How are you today?" I asked as I plopped down at this table.

He said he was starting to feel better. He had met two young people from the Hungarian basketball team in the pilgrims' albergue last night, and they doctored him up with some strange natural remedies that surprisingly worked.

I asked if I could join him, although I already had, which he gladly welcomed, then I went inside the café to order my favorite, an egg bocadillo and a Coke.

I wandered back outside and sat down, asking Camino Patrick if he had gone in to see the cathedral yet. He hadn't. He didn't even seem that interested.

I was surprised. My connection to this place was powerful and this was a highlight of the Camino so far for me. He seemed to have no connection to it at all.

We sat for a while, not saying much, and then he asked if I would watch his backpack while he went to visit the cathedral.

He walked off and was back less than five minutes later. I asked what he thought of it, to which he said, "Eh. It's okay. I wasn't all that impressed."

I laughed. To each their own Camino.

We sat for a while and watched as other pilgrims came and went. Soon I saw John with Alexia, as he hobbled down the cathedral stairs. Apparently he had decided to walk today after all, though he looked as though he were in pain. When they saw us they came over to say hi, but said they were moving on. Camino Patrick asked me if we could walk together to Carrión. I hesitated because I really preferred to walk alone and in silence. But we weren't that far away, so I broke my rule and agreed. A few hours wouldn't make that much of a difference. Besides, everything on the Camino happens for a reason. I felt walking with Patrick was part of that reason today.

It did help me forget my burning feet to be distracted by his company. We were soon on our way. As we walked I asked him more about his life. He told me that he loved to pray and that it was a big part of his life. He had originally wanted to be a priest, but that plan got sidelined and he ended up becoming an engineer instead. He lived on a small island off the upper peninsula of Michigan, and the parish priest there had ruined his experience of going to church with his caustic energy and rotten, angry attitude.

He decide to do the Camino because he had seen the movie *The Way* with Emilio Estevez and Martin Sheen a few years earlier and wanted to have the same life-changing experience as the people in the movie had. Then he asked me if I had my rock to carry to Cruz Ferro. I told him I didn't know about the rock or Cruz Ferro. I hadn't seen the movie.

"Oh, Sonia, it's a big part of the Camino," he said. "It is the place where all the pilgrims leave their burdens behind. You have to find a rock that represents your burdens and carry it to Cruz Ferro so you can take part in that tradition."

"How big is the rock you are carrying?" I asked him.

He said, "Not too big."

"I'm going to find a big rock," I said. "I want to leave all my burdens behind."

He laughed. "Are you sure you want to carry a big rock?"

"Absolutely! I am transporting my bag, so I can carry a really big rock."

I looked around as we walked and my eye was soon drawn to a big rock alongside the road. I bent down and picked it up. It was fairly hefty. This was it. This was my rock, and it needed to be from this place on the Camino, at the point of my letting the past go.

"Yes, that is quite a big rock. Are you sure it's big enough, Sonia?" Patrick asked, amused.

I thought for a moment as I held it in my hand. "Yes, it feels right," I answered. "This is the one."

I put it in Pilgrim and we continued on.

We walked and talked—it was a nice change to enjoy Camino Patrick's company. But not too long after I found the rock, I started feeling lousy, like I had a fever coming on. I started to cough. In no time a massive headache descended upon me and I lost all my energy.

"Oh no, Patrick, suddenly I don't feel well."

He could see it in my eyes and said, "Maybe you are getting what is going around."

"I might be," I said. "Where are the Hungarian basketball players who helped you?"

"I haven't seen them since this morning," he answered. "Here. Let me carry your bag for you."

"Aw, Patrick, I just put that big rock into it. It'll be too heavy. You have your own to carry."

"No, it won't, Sonia. Let me carry it."

Because the Camino funk had hit me like a ton of bricks, I was actually grateful to hand off my bag. I suddenly felt weak and was getting chills. Before I gave him my bag, I pulled out all the layers of clothing I had shed this morning and put them back on.

"Thank you so much, Patrick. I am so grateful for the help."

I was going down fast. It was weird. I was relieved Patrick was there to help keep me moving.

"How much farther do we have to go?"

He said he had just seen a marker a few minutes back that said four kilometers.

The rest of the walk was a blur. We chatted a little, but it was hard to concentrate because of my headache. I felt badly that I wasn't better company for him.

Patrick was so kind and told me not to worry about it. Eventually we made it to Carrión and he said he needed to find a pilgrims' albergue in which to stay. I told him the name of my hostel and he said he would meet me there for dinner at 8. I took Pilgrim from him and gave him a hug as he set off to find a pilgrims' albergue.

I wandered farther into town. It was the most charming town I had seen since Santo Domingo. The streets wound around and it looked inviting to explore, so I was especially disappointed that I felt so lousy all of a sudden.

It was siesta time, and that meant stores were closed from noon to 4 P.M. It was almost four, so I walked slowly because I wanted to go to a pharmacy and get some lozenges for the sore throat I felt coming on. As I walked, I ran into Charles and Lawrence from a few days back and found out they were staying at the same hostel I was, which they informed me was a fantastic refurbished monastery. Charles loved it; Lawrence said it felt a bit heavy.

They had arrived two hours earlier and were now on the way back to town to look around. I had to walk another two kilometers to get there.

Once I arrived at the hostel I was charmed. It was a regal monastery, surrounded by gorgeous gardens. The guest rooms were old monks' quarters refurbished to elegant standards. The walls were paneled in thick dark wood, polished to a high shine, with marbled floors, and carved windows covered in heavy velvet curtains, which fell all the way to the floor. I was really relieved to be welcomed into such a grounding place, given that I felt so ill.

Dinner was at 8 and it was only 4:15. Great. I could lie down until then. Patrick had promised he would be there tonight and we would eat together. I wondered if he would actually walk the extra way or just stay in town.

By now I was certain I had a fever, so I took some more ibuprofen and hoped my headache and chills would go away. I was so congested I could barely breathe and it became worse when I lay down. So I took my nap sitting upright in my bed. It sort of worked.

I woke up at 8:15 and hobbled down to see if Camino Patrick was waiting for me. He was nowhere in sight.

Disappointed, I walked to the restaurant alone, but then saw Charles and Lawrence sitting in the corner at a table. I was seated at a small table right next to theirs, and the three of us had a wonderful conversation over dinner, in spite of that fact that I felt worse than ever.

Charles offered me a decongestant because I told him I couldn't breathe. Desperate for relief, I took it. Given I'd had a few glasses of wine, it all but knocked me out right there at the table. I had a long walk back to my room, as the monastery was very big and it wasn't easy to find my way around. As I wandered the halls I felt I was walking with the ghosts of monks passed. The monastery was dimly lit and had many side doors and strange hallways and corridors.

After a time, I found my door. I was a mess and needed to go to sleep, which I promptly did.

Day 17
(17 km; 11 mi)

Carrión to Calzadilla de la Cueza

I woke up with a chest cold and a strong cough, and felt like I had a fever. I had gone from burning up to freezing cold all night long, and every muscle in my body was now stiff and sore, both from walking and now from this new state of affairs. I felt sorry for myself and didn't want to get up because I was so miserable, but I could feel Gumby staring me down in the dark, and I knew he didn't want to hear my excuses.

"You don't even have muscles, Gumby, so don't give me that look," I snapped at him as I threw my sleeping bag off of me, and let out a loud groan. The doors in this hostel/monastery were so thick I was pretty sure no one heard me.

"I'm up!" I screamed in defiance to no one as I shuffled into the bathroom and turned on the light. I had no idea what time it was because my room had wooden shutters on the windows, so it was pitch-black. I turned on the shower and looked at my watch. It was 7:30.

I stepped into the shower and let the water run over my head and shoulders for a long time, hoping it would ease the congestion in my lungs and quiet my cough. It didn't.

Next, I shuffled over to the window and opened the shutters, wondering if I were doomed to shuffle for the rest of my life, given how much pain my feet were in. Once the shutters were open, I was surprised to be greeted with the most beautiful, sunny day outside. I knew the day ahead was shorter than usual, as I only had to walk 17 kilometers to my next destination, which by Camino standards was not much more than a short stroll.

"I can do this," I said aloud to myself, rising to the occasion. Continuing to think aloud I said, "I hope the breakfast here is decent. I need strong fresh coffee if I'm going to make it today." Gumby seemed to offer a wink of approval as I finished getting dressed and packed up Cheater. "I don't need your approval," I snapped back at him, stuffing him into my pocket as I did. "You are only going along for the ride. I'm the one doing all the work here, so keep your opinions to yourself."

I checked to see if I had my small purse around my neck, with my pilgrim's passport handy so I could get it stamped downstairs. I had almost forgotten to get a stamp two times along the way so far, so I decided to keep my little purse out of Pilgrim and visible so I wouldn't risk forgetting my stamps in the future.

I wasn't quite ready to bother taking all my stuff downstairs just yet, so I decided to eat breakfast first, and then come back later for my things. Perhaps then I would feel better and have more energy.

I found my way to the dining room and was welcomed by a fairly decent breakfast buffet, which made me happy. Then I noticed that the coffee was in thermoses and was not freshly brewed with steamed milk the way I wanted, so I found the waiter and asked him if he would do that for me.

He could tell I wasn't feeling well (and I admit I played it up a bit for persuasion), so he took mercy on me and set off to make it happen. I was not inspired to eat as much as I first thought I was, because when it actually came time to put things on my plate, none of it looked as good as it had only a moment ago.

I picked up a small bowl, filled it with plain yogurt, and added some cornflakes to it from a plastic container, then filled a tiny glass with fresh orange juice. Then I sat down. Charles and Lawrence wandered into the dining room just then and greeted me. They were in tip-top shape, probably due to the fact that they had only been walking for a few days and missed most of the rain that had been following me for the past few weeks.

Charles saw how little I was eating and told me I had better load up on food before I left, as his guidebook warned that there were few, if any, stops along the way to get a snack or a coffee before arriving at our destination. I took his advice and forced myself to eat a large piece of toast with butter and jam, and washed it down with my now second cup of delicious, steaming, hot, fresh café con leche.

"I have PowerBars," I assured them, appreciating their concern for me. "I'll throw a few in my pocket just in case I run out of gas."

I finished my breakfast and wished them a "Buen Camino," as they said they were not leaving for another hour or so. They wanted to take their time this morning, as this was their last day before they had to go back home, and they wanted to savor every minute.

I went back to my room, got my things together, and headed for the prized elevator down to the lobby. When I arrived I was handed a letter addressed to me. It was from Camino Patrick. Apparently he had come to the hotel last night to have dinner with me, but when he didn't see me in the lobby, he figured I was sleeping. He didn't want the receptionist to ring my room and disturb me because he knew I felt so lousy, so he waited for a few minutes and then went back to town.

Rats, I thought, feeling badly that he had walked all this way and we did not have dinner together. I wondered if I would see him today. I couldn't remember how far he was walking, but I did know that he usually left very early in the morning so he would get to the next town in time to find a pilgrims' albergue with open beds. That meant it was unlikely I would run into him.

I handed over Cheater to the receptionist to be picked up by the transport company and had my passport stamped. Then I stuffed it back into my little purse. Next I slung Pilgrim over my shoulder and headed outside. As I stepped out, I noticed a huge tour bus with dozens of hotel guests getting on board.

"I wonder where they are going?" I asked myself, hearing them speak German. "We are pretty much in the middle of nowhere."

They were happy and seemed to be having a wonderful time and many wished me a "Buen Camino" as I walked past them in search of the next yellow Camino arrow.

It was warm outside for a change and the birds were singing like crazy as I found my way onto the path. The sunshine felt good on my face as I moved slowly along. I was so grateful for the poles that Camino Patrick let me have, especially on a day like today when I felt like crap. They kept pulling me forward even though my body was dragging.

> *Holy Mother God,*
> *Please give me the energy to keep moving.*
> *Thank you, and amen.*

The path was very flat and lined with few trees as it followed the ancient Roman road to a town ahead called Astorga. I was grateful that the terrain didn't physically challenge me, as I had so little energy.

The Camino was desolate today. I walked for hours and didn't see a single other person. It was so quiet I even began to worry that I might have taken a wrong turn, although there were enough yellow arrows and Camino shells to assure me that I wasn't lost.

Maybe it was because I was feeling so sick today, but I suddenly no longer had any desire to continue being as hard on myself. I knew in my heart that I had been trying my best to be a loving, kind, generous person for as long as I could remember, and whatever negative karma I had carried into this life with me now felt over. In its place I felt a genuine tenderness for my spirit that I had never, ever felt before.

I knew this feeling had to do with the closure I experienced at the Templar cathedral yesterday. In my heart I felt something dreadfully old and heavy and filled with shame had just lifted from the core of my being. Underneath it lay an entire matrix of deep-seated and well-hidden insecurities that had controlled so much of my life.

I had never openly admitted to myself, or to anyone else for that matter, that I was insecure. Well, not as insecure as I really was. Instead, I threw myself into self-improvement, self-development, and hard work in order to stay one step ahead of these insecurities before they took over.

I could see how my efforts drove me to try to be my best at all times, but I was also acutely aware of just how much shame I had carried in my being and tried my hardest to hide. Now I realized that I had always felt that there was something inherently wrong with me for as far back as I could remember, and that whatever it was, as hard as I tried, I could never really rid myself of it.

It was not rooted in what I did or didn't do, or how I performed or didn't perform. It didn't have to do with how I looked or where I was from, or anything that I could put my finger on. It was much deeper than that. It wasn't a feeling that I could trace back to my childhood. I felt I was born with it. It was part of my soul's blueprint. And it was a feeling I came here to erase, not only in myself, but in as many other people as I possibly could touch, as well.

This insecurity and shame was tinged with some sort of guilt and remorse, and was something I felt I could only ease if I devoted my life to the service and healing of others. I weirdly knew this from the earliest age, not only wanting to help my mother and family, but also anyone else who came into my path. Moved more by instinct than by conscious thought, I spent hours and hours at the local library learning about spiritual things beginning when I was ten years old. These were not related to the Catholic teachings I was introduced to at school, but rather metaphysical lessons not taught or even allowed at school.

Reading books on metaphysics became my passion, and I spent more time at the library than any other place. I went there both for the peace and solitude it offered me, as well as for the rich discoveries I happened upon, almost certainly guided by higher forces the entire time.

As I walked I actually marveled at how clear about my path I was at such an early age and how much responsibility I took on in being an intuitive guide for others when I was only a kid myself.

As I walked I felt a certain pressure in my heart begin to ease. The compassion for myself was growing. I only wished that the guidance I shared with others could have spared me some of the heartache I had experienced myself. I had somehow erroneously thought that if I was clear enough for them, I could somehow by-pass some of the soul lessons I was here to learn for myself.

Then again, maybe I had bypassed some of them. Maybe I could have suffered a whole lot more than I had. In so many ways my life was miraculously wonderful. I loved and treasured my daughters and felt they were the best gift of my life. I also felt certain I was on a true path of service in my work. And even in the midst of these challenges, there was a great deal of love in my heart for everything and everyone I was struggling with, even Patrick.

If anything, it was because I had grown as much as I had through my mystical studies that I now had the strength and courage to ask every aspect of my life to move into harmony with my spirit, no matter how messy it was. I wasn't afraid to ask for what I wanted and needed at the deepest level anymore. I was now willing to let go of everything I was attached to—even my marriage and family, my reputation, my home, my comfort—to live in the highest degree of integrity with my spirit as possible.

I felt I was at a point where I could face all the shadows and dark crevices of my soul with courage. I knew in my heart that I needed to forgive, release, and love even more, and mostly myself.

I blinked and came back to the moment and the hot sun.

I had a fever, so I had to rest. Thank goodness Charles told me to take extra PowerBars and water, as it was true, there was no place to stop and get any sort of refreshment. There wasn't even a place to sit along the path. As I rested on the ground eating my bar, I wondered how many remained after today. My supply was dwindling fast, and I was only halfway to Santiago.

I took my sun hat out and put it on my head. The bright sun was now beating down, and the last thing I needed was to get sunburned. I took out my sunblock and slathered it on my face, arms, and hands. Then I stood up and got going once again.

I was walking very slowly today, almost as though moving through molasses. Even though it was only 17 kilometers to the town where I was staying the night, it seemed as though it would take me all day to get there.

Just then I heard voices behind me and noticed the bus I had seen at the hotel this morning had just stopped and was now unloading the entire bunch of German tourists onto the path. At first I didn't understand what was happening, but soon figured out that they were only walking part of the way to get the Camino experience without having to take on the big Camino effort.

Seeing this made me laugh. *I don't feel so bad sending my bag ahead now,* I thought as I watched the jovial crowd descend in pairs off the bus and start strolling along. *At least I am actually walking the full distance and not just taking in bits and pieces of it.*

Just then I stopped myself from judging them. Some people would think I was just as bad as these people because I was not carrying my own backpack from town to town or staying at the local pilgrims' albergues. *Just remember, Sonia, to each their own Camino.*

Who knows? Maybe they've done the Camino many times before, and this time they're just coming back for the highlights.

It's funny how fast the mind compares and judges, just so it can feel superior. Why do I care that these people are having the tour bus Camino experience? I don't even know who these people are. If I were honest, in fact, I actually wished I could have approached the bus driver and asked for a ride today. It was too late. The crowd was slowly moving down the path with me and the bus was long gone.

I didn't know quite how to navigate this flash-mob scene I suddenly found myself in. I felt like the sausage in the middle of a German sandwich. There were about 20 Germans in front of me, 6 or 7 to each side of me, and about 20 behind me. I felt as though I had just wandered into someone else's movie and didn't belong there.

I had no choice but to speed up if I didn't want to remain firmly entrenched in the German experience. I didn't know if I had the energy in me to move fast today, but somehow I did. In ten minutes flat they were a good distance behind me, and I was back to my solitude.

Whew! That was weird, I thought. I was so grateful to get back to my silent, uninterrupted, no-talking, no-sounds-besides-nature Camino. While my heart was pounding from the effort, it was also pounding with relief. I wanted to be alone. I didn't want to be immersed in the stream of other people's energy. That was so clear to me that I had to laugh at how the Camino orchestrated this bizarre interlude just to remind me how important quiet time in nature was to me, lest I forget. I treasured and needed it. I couldn't surrender this to anyone or anything.

I kept up my pace to assure myself of the privacy I wanted to maintain. And before I knew it, I happened upon a makeshift oasis alongside the road, filled with other pilgrims drinking coffee, eating snacks, and sitting in the sun.

I blinked as I got closer to this spot. How on earth did these people get here? Where did they come from? Other than the Germans who were behind me, I hadn't seen a single soul all day long, and yet sitting here were at least 15 pilgrims.

I shook my head in wonderment as I cruised up to a little table and put my poles and Pilgrim down. My blood sugar was so low and my fever so high by now it was time for a cold Coke. As soon as I sat down to enjoy it, I noticed the tour bus just ahead on the road. Within minutes the Germans started walking by and boarding the bus. They probably walked about 5 kilometers from start to finish. Shaking my head at the different ways we human beings did things, I downed my Coke and ate another PowerBar. It was good to be me.

Day 18

(22 km; 14 mi)

Calzadilla de la Cueza to Sahagún

I made it to Calzadilla by 2:30 in the afternoon, which was record time for me. I was so hungry and drained by the time I arrived all I wanted to do was eat lunch and go to sleep. I was sure I had a fairly high fever, as my head was pounding and I had a bad case of the chills. Thankfully, the sun was out, and since the town was nonexistent, finding my way to the hostel was easy.

When I arrived I saw Cheater sitting right in front of the receptionist's desk waiting for me. I was so happy to see him, as I could hardly wait to settle into my room, get out my pillow and sleeping bag, take an ibuprofen, and go to sleep. The only saving grace about my fever was that it took my attention off my aching feet for almost the entire day, which was a welcome relief.

The receptionist was a warm and welcoming Spaniard who liked to touch a lot. He held my hand when he handed me my room key and rubbed my back when I reached down to pick up my day pack, which I had set down when I walked in the door. He was extremely gracious and offered to escort me to my room and carried Cheater for me. The elevator to the third floor, where my room was located, was very small. The two of us along with Cheater made for a tight squeeze, and for this he seemed particularly happy. We were nearly cheek-to-cheek as we lurched upward in the shaky lift, and several times he lunged into me when I knew he didn't have to.

Although it was weird and uncomfortable to be caged in with him like this, I was too tired to care. If anything, I had to smile at the way in which he managed to be in such close contact with me when it was entirely unnecessary. Given how dreary the town was, with obviously nothing to do but welcome pilgrims as far as I could tell, I had to admire how he used this overly gracious welcome tactic to break up the monotony. Once we arrived on the third floor, he guided me to the back of the hostel, away from the noise in the lobby and restaurant downstairs. He then gave me a big chest-to-chest uncomfortably long hug, which I had to peel myself away from by saying, "Muchas gracias, señor." Turning my back to him, I walked toward the door. He stepped back and watched me for a moment and once he saw I was in my room, he turned and left (thank God).

Once in my room I plopped onto the bed and closed my eyes. "Please don't let me get any sicker than this," I said out loud to the Universe. "I don't feel good," I groaned and allowed myself to relax, too tired to even take my jacket off, hoping I could just fall asleep.

But instead of dozing off, I immediately heard a fairly loud ruckus coming from downstairs. I kept my eyes closed as I listened, but couldn't quite make out what was happening. I didn't want to either, so I just lay on my bed trying to tune it all out.

I had no such luck. It was getting louder. I could hear all sorts of languages flying around and waves of laughter and singing. It seemed as though my little hostel had become the local pilgrims' landing, and with more and more pilgrims arriving by the moment came more talking, more laughter, and more singing. Giving up on all thoughts of an afternoon nap, I remembered that I was hungry, so decided to get cleaned up and go down and join the jamboree.

The minute I peeled off my boots, my feet started screaming at me again. I had been walking in my boots every day now because, as much as they still hurt my sensitive toes, it helped with the electric shock waves of pain I was now getting across my arches. I was able to use my limited amount of medical tape to wrap my feet tight for two days at a time if I was careful not to get my feet wet in the shower. The way I got around this was to wrap them in plastic bags and tie them around the ankle with hair ties, a rather ingenious solution if I say so myself. This had worked for the past seven days now, but I knew I would have to find more medical tape soon because I was running out.

After my shower I took three ibuprofen and wished I had some cough syrup because a chest cold was now moving in with a vengeance. Since I didn't, I decided to go downstairs and drown my misery in red wine.

Once there I saw just about every pilgrim I had passed on the Camino since the day I began in Saint-Jean-Pied-de-Port with the exception of Camino Patrick. I saw the Italians, and Colum and Alex, as well as the two Germans and one Austrian I shared a table with in the café days ago. I saw the pilgrim who had asthma way back at the beginning, and even the French people who walked with their wagon, which was now parked outside in front of the hostel. It was like a huge unexpected reunion. Everyone acknowledged everyone, celebrating that we had all made it this far.

As I am normally quiet, I sat down at a table and just smiled at first, but soon it felt as though I were with a group of my best friends. The ruckus was mostly coming from the Irish pilgrims who were drinking large quantities of beer and singing, but there were also two rambunctious Dutchmen and two guys from England who matched them, beer for beer and song for song.

There were so many bottles of wine on the tables that someone thrust a glass in my hand and filled it to the brim, saying "Buen Camino" before I could object, so I clinked glasses with everyone and joined in the festivities.

After two large glasses of wine I felt tipsy and knew if I didn't add at least some bread to the mix, I might pass out, as I was already feeling light-headed when I first sat down. I got up and went to the bar and asked for an egg bocadillo, which was promptly served up as I watched the waitress cook it in front of my eyes. It was huge and I didn't think I could eat it all. But I surprised myself, and inhaled it in a matter of minutes, licking my fingers and marveling that it had all disappeared.

The party had now grown to at least 30 pilgrims, and as fun as it was to be there, I had to throw in the party towel and go back to my room. Between the wine, my now sore throat, and my full stomach, I had no more "oomph" in me to carry on.

As I headed to the elevator, I passed by the receptionist's desk once again, only to notice that Lover Boy was now signing in another guest, this time a middle-aged man from Canada. He slapped his room key down on the counter without so much as looking up at him and nodded in the direction of the elevator with a smirk. It was such a departure from the royal welcome I had just received that I was surprised. Shaking my head as I proceeded to the elevator, where the Canadian was also now getting in, I overhead him saying to himself, "Geez. What a jerk that guy was!"

He pushed the button for the third floor, and we both headed up. When he got off he looked at his key and saw that his room was right off the elevator overlooking the very loud lobby. He groaned again, as the noise was almost out of control. I looked at him and said, "If you can't beat 'em, join 'em."

"Guess so," he answered. Then we both said "Buen Camino" at the same time and went our separate ways.

I slept until the next morning, almost 14 straight hours. It was fitful sleep, and I was freezing cold and coughed most of the night, so I didn't exactly feel rested when I woke up. Still, I got up and decided to take a hot shower and get going. I just wanted to push through and be done with this Camino experience. It seemed long.

After my shower, I packed up Cheater and stuffed Gumby into my pocket. All was quiet downstairs as I entered the elevator and pushed the ground-floor button.

A different receptionist greeted me this time, a quiet young man whom I assumed to be the son of the man who checked me in yesterday.

He asked if I slept well and said I could find breakfast in the dining room adjacent to the lobby. He was the opposite of his overbearing, touchy-feely father and I wondered if he ever thought about walking the Camino himself just to get away.

Soon my thoughts drifted away from him and on to the buffet. There was cereal, yogurt, large slices of bread with butter and jam, fresh orange juice, and thermoses of coffee. As good as it looked, I stuck with yogurt and juice, as I had woken up with a severe sore throat.

I looked around and noticed the room was filled with pilgrims this morning, but they were very quiet. Honestly, most of them looked hungover. *Well, it's nothing they can't walk off today,* I thought, hoping the same would be true for my sore throat.

The coffee was bad, so I finished my yogurt and went out to the lobby bar, where I noticed an espresso machine. I ordered a large café con leche and sat on a stool while the barista made it. Then I remembered to get my pilgrim's passport stamped, so I took it out of my small shoulder purse and gave it to her for the prized acknowledgment that said, yes, I made it this far.

The sun was out, but the wind was kicking up debris and I just knew it would be another cold day. I decided I was not dressed warmly enough to brave the cold, so I walked over to Cheater, opened him up, and pulled out a second long-sleeve wool shirt to put over my first long-sleeve wool shirt. *This feels better,* I thought, attempting to fight off the chills that had taken over my body.

I sipped my last delicious drops of coffee, put my day pack on, slung my little purse over that, stuck Gumby in the front looking out, and headed for the door. I had overheard that there were few places to stop along the way for a snack or coffee, so I made sure my water bottle was filled to the brim and that I had at least two PowerBars to keep me going.

I stepped outside and was hit with freezing-cold air but a bright sun. I then put on my hiking gloves, donned my Foreign Legion/burka sun hat, extended my walking poles, and was off. My feet took a few minutes to cooperate, testing my resolve to keep moving by sending extra-strong electric shocks along the sides of each foot, but I was not to be slowed down or dissuaded from the adventure ahead.

"Ultreya!" I said aloud, which means "Onward" in Spanish. In spite of my sore feet, and increasingly sore throat, I was a pilgrim and had to keep moving.

Holy Mother-Father God,
Please give me strength today because I don't feel that well.
Thank you, and amen.

Thankfully, the path was flat today, and the wind died down a bit after about an hour. I got lost in my reverie, realizing that as I walked, I entered an almost dreamlike state of consciousness, drifting from the moment and the beauty and strangeness all around me to my life back home and the discomfort of what I had to face when I returned, to past lives and unlived dreams, and back again.

The rhythm of my footsteps took me into a deep state of meditation and for hours my mind became silent as I slipped into a resting place with God. I could tell that as I walked I was peeling off lifetimes of pain and sorrow and sin, and that I was purging myself of darkness and wounding, both self-inflicted as well as at the hands of others. The feelings of anger and grief I had started out with had all started to lift, and in their place I was feeling an interesting blend of confusion and curiosity, wondering, like the Talking Heads song so poignantly asks, "How did I get here?"

There was not much to look at as I walked, beyond the occasional Camino shell, yellow arrow, some stone configurations, and a sign explaining that the path I was walking was once walked in the 9th century. That amazed me. The *9th century!* That was 12 centuries ago. That is how long this route under the Milky Way has been traveled.

As time passed I felt, once again, as though I had entered an alternate universe. Maybe my physical body was in the here-and-now dimension, but the rest of me had stepped into another dimension, another time and place. My ego identity faded away, and I began to witness my life from a more detached state than ever before.

I knew the journey to Santiago was a metaphor for the inner journey back to the heart and soul of my spirit. I knew that I was walking off old karma, letting go of my attachment to my old stories, releasing my wounds back to the earth, while being restored by nature as I walked back into my pure and sweet essence.

And yet, I also understood the need for this journey. To simply say to myself or anyone else, "I am forgiven" or "I forgive" could not shift my past karmic energy as well as walking the Camino. I was walking myself out of trauma and grief and anger and shame and righteous indignation and feelings of worthlessness and over-thinking and every other faulty human perception that blocked the truth of my being from shining through.

I loved the journey even though it was hard, painful, extremely uncomfortable and challenging, and at times seemed endless and to make no sense. The Camino was about coming back to myself, to blessings, to forgiveness, to trust, to discipline and prayer and faith.

I breathed and sat down. It was time for a PowerBar. My energy had just dropped and I felt like passing out. As I swallowed hard I was now in a full sweat, with a sore throat that felt as though it were on fire. I knew something more than a chest cold was happening. I peeled off my second wool shirt and wrapped it around my waist. I also wrapped my jacket around my waist and pulled off my walking gloves, as even these were too hot to keep on. I lay down on the ground and rested. All I could think of was that at least I didn't have any blisters on my feet. Not one. I had enough blister treatment in Pilgrim and Cheater to open a foot clinic and yet had only suffered the slightest blisters way back when I wore my clown shoes. Closing my eyes I thought I must be delirious to be thinking about this as I lay on the ground.

I didn't care. The ground felt cool and I was so hot. I stayed there until I, too, cooled off. Once again up, I looked around and saw nothing for as far as I could see. The sun danced across the plains, and I could see wavy lines that revealed the energy of the sun reflecting off of the earth. I wondered how much farther I had to go before I came to a town.

It didn't matter. I would get there when I got there, so I kept on going. Walking the path today I could really sense the Templars' protective, yet warrior-like, presence. The villages that did remain were mostly left in ruins, but this area had once been a Templar stronghold and their energy still hung in the air. I wondered what their lives were really like.

I heard my spirit answer, "Certainly not much fun."

That made me laugh. "Certainly not."

The more I walked, the more my fever burned me up.

Slowly pushing ahead, I suddenly screamed out, "Help! I am burning up."

Just then, a whoosh of energy flooded through me, and I saw myself being burned at the stake during the Inquisition.

This vision left me speechless, and a little freaked out. It wasn't a thought. It was a flashback!

The sweat was pouring down my face as I whipped my sun hat off. I was so hot that I actually thought for a moment of taking my pants off, as well.

I started to pray, and what came out of my mouth was, "I forgive me. I forgive them. I forgive everybody. I forgive everything. I forgive all of us."

I was crying and probably a little delirious with fever under the burning sun, but after only a few moments, the wind kicked back up and everything started to cool down again. I was back to the Camino. I was even getting a little cold. I noticed a sign that said Sahagún was just ahead. I just kept walking.

In what seemed like time travel forward, I found myself suddenly on the edge of Sahagún, walking along a train track leading into the center of the town. It felt like I was entering a town in the old Wild West. Once I crossed the tracks, the feeling of the place charmed me. It was a Sunday and the local people were all dressed up, strolling around, eating ice cream, and walking arm in arm. Farther on, I happened upon the town square, lined with restaurants and cafés, where it seemed the entire town was enjoying

Sunday lunch together. Kids in their Sunday best were dancing and running around in the square, and in one corner was a shrine to Mother Mary. On it was a nearly life-size doll dressed in a purple cape, complete with makeup and wig, on top of a table filled to the brim with flowers. It was a bit surreal, but I enjoyed the sense of theater. I kept on walking, looking for my hostel, when I noticed a sign for the local emergency room. Without thinking I headed straight to it. When I rang the doorbell, a young woman answered and I pointed to my throat.

She motioned for me to sit down and said the doctor would arrive in a minute. To my surprise, she did arrive in a minute, and even better, she spoke a little English.

I told her I had a very bad sore throat and maybe a fever. She took my temperature and said I had a 103-degree fever. Then she took a look at my throat and immediately said, "You have a throat infection, maybe strep. It looks very bad. You need medicine."

I agreed. I felt very bad, and I did need medicine.

She wrote me a prescription and then gave me the address of the pharmacy.

"Open today?" I asked, knowing it was Sunday.

"Sí, until 2 P.M.," she answered.

I thanked her for the help and asked her what I owed her, hoping it wouldn't be too much as I had very few euros on me.

"No charge. You are a peregrina. Go with God," she answered.

"Thank you," I said, so grateful for her help and her kindness.

I took the prescription and left to look for the pharmacy. That took longer than I wanted it to, but eventually I found it. The pharmacist gave me some penicillin and some throat lozenges and told me to rest. I threw some medical tape onto the counter, happy to have that, as well.

I paid, then walked out and started toward my hostel. It was five minutes away. On my way there I ran into Clint from Roncesvalles. I hadn't seen him since then. He was surprised and seemed happy to see me. He introduced me to two other pilgrims, Victoria and her son, Eric, who were sitting with him and invited me to join them. She had a strong, determined face, lined with deep wrinkles far beyond her years, telling of life mostly lived outdoors in the sun. Eric, her son, looked as though he was around 30 or so, earrings in both ears, a wimpy ponytail fighting a now balding pate, and a defiant look on his face. Too tired to wonder about them at the moment, and ignoring the obvious tension between them—and in need of reinforcements for my now totally depleted energy—I stopped and had a glass of freshly squeezed orange juice with them before I went on to find my hostel and check in.

"I made it, and so did Cheater," I sighed in relief as I headed to my room. I took my penicillin and lay on the lumpy single bed, thinking about the flashback of being burned at the stake I had had a few hours earlier. It seemed almost as though it hadn't happened. Certainly, the thought of this had never crossed my mind before today. And yet, I knew it was real and I also knew that another big piece of the past had been released and cleared, literally burned off with my fever.

Day 19
(17 km; 11 mi)

Sahagún to El Burgo Ranero

Aw, crap! Sore throat! The minute I woke up I realized I was no better off than yesterday. I started singing in my head the Alicia Keys song "Girl on Fire" because my throat was. Before I left for the Camino, I decided that this would be one of my theme songs for my journey, but I hadn't intended to take it to this point.

"Water!" I gasped, seeking relief as I reached for the light, hoping Gumby could help me out. I couldn't even groan because my throat hurt so much. "Oh well, just burning off some more old karma," I whispered out loud to any invisible spirit helpers in the room, trying to look on the bright side of things.

At least my fever was gone. I woke up in a full sweat, but I no longer had a headache, so that was progress. And I was hungry. I took a hot shower to both wake up and warm up, as the room was dark and freezing cold, and happily found that it helped ease some of the pain in my throat, as well. I dressed quickly, packed up Cheater, stuffed Gumby in my pocket, threw my Pilgrim and small purse over my shoulder, and headed downstairs. It was Camino time!

Right next to the reception area was a small café and on the counter were prearranged plates with one slice of toast, a small glass of orange juice, and a tiny yogurt on each. I was disappointed that this was all that my pilgrim breakfast offered, as I was really hungry. Then I remembered the café where I had sat down with

Clint yesterday afternoon and decided to return after I checked out of the hostel and order a second breakfast before I got going.

I slurped down my delicious cup of café con leche (at least that was not disappointing) and ordered a second cup because it tasted so good. The warmth felt great on my throat. Then I downed the penicillin I was prescribed by the doctor, had my pilgrim's passport stamped, left Cheater with the receptionist, and skipped out the door. I wasn't sure why I was in such a good mood today given that I didn't feel great, but I suspected it had something to do with freeing myself of yet another huge load of negative karma yesterday, which lightened my spirit immensely.

I looked at my watch and realized it was already 9 A.M., so the early-morning pilgrim rush hour was most definitely over. Since I didn't have that far to go today and there was no reason for me to hurry, I decided to poke around the town a little after breakfast number 2 before I headed out.

> *Holy Mother God,*
> *Help me walk away from this illness today.*
> *Thank you, and amen.*

Unlike yesterday, it seemed more like a ghost town today, at least at this early hour. Once back in the square I was disappointed to see that Mother Mary, with her cape and wig, had disappeared, and that most of the little cafés were closed down, leaving the square feeling sad and abandoned. I looked for the church but didn't see it, so decided I would just keep going, as there is an unspoken rule on the Camino that says you don't go backward, although I wondered if I were the one who made up that rule.

The passage out of town wound through several little streets. I saw the Templars' red cross painted on the corners of various buildings here and there as I moved through the remainder of the town, but eventually my eyes were drawn closer to the ground and the yellow arrows guiding me back to the Camino. As I walked along, I started silently singing "I'm Off to See the Wizard" once again.

Walking the Camino was a lot like walking to the Emerald City in the sense that it was an epic journey back to a more authentic and holy state of being. Each day presented another obstacle and a gift, and it was like a treasure hunt to discover the gift without getting thrown off course by the obstacle, just like Dorothy and her friends had had to do.

It was cold but sunny as I made my way along the senda, or route, which was mostly barren and flat, with the exception of a few trees lining the path. The path itself was wide and ran parallel to the highway, but I didn't mind because it was easy to walk.

I was glad I'd remembered to put a PowerBar in my pocket this morning, even though I'd had two breakfasts, because I was starving again after only two hours of walking. As I sat and enjoyed my bar, I noticed quite a few pilgrims on the path today that I had never seen before and wondered where they came from. Maybe they took the train to Sahagún and started from there. I had overheard what looked to me like a 50-year-old pretty blonde woman at the hostel two days ago who had arrived in Sahagún and then taken a taxi to Calzadilla in order to begin there. She came to complete the Camino at the point where she and her husband had left off three years earlier.

They had planned to come back and finish this year, and had the tickets and everything ready to go, but then her husband unexpectedly died in a freak skiing accident. She was devastated and hoped that walking the rest of the way on her own would help heal her grief.

As I walked, I wondered what it would be like to have Patrick suddenly die like that, and the thought made me shudder. I knew our marriage had died, but I, too, would be devastated if Patrick suddenly died the way her husband had. He sounded a lot like Patrick, in fact. He was an adventurer and loved to bike and ski and travel—all the things Patrick liked to do.

She said they had so much fun together even though he didn't like his day job as a high-school chemistry teacher, and they went on all these adventures to create a more interesting life than the one he had carved out for himself at work. Now that he was gone she said she was very lonely and felt she had nothing more to live for.

She wasn't talking to me when she shared all of this. I just happened to be sitting within earshot. She also said, at least five times, that she felt that now that she was 60 years old she was too old to ever find another man to love her. In fact, she was absolutely convinced that without her youth no man would be interested in her ever again, so what was there to look forward to?

While I had a lot of compassion for her, it irritated me to listen to that. I suppose that many women feel a certain amount of pressure to stay young and beautiful because our world is so youth obsessed, but to hear a woman actually invalidate herself due to her age and accept her fear of failing to ever again attract a man as a fact was disturbing to me. It took everything in me not to jump up and tell her she was beautiful and crazy for thinking that as she aged she lost all value and could only expect to be rejected—as if being loved by a man were the only reason for living in the first place. I would have, but it didn't seem right at the time. I knew she wouldn't hear me.

So I just listened and felt the defeat in her spirit. Of course, I knew she was still in grief and with that comes all kinds of fears. I understood that because I, too, had wondered if I could ever have a love life beyond Patrick. Yet, while I was not feeling open to it at the moment, I certainly didn't believe that it was out of the realm of possibility because of my age, nor did I feel it was the only thing worth living for.

But then again, I thought as I finished my bar and got up again, maybe I had to hear her just in case I might secretly share some of those fears. After all, I am just as invested as the next woman in making myself look beautiful, and yes, youthful. Or at least I am when not walking the Camino. Even here, though, I still took care of my skin and protected it from the sun so I wouldn't get wrinkled. So was I really any different from her? Did I drink a sip of the same poison cup of bullshit that suggests I am only as valuable as how attractive I am to a man or how young I look?

Maybe I did, because listening to her made me feel so uncomfortable. So much so that I moved away from her as soon as I could because her energy bothered me so much.

Maybe I overheard her because the Camino is now asking me to look at my own fears about aging and needing male approval, I thought. Maybe it's time I embrace the crone in me, stop running away from her, and approve of my aging self. Maybe with age comes wisdom and inner beauty that is unsurpassed and powerful. Maybe it's time I let myself connect to this.

I thought about what I believe is beautiful. I know how much I love and need beauty, and how much I try to create it in my life. I have a beautiful home. I create beautiful feelings in my students when I'm working. But did I feel beautiful?

I mostly did, and yet, with all the loss and grief I had been feeling in the past few years, I didn't feel as beautiful as I wanted to feel. I also felt that being angry made me feel less beautiful. Not that I believed that anger was not okay. Sometimes the lightning bolt of anger beautifully shatters what harms us and frees us from its grip. That anger is beautiful and bold and brilliant.

But that wasn't the anger I was thinking of. The kind of anger that isn't beautiful is static and stagnant. Stuck anger. Anger that resents and blames and acts like a victim. That isn't beautiful. That kind of anger is ugly and steals away the beauty of life. I suffered that loss of beauty when I was languishing in those stuck feelings. At least now (thank goodness) I was liberating that stuck anger and returning to the beauty of my spirit as I walked every day.

"Thank you, Camino," I said aloud in gratitude. "Thank you."

I also thought of that woman's other dominant energy, fear. Her fear was palpable. She was swimming in it. I prayed for her to find her way to center and away from this dark feeling of fear that engulfed her. How awful to feel so powerless to overcome it.

As I thought of her, I wondered if I, too, had some of those same fears in me. Maybe that woman, so afraid of aging and fearing that she would never be loved again, was more courageous than I was because at least she was open and honest about it. She announced her fears while I hid mine away in the shadows.

More thoughts came cascading forward. Maybe the point of walking the Camino was to stop and look at all the feelings and fears I hide from because they take me away from my power and beauty. Maybe it was time to stop judging even these dark parts of myself, and just acknowledge and accept that I have some of these fears at times, just as she did. I wasn't possessed or obsessed with them, but they were there. And maybe now it was time to bring my fears to the light so they, too, could move on, just as she so courageously had.

Was I ready to release my fear of getting older and giving up the glow of youth for the inner light of wisdom? Honestly, not yet. I still wanted to feel young. I wanted to be young. But what if I did give up those attachments? What if I fully embraced myself, an aging woman, and no longer carried the fear of becoming the crone? What then?

Could I simply be comfortable in my own skin and love myself for who I am today? All of me and all of my years?

I wanted to say "yes" to those questions. More than anything I wanted to say, and mean, and believe that "yes" with every cell of my being. But I wasn't fully there yet.

I also knew that all the grief and sorrow I carried in my bones around my failed marriage and other failed relationships stemmed from me not being there yet. As much as I hated to admit this, I knew it was true.

When I saw that other woman reject herself, it felt sad, like a tremendous loss to herself and the world. I didn't want to lose any part of myself or deny any part of myself to the world. I wanted to embrace, celebrate, fully love, and share all parts of me.

No wonder my throat is on fire today, I thought. *My own words, and more important, my own thoughts and beliefs, have not loved and honored me. It isn't that Patrick didn't love me. It's that I didn't love me, then blamed him.*

My fiery throat was purging all that had me by the throat, all that made me feel as though I was not enough, never enough. It was time to free myself from all that caused me to reject myself and instead, fully love my beautiful self. I prayed to arrive in this place in me. *That is my Santiago. That is where I am going.*

As these thoughts flooded my mind I remembered a Native American blessing that says, "May you walk in beauty."

I decided right then that I would do just that. I would walk in the beauty of me today, all day. And I did, silently singing, *This girl is on fire!*

Day 20

(19 km; 12 mi)

El Burgo Ranero to Mansilla de las Mulas

When I arrived at the hostel, I once again ran into many familiar faces, people who were now becoming my Camino friends. There was Linda, who had started her Camino in Le Puy, France, and had been walking for three months now. There was Petra from Holland, and Hans and his friend Peter from Germany, and Clint and his new Camino partner Dean, a 40-year-old pilgrim from England whom he had met a few days earlier. The one I most appreciated seeing, however, was my gentle Canadian friend Colum, from Vancouver. Alan, his traveling mate for a time, had gone ahead and so Colum was now on his own, and nearing the end of his Camino journey. He would finish when he arrived in León in two days.

We sat at the bar in our hostel and had a few beers and talked about his life. He told me he had run away from home in Ireland when he was 16 and hadn't been back or looked back since. He said he left because his mother was such a gloomy, negative woman that he felt she was killing his spirit. He came to America and became a citizen, but then got drafted, so he married a Canadian woman and moved to Canada to avoid Vietnam. He had two daughters and three grandchildren, one of whom he loved dearly. He said he had no connection to the other two and thought the "lights of their spirits" were out, and he couldn't relate to their "dim" world.

I felt so enchanted by his company. I talked to him a little about Patrick and he said to beware of the Irish. "There are certain Irish people who dwell in misery and can't see or feel the wonder of the world. Dreary folks, they are. Good to get away from them."

I told him Patrick's birthday was coming up in a week and I was wondering if I should contact him to wish him a happy birthday.

"No," he said, without missing a beat. "He doesn't sound like he would be able to receive the gift of your blessing, so don't bother. Those Irish like to suffer and hold grudges and be wounded forever. Leave it. Move on."

I appreciated his perspective even if I didn't necessarily agree with it or feel it was the right advice for me. There was, however, truth to the wisdom of letting go of those who didn't want to open their hearts and receive your love. I certainly know you can't make people do this. I tried and failed. He was right about not wasting time on vain efforts, as well. Colum was a special soul. He had the poetic spirit of the Irish in him, and that I loved. He said he read a poem and wrote a poem every day. I asked him if he would share one of those poems with me, and he laughed and shook his head.

What I appreciated most about Colum was his clear and unapologetic spirit. He said what he felt and didn't beat around the bush. He didn't qualify his feelings or tone them down. He just put himself out there, as if to say, "Take it or leave it." He truly didn't care what anyone thought about him.

I asked him if he had always been this way. He thought for a minute and then said, "I learned early on that I might as well be dead rather than live for the approval of someone else. So yes, I have always been like this. Why not? No one else takes care of me, so why should I care what anyone thinks? I'm a good man. I know myself and I like myself. I love life, and if I ask for approval, I give a bit of my life away. And I don't want to give any of it away, ever. My life belongs to me."

I asked Colum how old he was. He said, "I'm 73 and going strong." That was for sure. I admired his calm sense of self. I wanted to feel that as well.

"You know, Colum, I'd like to be more like you." He laughed and said, "Good luck with that. Now I'm off to take a nap." That sounded like a good idea to me as well, as dinner wasn't served until eight and it was only three, so I followed right behind him.

The hostel was simple, but my room was surprisingly large and had a tiny bathtub, so I was able to open up Cheater and wash some clothes, which I sorely needed to do. Then I took a long tub bath and had a nap myself.

Later I went back down for dinner but wasn't feeling very hungry. My fever had broken, but I still felt lousy and had an extremely sore throat. I saw Colum sitting and drinking a beer with some other pilgrims, but I wasn't feeling social, so I kept to myself, eating a bowl of soup then retiring for the night.

The next morning I looked around for Colum, but he was already gone. I would miss him. I decided to once again take my time leaving town and sat down to breakfast. It was fantastic. I had an egg and potato omelet and two large glasses of fresh orange juice, several fresh-baked croissants, and a large café con leche. I felt as though I were in a five-star hotel, even though it was really the simplest little lodge. It's just that all was made and served with such love that it left me feeling so pampered. I left with my pilgrim's stamp and a thoroughly refreshed sense of myself.

> Holy Mother God,
> Thank you for the good company of Colum. And the delicious breakfast I was served this morning.
> I am grateful.
> Amen.

The walk today was short enough, only 19 kilometers, and the entire length of the path was relatively flat again. As I started out, I was drawn into a peaceful reverie, free of thoughts, free of revelations, and fully centered in the present. The birds were singing so loudly that I felt, at times, as though I were being personally serenaded. I didn't know birds could sing that loud.

I walked slowly because the electric shocks along the sides of my feet made it difficult to walk at all. I wondered why I'd had so much trouble with my feet since the beginning of the Camino, but no sooner did I start to question this than I knew it was a reflection of how little support I had felt under my feet for some time, and how little importance I had placed on having the kind of support I needed in my life. I trained myself to ignore what I needed and now it was catching up to me.

Nearly crawling along the Camino at this point, I realized how my feet were demanding I notice this lifelong self-sabotaging pattern and stop it once and for all. "I get it," I said out loud to the Camino. "I hear you. I don't want to be electrocuted with the message!" I was now getting irritable.

The longer I walked, the more evident it became that recognizing my need for support and knowing in what way I needed support would make a huge difference in bettering any future relationships. If I was not in touch with my needs, then how could anyone else meet them? No wonder I got so frustrated with Patrick. I was such an over-giving martyr. Yuck!

Up until now, my needs only became evident to anyone, including me, when I exploded after depleting myself completely. The more the sun beat relentlessly into the back of my head, the more clearly I could see how quickly I took on the role of superhero with others—giving, doing, rescuing, saving, solving, creating whatever they needed—and how I genuinely thought that I had to do that from the time I was a child growing up in my crazy, overcrowded home. I also saw how easily I became out of touch with myself, and especially my body. I overworked, over-traveled, over-consulted with others, and took on so many responsibilities for so many people without even stopping for a moment to consider whether I should be doing that, wanted to do that, or had the energy to do that. I just did it.

And to be honest, I liked how much I could accomplish at once. I was impressed with my superhero powers. But it always happened that just when I thought I was flying high, some very small thing would send me hurtling down to the ground.

That happened just before I left for the Camino. I was working way too many hours a day, as well as teaching every weekend and traveling from one end of the country to the other. While it seemed from the outside as though I were effortlessly flowing along with all of this, on the inside I was slowly being drained—and didn't even know to what extent that was happening.

It became abundantly clear just how on empty I was when I got off a flight in Chicago and started to drive home from the airport one day. Stuck in bumper-to-bumper traffic on the highway, I noticed that my car was nearly out of gas and there was no exit or gas station in sight. Rather than dealing with this stressful moment like a grown-up, I got really upset and started yelling at my car and the traffic and myself, reducing myself to tears because I was so depleted. By the time I coasted into the station on gas fumes, I was an emotional wreck. My only saving grace was that I was alone so no one witnessed me in such a sorry state.

I came back to the moment. The sun was intense and, save for the rare tree, there was no relief from it at all. I also found no relief from the memories of other occasions when I had run myself into the ground, or become so depleted from trying so hard and doing so much for others. This was an unrelenting pattern in me, and that realization made me all the more upset.

I wanted to enjoy the singing birds and go back to my peaceful reverie. Where did that go? When and why did I turn down this tunnel of emotional hell?

I was surprised at what was churning inside me, because some of the feelings and experiences rolling around in my body were so old I couldn't believe it. I remembered feeling so drained and acting so self-denying clear back to when I was only five or six years old. "Really, Sonia?" I asked myself. "You need to dredge this shit up?"

I had thought I was done with the past. I had thought I was done with being angry and upset and yet here I was, all over again, feeling enraged. I was enraged with myself for becoming a martyr. I was enraged with every person in my life who allowed me to act like a martyr instead of insisting that I relax, by assuring me that I was not responsible for them. I was enraged that I felt the only person I could trust to be responsible for anything was me. And that upset me even more because that was such a martyr attitude and so clearly not true. Most of all, I was *really* enraged that I was so completely depleted right now, that my feet hurt so fucking much, and that in spite of all my efforts and all the damn money I had spent, I felt no relief from any of this at all! Finally, I was so overwhelmed that I just stopped and screamed out loud, at the top of my lungs, "AAWWWWWRRRGGGG!"

Fortunately, there was no one around to hear me, but I wouldn't have cared if there were. Then, with the very next breath, a bone-deep inner calm swept through my entire body, as though these long-held trapped emotions had finally been jarred free. The next sound that escaped from me was a quiet, "Ahhhhh."

My mind became silent after that, acutely aware of the newly freed-up space in my body, in my bones, in my lungs, in my cells now that I had let all that old, dead energy out. I now felt I had more room to breathe, more room inside me to be me.

Day 21
(19 km; 12 mi)

Mansilla de las Mulas to León

I arrived in Mansilla de las Mulas shortly before 1 P.M. only to find a glorious open market in the center of the square, with hundreds of people milling about selling fresh fruits and vegetables, cheeses and hams, and clothing, while musicians played in one corner, and others sat in cafés drinking beer and wine and relaxing under the warm sun.

After wandering through the market and buying some fresh fruit, I decided to look for my hostel, which was located on a side street a few blocks off the town square. When I arrived, I was met by a surly, indifferent, tattooed teenager who was watching a Spanish soap opera and left me waiting for a commercial to come on before acknowledging my presence.

When I told her I had a reservation, she rolled her eyes and shook her head as if that wasn't possible and then disappeared behind a door into what was apparently the kitchen. After a full ten minutes had passed, I actually wondered if she had gone off to have a siesta and just left me standing there until her nap was over. I rang the receptionist's bell again, this time loudly, either to wake her up or to get someone else to come out from behind the door and help me.

A good five more minutes passed before she reemerged from behind the kitchen door, reeking of boredom and disinterest in everything, including me. Yet she did reach up, get a key, and start walking toward another set of doors, leaving me to guess that I was to follow her.

"Wait," I said, looking around for Cheater. She turned and stared at me as I pantomimed that I was looking for my bag. Apparently understanding me, she shuffled over to another door, opened it, and pointed inside, without making any eye contact with me whatsoever. Her affect was so over-the-top that I burst out laughing.

I now had to struggle with Cheater, my poles, and Pilgrim. I foolishly looked up to see if she would lend a hand. What was I thinking? She was ten feet ahead of me, watching me juggle my stuff without moving a muscle.

Realizing she was not going to help, I took my time as I carried first Cheater, then Pilgrim and my poles, up the stairs. I repeated this ritual in two separate trips up the four flights of stairs we had to climb as she watched and waited with indifference.

Finally, we stepped out onto a small terrace, with my room just off to the side. As we walked by, she nodded to a washing machine to the left of us. What a beautiful sight to behold! I then followed her to my room, as she opened the door and let me in. Following her right back out, I walked over to the washing machine and saw it took a few euros. I asked her for laundry soap. She said "Sí" in a dull monotone and started walking back downstairs.

She disappeared back into the kitchen and left me standing at the counter just as she had when I first arrived, which by now was ticking me off. Soon another woman came out of the kitchen, who I was sure was her mother, as she had similar features and the very same monotone affect. I smiled and said, "Soap?" and pointed to my clothes and pantomimed washing them.

"Sí," she said and left once again. I looked around and wondered if I had wandered into the Twilight Zone, as these women were acting like zombies. Yet, to my surprise she stepped back out after only a minute, with two small boxes of laundry soap and asked me for two euros.

I then took the soap and marched back upstairs. I threw Cheater open, gathered up my laundry, and headed straight to the washer. Once that was under way, I looked around and noticed how beautiful the terrace was, filled with gorgeous plants and flowers along with comfortable lounge chairs in which to sit and relax.

Up until now it had been too cold to sit in the sun, but the last two days were actually pretty warm, so I curled up in one of the chairs and promptly fell asleep. I woke up to other pilgrims stepping out on the terrace and then jumped up to check on my laundry. The washing cycle had just ended, so I shook out the freshly washed clothes and put them on a drying rack in the corner. Then I headed downstairs to go look around the town.

When I got back I ran into my friend Petra, as well as Hans and Peter, who had also just checked in. They both said something to me about the zombie mom-and-daughter team and I just laughed, saying, "Camino test."

That night I was invited to join about ten other pilgrims at a restaurant that Petra had heard was good. On the way there, I passed by the local church and went inside. It had been days since I had been inside a church, and it felt good to sit quietly and pray. You could really feel the history and power of the Camino in the churches. So many pilgrims for so many centuries had passed through these doors, all with the same intention as mine, to forgive and be forgiven in order to move on in peace. I said a rosary and thanked God for getting me this far. I was two-thirds of the way to Santiago by now, and even though it was hard to walk, miraculously, I was still moving.

I met up with everyone afterward, but by then the group had grown to nearly 20 pilgrims, and the minute I sat down I regretted being there. It wasn't that I didn't like everyone. It was just too much confusion to deal with right now. I wanted to stay quiet and contemplative, and the crowd was really loud and boisterous, and with only one waiter for our entire group the service was really slow.

I left after only soup and salad because I had already been in the restaurant over three hours and I was fried. I was so grateful for the term "Buen Camino" because that was all I had to say to bow out and everyone got it. Twenty "Buen Camino's" came right back at me as I waved and headed out the door, followed by five other pilgrims who felt the same way I did.

The next morning I headed down the street then entered a little café where, as I passed by, I had heard a man singing at the top of his lungs. When I walked in, he cheerfully greeted me, "Buenos días." I ordered my favorite breakfast, an egg bocadillo and café con leche, of course. Then I remembered I hadn't gotten my pilgrim's passport stamped at the hostel before I left, so I asked the waiter to do it, which he gladly and rather ceremoniously did. I left happy, in really clean clothes, and ready to get on to my next stop: León.

Walking out of town I was happy to get back into my own peaceful, private, quiet, Camino flow and away from everyone else's energy. I wanted to be alone with my thoughts, my feelings, my spirit, my guides, and my insights; and I found that this quickly disappeared when I was with too many others for very long. Everyone's Camino is their own creation, and the Camino I needed was one of solitude and quiet.

As much as I longed for a meditative journey, however, this was not the Camino I encountered. Apart from a short peaceful walk out of town, the Camino today was the greatest walking challenge so far. Long parts of it ran along a very busy highway, and there was a moment when I had to make a mad dash across four lanes to get to the other side. Yet between my aching feet and my still very sore knee, a mad dash was physically impossible. All I could manage was a sort of hop-along maneuver, which planted me head-on with a semitruck that blasted its horn at the sight of me, then swerved, scattering my nervous system all over the road.

I regained my composure only to walk through an endlessly long stretch of ugly warehouses and commercial buildings that drained the remaining life force out of my body. The only miracle in all of this was the speed at which I arrived in León. In five hours flat, I was standing in front of the cathedral in the central square, amazed by the majestic beauty before me. As I entered the church I felt a wave of pride at having braved the crazy elements and circumstances I had faced this far. I was also grateful I was still hanging in there, and hadn't gotten killed by a truck today.

The church was awesome. Between the architecture, the intricate stained glass, the multiple altars, and the arched ceilings, all I could do was marvel at the craftsmanship of the people who were able to create this so long ago. It was nothing short of a miracle as far as I could see. A warm, golden light flooded the entire place through the stained-glass windows, adding to its glory.

As I walked around the church, I felt as if I were being watched. Several times I was sure someone was standing right behind me, only to turn and see that no one was there. "Whoever you are watching over me," I whispered under my breath, "thank you for saving my life today."

After my visit I went back outside to explore. The city was vibrant and busy, light-years away from the Camino. Just off the main square I happened upon a place that offered healing foot massages for pilgrims, and on a whim I decided to go in. I needed help.

The massage therapist was a wiry, welcoming, and serious man. He was about 5'6", with black hair, wearing a doctor's white coat and a big cross on a leather cord around his neck. He smiled some, but he didn't speak a word of English. I pointed to my feet, and he nodded and pointed to the massage table. I took off my socks and shoes and he gestured to me to lie facedown. I did, but didn't understand why. So there I was, lying facedown, when he started to massage my shoulders. It wasn't my feet, but it felt so good that I didn't stop him. Maybe he was just warming up for the feet.

Then, suddenly, it didn't feel so good. He started to pound and beat on my back and knead into it with his elbow and knuckles with so much force it knocked the breath out of me. I kept saying, "No, feet," with my face smashed into the table, while he kept digging harder and deeper into my neck and shoulders, completely ignoring my pained objections. I tried several times to turn over and point to my feet, but he kept pushing my face back down, saying, "Moment, moment," as he dug his fingers into my ribs and back. I screamed out loud for mercy. The more I screamed, the louder he said, "Moment!" and the harder he pounded.

Finally, after a half an hour or so, he stopped. He never once touched my feet, but given the beating I just took, I was glad. I still had to walk another 12 days, and with his technique I wouldn't be able to walk out the door.

Right before he finished, he began to pray over me out loud in Spanish for about a minute and then threw holy water all over my back. Then he turned me faceup (finally) and said in almost perfect English that I was blessed and was a blessed pilgrim. I left feeling unsure of whether or not going in there had been a good decision. With the exception of my feet, I did actually feel better after all that.

After this intense interlude, I eventually found my way to my hostel, happy to discover that it was a medieval monastery turned elegant hotel. My room was small but nice—exactly what I needed right now.

After I checked in and grabbed Cheater, I went to my room and took a long nap.

When I woke up, I went to a nearby café and treated myself to a large pizza and salad, and a glass of the best red wine in the house. I sat and relaxed for a while before taking another long stroll around the main square, and then went in to bed.

All I could say as my head hit the pillow was, "Thank God I'm still going strong!"

Day 22
(24 km; 15 mi)

León to Mazarife

I woke up to gray skies and pouring rain, the sunny warmth and clear blue skies of yesterday long gone. I lingered in bed and contemplated taking a taxi today, as nothing in me wanted to face the nasty conditions outside my window. I needed a break. I was tired. I hurt. Still debating whether or not I would succumb to temptation, I shuffled toward the shower, my feet clearly casting a vote for the taxi. I looked in the mirror and asked myself what to do. I was surprisingly bright-eyed in spite of my resistance as I answered, "You'll know after breakfast."

I replied, "Fair enough," and then took a long, hot shower. I packed up Cheater and counted my remaining PowerBars. I had 13 days and eight bars left. Then I dressed warmly, pulling out the long underwear, long-sleeve wool shirt, and headband I had thought I would no longer need. The pain in my toes was starting to ease up a little, in spite of what was now an obvious infection breeding under my nails, but the shooting pains I felt along the sides of my feet were constant. "I hope I haven't permanently trashed my feet," I said aloud, admitting the anxiety I had felt for days.

Still, all I could do was keep walking, and for the moment that meant as far as the dining room for breakfast. I searched the corridors, following the smell of coffee, and had to marvel at how beautiful this old monastery was, even if it did feel a little haunted by the heavy spirits of the past.

It took a while to find what I was looking for, but eventually I did locate the brightly lit dining room, already teeming with happy pilgrims fortifying themselves before starting their day. It didn't take long to discover why. The buffet was out of this world. Fresh-squeezed juices of all sorts, freshly baked pastries and crois- sants, toast, yogurts, dried and fresh fruits, cheeses, and potato and egg omelets were laid out in a lovely array, refreshed regularly by a delightful Spanish woman who greeted us with such warmth that it couldn't help but lift a person's spirits. What a departure from yesterday's den of misery!

I loaded up my plate to overflowing with food, and then filled up three glasses with different fresh juices before I settled down to eat. Then I looked around to see who else was in the room. There was a group of five Italian bikers, a hardy-looking French-speaking couple, a young Englishman, and a Russian woman, all appreciat- ing their breakfast as much as I was.

Buoyed by the food and the positive energy in the room, I decided to stop fighting the walk ahead and go for it. But, just to make it through, I did go back to the buffet and grab three more hot apple pastries, two bananas, and some cheese and bread. I wrapped it all up in a napkin to take along with me, wondering if I was being a thief or if this was an acceptable pilgrim thing to do. I didn't care. I wanted backup on the Camino, and I would much rather have this than another PowerBar later on.

I headed back to my room and loaded up Cheater, who was getting lighter by the day. Then I headed downstairs, Gumby hanging off Pilgrim, my little purse tucked inside. Once I arrived at the front desk, I was informed by the receptionist that the hos- tel where I stayed yesterday had called and said I had left a pair of pants, some socks, and one of my wool shirts on the drying rack on the terrace, but they would hold them for me if I wanted to go back and get them.

"Rats! My stuff!" I totally forgot about it yesterday. I sighed, not wanting to visit the Zombie Palace ever again. Besides, it was the Camino! You don't go backward. You just keep moving for- ward. So I said to the receptionist, "Tell them to keep it or give it to another pilgrim. I'm moving on." I then asked her for a pilgrim's stamp for my passport, draped my rain poncho over my head, and said, "Ultreya." Then I headed out the door.

The Camino shells, which I had to follow to get out of town, were embedded in the ground and were tricky to find, so I had to pay extra-close attention if I wanted to stay on course. I had to walk for over an hour and a half through the same dreary suburbs as yesterday before I returned to the natural beauty of the Camino.

I wondered what day of the week it was, having lost all track of time. I kept a sharp eye out for the yellow arrows, as twice this morning I had already veered off the path and onto the wrong road by mistake and had to backtrack. Finally I arrived at a small town called Virgen del Camino and slipped into a café to dry off a bit and enjoy a mid-morning break. As I sat with my coffee, I closed my eyes and said an earnest prayer to feel true love for myself today.

> *Holy Mother-Father God,*
> *Please open my heart to see the goodness of me and help me forgive and release everything that blocks my feelings of self-love and gratitude for the gift of this life, which you have given me.*
> *Amen.*

The walk was mostly flat, running parallel to the highway, peppered with occasional storks flying overhead to break up the otherwise monotonous scenery.

The storms in my mind of the past few days were starting to subside as well, and I intuitively sensed (or maybe just hoped) they might not return again. My mind was quiet and clear, allowing me to listen as the Camino talked to me.

Do you see how your life has unfolded as it has because of the choices you've made? it asked me.

Looking backward, I could see exactly how my own choices got me to where I was today. I chose to try too hard in my relationships. I chose to do too much. I chose to be willful and try to make things work out even when they weren't. I chose to react to

Patrick rather than respond, and I chose to be frustrated with him rather than try to understand him.

"I do, but I'm only human. I did what I knew at the time," I justified myself to the Camino. Then I paused. "Okay. It's true. I also chose to do a few things I knew better than to do," I admitted. "I chose to fight. I chose to hold grudges. I chose to stay upset."

It felt good to acknowledge these things. It helped me realize that I was not a victim of anything; rather, I was responsible for my own unhappiness.

Yes, I am glad you can see that now, the Camino seemed to suggest with the faintest rays of sunlight flashing across the plains as I walked.

Are you aware of how you've bound yourself to your own choices and them blamed others as if they had forced them upon you? the Camino asked next.

"In what way?" I responded. "I'm not sure I understand."

Are you sure you don't understand? it challenged me.

"I guess I chose to work as hard as I did because I loved what I was doing, but when I overworked and burned myself out, I blamed Patrick for not working hard enough to keep up with me."

Yes, you did.

"I guess I chose to keep trying to please my father long into adulthood instead of telling him I wouldn't do that anymore, and then blamed him for not changing."

That, too.

The longer I walked, the more I could see how my own choices determined everything I was feeling. I didn't choose every external situation, of course, but I did choose how I would respond to those situations.

And the truth is that many of my choices had been fantastic. I chose to follow my intuition and teach others to do the same. I chose to travel the world with Patrick and our daughters, and that choice was one of the best of my life. I chose to write books, which I loved doing, even though my first editor asked me if English was my native language. I chose to stay married and raise our daughters with Patrick, as he was a good dad. These were all great choices, and I was happy I made them.

Other choices were not the best, and I could clearly see how those choices caused me the pain I was in. The choice to believe that I was hard to love, for example, made me try way too hard in all of my relationships to prove myself lovable by doing so much. Then I would feel taken advantage of or unappreciated. I definitely needed to reconsider that choice because it wasn't serving me. I'm not difficult to love, even if I can, at times, be difficult to be around. Who isn't? We all have our light and shadow sides.

I also chose to believe that Patrick was not a nice person. That choice made me angry and defensive, and I could see now how I provoked him into not being a nice person. Patrick certainly had his issues, and, yes, he could be not so nice at times, but it wasn't as though that was all he was. He could be very loving and kind, and was there for people in need.

I could also see now that I wasn't bound by those decisions forever. In fact, the more I walked, the clearer it became that it was time to make some new choices, the first being to stop feeling victimized by people and start letting go of the sense of powerlessness I had been feeling.

I was so deep in concentration over all of this that I walked into Mazarife, where I was scheduled to stop, and then out of town without noticing. Once I did, I circled back and went to find my hostel. I walked around the town and the church three or four times looking for it, but had no luck. In fact, apart from one small pilgrims' albergue/restaurant across from the church, there was nothing else in the town. Frustrated, I walked into the pilgrims' albergue bar and ordered an egg bocadillo. Then I asked the waiter if he knew where my hostel was.

He shook his head and said there was no such place in Mazarife. I looked at the paper with my itinerary once again, and then showed it to him, and he still shook his head.

Having learned by now not to get too upset by a bump in the road such as this, I asked him to ask others who worked there if they might know where this hostel was located while I ate my sandwich.

He disappeared into the kitchen. Five minutes later a short, heavyset woman came out from the kitchen and said my hostel was another ten kilometers down the road. I almost choked. "No, I don't want to walk that far! I can't. Not today!" I cried.

Nearly breaking down, I asked if I could call a taxi. She shook her head and said there were no taxis in Mazarife. I believed her. There were no people in Mazarife, so why should there be any taxis?

"You can stay here," she offered.

"I wish I could," I answered, "but my bag is waiting for me at the hostel. I have to catch up with it."

"Crap," I swore under my breath. "This sucks."

Embarrassed by my poor reaction, I apologized immediately. She said, "No worries. I will call them and tell them that you are tired."

"Okay," I said, not expecting that to change a thing.

I ordered a Coke from the bartender as she dialed, thinking I would need as much sugar and fuel as possible if I were going to make it as far as I had to go, especially now that the rain was once again coming down outside the pilgrims' albergue window. Meanwhile, she chatted excitedly away to someone on the other end of the phone, punctuating her conversation with numerous "sí, sí, sí's" while glancing my way, with a look of pity in her eyes.

When she finally hung up, she looked at me and said, "Is okay! He is come to get you. One hour."

I was so happy to hear that I would have waited all day. I thanked her profusely for helping me out, then sat back and relaxed. I needed this today. I was tired of soldiering on. I wanted to be carried. Mercifully, I was going to be.

"Perfect," I said, thanking the Camino for this new turn of events. Letting myself be helped was a new choice for me and one I sorely needed to make right now.

An hour and a half later, I found myself sitting in the most comfortable old farmhouse, my feet up, relaxing in front of a roaring fireplace, with a glass of delicious red wine in hand, hosted by the loveliest people I'd met at any hostel so far along the Camino.

The wife, Marcella, a quiet woman of around 50, with warm brown eyes and a kind smile, insisted I give her all my clothes to wash, and then encouraged me to take a nap and meet them at eight for dinner.

Feeling so welcomed, I relaxed, slept, and then had the most delicious home-cooked meal of fresh fish, steamed vegetables from their garden, a tossed green salad, homemade bread, cheeses, and delicious cake and chocolates.

Falling asleep that night, I thought, *How wonderful to receive this love and generosity today. I needed it!*

Day 23
(30 km; 19 mi)

Mazarife to Astorga

I woke up to the smell of freshly baked bread and hot coffee, so it didn't take much to draw me out of bed and downstairs, not even bothering to change out of my nightclothes. Once downstairs I was thrilled to find a delicious Spanish omelet with fresh stewed tomatoes, served alongside a basket filled with still warm bread and homemade jam, and a steaming hot café con leche waiting for me on the dining-room table. Moments later, my wonderful host, Marcella, entered the dining room and after wishing me a cheerful "Buenos días," handed over my freshly washed and folded laundry and asked if there were anything else she or her husband, Miguel, could do for me before I set out on the Camino today.

Thinking about my few remaining PowerBars, I asked if they would mind if I took a little bread and cheese with me for the walk. Ten minutes later I was handed a carefully packed picnic, complete with bread, cheese, fruit, jam, ham, and chocolate. I happily accepted their offering and stuffed the package into Pilgrim, grateful to have something new to eat today. Receiving was getting easier by the day.

I went upstairs and took a long, hot shower, then packed up Cheater and got ready to go. As usual, it was raining and cold, so I threw on warm clothes, glad that I hadn't left my long underwear behind several days ago. Then I went back downstairs to enjoy one more cup of coffee before I set out for the long walk ahead. It was so cozy at this farmhouse I wanted to say for a week.

A few minutes later, Miguel carried Cheater down to the first floor for me and assured me that someone would soon be there to pick him up and deliver him to the next hostel. I was grateful not to have to carry Cheater down myself, even though he had lost a considerable amount of weight since we started out on this journey together. I had too, it seemed, because I'd had to take the shoelaces from my (useless) lightweight hiking shoes and tie my belt loops more tightly together this morning, as my pants were beginning to fall off. Lingering a bit longer, I asked them to stamp my pilgrim's passport, then took some photos of them, wanting to remember their kindness long after this adventure was over.

It was now time to go, so I asked them to point me in the direction of the Camino, delighted to find out that it was directly out their back door. I gave them both a big hug as they wished me a hearty "Buen Camino."

Once on the path, my heart was peaceful as the Camino led me through more flat farmland along the railroad tracks, under rainy skies. I was so grateful for the simple kindness and love shown me last night that today I felt as though I were the luckiest and most blessed person alive. Even my white hiking shirt was not only returned to me freshly washed, but also ironed, for heaven's sake. They treated me with such respect for making this pilgrimage— I couldn't believe it! The love I felt was so healing that much of what had troubled me over the past few days ceased to matter. It felt good to step into this higher vibration and keep moving.

Eventually I came across an incredible stone bridge leading into the next town. I stopped and read about it on a sign. Called the Puente de Órbigo, it was one of the longest and oldest medieval stone bridges in Spain, dating back to the 13th century, and built over an even older Roman bridge that existed for centuries before. It was considered one of the great historical landmarks on the Camino, and I could see why. Its 20 arches led me across the Río Órbigo along what was known as the Paso Honroso, or Passage of Honor, because of a famous jousting tournament that took place there in 1434.

According to legend, a knight from León named Don Suero de Quiñones, scorned by a beautiful lady, threw down his gauntlet to any knight who dared to pass as he stood defending the bridge, and also his honor. Knights came from all over Europe to accept his challenge, yet he successfully guarded the bridge from passage for 30 consecutive days. Then he continued on to Santiago to say prayers of thanks for his newfound freedom from the bondage of love that had held him in misery, now feeling that his honor had been fully restored.

I thought about the knight Don Suero and the bondage he had felt to the one who had scorned him. It's true that we bind ourselves to the ones that hurt us if we cannot forgive, and because of that we continue to suffer long after the wounding has occurred.

That is what forgiveness is all about in the end, isn't it? I thought. *Releasing ourselves from what holds us in bondage?*

I, too, wanted freedom from bondage, I thought, as I walked over the bridge. And like the knight Don Suero, the only way to achieve it was to fight what had stolen it away. I had to fight off regret and bitterness. I had to fight off confusion and judgment. I had to fight off shame and embarrassment. But what I had to fight off most of all was the isolating and distorted "victim" perceptions of my ego.

It was time to release myself from these dark feelings, because nothing good came from them. Nothing. They didn't bring me peace. They didn't lift my heart. They didn't make me feel better. They just made me feel sad and worthless and unloved. It was the worst kind of bondage a person could be in, and I wanted no more of it.

As I walked I also came to realize that to truly forgive, I needed more than to just understand why things had happened as they did, although that did play an important part. I understood all along in my marriage that I was facing my own karma and my own spiritual tests. I also understood it was my choice to be born into the family I was born into, for the spiritual lessons and opportunities this family offered me. I even understood that it was I who chose all the relationships I had been involved with in my life in order to learn certain soul lessons for my own spiritual growth.

I had even mentally forgiven everyone who had hurt me, and wanted them to forgive me as well. I didn't want to be bound by my ego's perceived injuries anymore. It's just that in spite of my understanding, I was still in pain.

What I wanted now was to turn it all over to God and be relieved of the pain in my heart and soul. I wanted to be forgiven for holding on to the pain. I wanted to release all of it so I could fully feel and receive all the love available to me now. I wanted to forgive myself for cutting myself off from the love that God and my Higher Self had for me. That is what this Camino was about. That was the forgiveness I sought.

I came back to the moment. The bridge spilled into a medieval town. The rain had subsided to a light drizzle, so I slid off my poncho hood so I could better look around. It felt as though I had stepped back in time, and once again I flashed on the Knights Templar. I felt as if I had been here before. It wasn't even a thought. It was more like a déjà vu. I had crossed this bridge and might have even been part of building it.

I walked off the bridge and into the center of the town, named Hospital de Órbigo. It was very early in the morning, so the entire town was shut down and there was hardly a soul in sight. I did notice, however, a funny-looking little man riding up and down the small cobblestone street next to me on a bicycle that appeared way too small for him, wearing a bright yellow-orange vest that said "Security," which seemed a bit out of place since there was no one around that seemed threatening. But then again, I had come to realize that every single thing that appeared on the Camino had a message for me, and if that was so, his appeared to suggest that I was safe and protected.

He rode past me several times, catching my eye and glancing at me sideways with a slight smile. I started to wonder if he might be an angel. The thought dropped in from out of nowhere, but the minute this came to mind, I got a chill all over my body. I looked around to see where he was, but he had disappeared. I sat down to eat my picnic lunch and waited for him to return, but he never rode by again. "Okay, Camino. I got the message. All is well. Thank you," I said aloud.

I packed up Pilgrim and stood up. The rain started up again, so I grabbed my poles, pulled my poncho back over my head, and got going.

Soon the path began to change. It was no longer flat, and I found myself climbing up and down rolling hill after hill. The ground was covered in round, wet rocks that were as slippery to walk on as ice, causing me to fall down again and again.

In addition, there were deep rivers of muddy sludge all along the path, no doubt caused by the weeks and weeks of rain that had been coming down. It took my full attention to navigate every step, as I didn't want to fall flat on my face and get soaked in the muck more than necessary.

I found myself jumping from side to side, leaping over little rivers of mud, reaching for tree branches for balance in order to avoid stepping into the ankle-deep puddles, as I slowly inched my way along, feeling as though I were playing a solo game of Twister as I went.

I couldn't lift my eyes from the ground in front of me, as one false move could potentially throw me to the ground. I walked this way for quite some time, eyes glued to the path. One time, I slipped off a rock and onto my side, jabbing my rib with my pole. Pilgrim flew off my back, catapulted ten feet from me by the weight of my big rock inside, and landed squarely in a pool of mud, Gumby ten feet farther. Because I had on my rain poncho and rain pants, I instantly became a human Slip'N Slide, bumping down the path for several feet before I ran smack into a tree stump lying across the path. I sat there stunned for a few minutes before I first cursed, then laughed, then stood up and went back to collect my strewn-about stuff.

Once I composed myself I set off again, the round rocks thankfully giving way to jagged flat ones as the ground evened out again, leaving me to return to the serenity of the morning. Orchards dotted either side of the path; the tree trunks were covered in moss, a dense mist swirling all around as if dancing through them. I could sense the nature fairies and sprites watching me as I continued slowly onward.

I was being pulled back into that other reality I had fallen into again and again. I wondered if the Camino pulled you into this other realm, or if I allowed myself to enter another realm as I walked. It didn't matter. I was in it and it was enfolding me completely, as if I were being wrapped up in a warm, comforting blanket.

Eventually I came upon a makeshift pilgrim shrine. To one side was a full-size homemade statue of a pilgrim, with a mask for a face, fully dressed in real clothes, wearing a hat and carrying a large walking stick. Next to him stood a large metal cross sitting atop a small mound of round stones left by previous pilgrims. He felt like an energetic gatekeeper, marking the entry to an entirely new dimension of the Camino. I looked around and found a large round stone and left it amidst the others, marking my own passage through here.

The path was made of red dirt and stones, flattened out even more, with occasional bluffs here and there. The weather had lightened up considerably, and it was now sunny but cool. Even so, I stopped and pulled off the several layers of clothing I was wearing and stuffed them into Pilgrim, as I was now drenched in sweat.

The mud on the path had dried up and while the stones were still tricky to walk on, I wasn't as bound to watch my every step as I had been a few hours earlier. I could now look up and out and see the expanse before me. I was starting to feel lighter and happier. At the moment nothing mattered. Not the past. Not the future. I was fully present, and my spirit was peaceful.

I felt as if I were part of nature, not just looking at it. I was connected to everything, not alone. My ego was watching, but it was silent. I felt fully awake and alive, not burdened with my stories or my wounds.

At around 3:30 I found myself at the end of the ancient Roman road as I came to the edge of Astorga, my destination for the day. I crossed over the train tracks, then came to a simple church. I entered and found myself awed by the stunning interior. Mother Mary looked down upon me from the altar, and I said a prayer of thanksgiving for having made it yet another day. Then I remembered that it was Patrick's birthday.

> *Holy Mother God,*
>
> *I thank you with all my heart and soul for overseeing me this far. I also want to say a special prayer of thanks for all the gifts I have received from Patrick. Today is his birthday, and for his present, I release him from my anger and resentment, and pray with my whole heart and soul that he may find his happiness and inner peace. I am grateful for all the help you have given me to arrive at this present state of mind. I pray that he has the happiest birthday he can possibly have.*
>
> *Amen.*

I went to the front of the church and lit a birthday candle for him and sent him unconditional love. "Thank you, Patrick," I whispered. "Happy birthday."

I sat for a little while longer and said a rosary in thanksgiving for all that I had experienced so far on the Camino. Then I got up, grabbed my poles, and continued on into town, until I came upon a beautiful plaza at the top of a hill. I saw my hostel right away, thank goodness, as the minute I spotted it thunder and lightning suddenly crackled in the sky, followed by a huge downpour, the biggest one yet of the Camino.

Day 24

(19 km; 12 mi)

Astorga to Rabanal del Camino

I woke up early, ready to get going once again. I was about to head back up into the mountains and wanted to get an early start, as I knew it would be a long ascent. My body felt great, with the exception of my miserable aching feet. It worked well enough to keep going. I couldn't stop now.

I opened the wooden shutters over my window and peered out into the plaza below. It was still pouring rain and I could see pilgrims, their backpacks bundled under rain ponchos, looking like a pack of huge, slow-moving turtles, all headed in the same direction.

I hopped into the shower, enjoying the hot stream of water pouring down my back, knowing that the minute I stepped outside it would be cold and miserable for who knows how many hours. I then dressed as warmly as possible and packed up Cheater. Next I stuffed Gumby and my little purse into Pilgrim, keeping my passport out so I could get a stamp. Then I headed downstairs with Cheater in the elevator (*yeah!*) at the end of the long hall.

The restaurant was located next door to the hostel, so after I deposited Cheater with the front-desk receptionist, I took the coupon she handed me and headed over, starving. The breakfast was disappointing. The toast and coffee were cold, and the juice wasn't fresh, and as hard as I tried to enjoy it, there was nothing about it I liked. I knew from overhearing other pilgrims that it was a fairly gradual climb up to Rabanal, with several cafés along the way, so I gave up trying to like my breakfast, unzipped Pilgrim to make sure I had a few PowerBars to carry me over, and headed out. The rain had stopped and now the sun was peeking through the clouds.

> Holy Mother God,
> Thank you. Thank you. Thank you. I'm off once again.
> Amen.

I held my big rock one more time, before I threw it into Pilgrim. It was really heavy and I wondered if I had overdone it in choosing this rock since it was so hard to carry. No, I thought, it felt just right. I wandered through the town and back toward the Camino, following the other pilgrims instead of looking for yellow arrows. Soon I passed the magnificent cathedral at the other end of town and stopped to take some photos. A German pilgrim offered to take my photo, which I gladly accepted, then I took one of her. I approached the church doors to go in, but it was (not surprisingly) locked.

It only took a few minutes to get out of town and on my way. The scenery was as haunting as yesterday. There was a dense, knee-deep soft mist covering the ground for as far as the eye could see. I sensed the nature spirits peeking out from behind the trees, whispering to each other as I walked by.

Every few minutes I had to stop and take photos, as I couldn't believe how mystical this all was. I felt enchanted.

While there was fog and mist all around me, inside I was getting more and more clear. Today I felt so much compassion for every single person in my life that I cried for almost two hours as I walked. I could see how each person was only doing the best that they could, and how I had a pattern of continually asking people to be more than they were, and then becoming disappointed. I also was keenly aware of how much I didn't listen to others, and I felt so sad about that.

Perhaps it was because I grew up with a mom who was essentially deaf, due to a hearing loss she suffered during the war; and from her, I learned to listen to energy, to vibration, to my intuition

. . . but didn't ever put a great deal of importance on what was actually being said. I had never thought of that before. How frustrating that must have been for people in my life. In many ways, I had become as deaf as my mother was, filtering my awareness to listen to what I wanted to hear, and not necessarily to what others were communicating. That was one of Patrick's main complaints about me and now, finally, I recognized that it was true. I didn't listen to much of what he said. No wonder my relationship with him got into so much trouble.

"I'm sorry, Patrick," I said aloud, hoping that his spirit would hear me. "Part of what heals the spirit is to be heard, and I didn't do that very well with you, did I?"

I also became more aware of all the wonderful things he had brought to my life, like all the wonderful meals he had so lovingly prepared for me and our family, and the gorgeous gardens he created for our home. And the ways in which he introduced me to camping and biking and canoeing and how to pick out and put lights on the best Christmas tree. And, of course, our two beautiful, amazing daughters. My father taught me great lessons, too, for that matter. He taught me how to stay focused and finish any job I started, how to fix just about anything that broke, and how to be resourceful and resilient and not allow life to beat me down, ever. I had been given so much by both of them, much of which I had completely missed or wasn't able to receive because of my wounded and defensive ego. The exciting thing was that in recognizing what had happened, I felt as if I were actually receiving these gifts now.

It wasn't too late to receive the love of others, even if my marriage was over, or my father had passed away. The love they had for me hadn't gone away. It was still present and real.

If that were the case, then, all the love I had ever shared wasn't lost either. In fact, I suddenly realized that love is never lost. It doesn't go away. It waits for each of us to receive it when we are ready to.

So much of what I had suffered felt like a lack or loss of love, when, in fact, it was my inability to receive love because I was so overwhelmed by the painful ways in which my ego had cut me off from it that was the real problem.

I was loved. We all are. And have been. And will be. All of us. Always.

I looked around as I walked, feeling love everywhere. Everything around me was breathing in love and breathing out love. The trees. The birds. The flowers. The rocks. And me. I had been the entire time. I was love, even if my mind took me far away from that truth. It was such a sublime feeling that I was afraid to think about it too much for fear it would go away.

It got colder and colder the higher I went, and after a while I had to look for a café just to warm up and rest. It took another hour, however, to find one. Finally I entered a little town called Cruces, where I stopped in a café for a café con leche. I was in such a contemplative mood that I just sat and stared into space as I drank, my dripping rain poncho by my side, Gumby at the table, and Pilgrim at my feet.

I was in a strange state of mind. I felt as if everything in my life were connected, like a weird matrix that was constantly shifting and changing. I felt the full impact of cause and effect, choice and result, throughout my entire existence. I felt this thread through my past lives, my present life, my family, my father and brother, my work, my daughters, my travels, my books and teaching, and my relationships, including and especially with Patrick. It was all connected. And moreover, it was all enveloped by absolute love.

This sense of dynamic interconnectedness had begun to become clear yesterday when I decided to ask God for forgiveness for not loving myself. It intensified as I walked, the path itself peeling away more and more of the old pain from my body, revealing a fresh new me underneath. My heart was returning to its original condition. I was healing and all was slowly being forgiven, by me, by others, and by God for all of us. Something amazing was taking place in me as I walked, and I knew it was the Camino itself that was causing this. The energy of the path was transforming me.

Slowly drifting back to the present, I began looking around to see who might be there. I noticed an older Spanish man at a table nearby struggling with his foot, and saw that he had a humongous blister on his heel and looked as if he were in tremendous pain. Since I carried a lot of blister remedies in Pilgrim each day, I approached him and offered my assistance.

He was reluctant to take any help from me, but once I showed him my huge array of blister bandages and creams, he quickly changed his mind. I carefully applied a little hydrogen peroxide on a cotton ball to his open wound, and then plastered the blister over with large moleskin that covered the entire area. He looked somewhat relieved, but I wasn't sure it was because he felt better, or if it was just the knowledge that he didn't have to walk any further with his raw skin rubbing against his boot. I then got up and wished him a "Buen Camino." I was on my way again.

The walk became steeper and steeper. It also got colder and colder, and I was freezing as I walked the last few kilometers. My rock felt heavier than ever and it pulled on my shoulders as I carried it in Pilgrim. Finally, I arrived in the tiny hamlet of Rabanal. I had only just entered and begun to look around when I came face-to-face with Camino Patrick.

We ran and gave each other a great big hug. I was so happy to see him. I thought I would never see him again. He told me that he had made such good time that he had been there for two days. I just shook my head. How did he do that? I was moving as fast as I could, and I could barely make it to the next town each day.

In Rabanal there was a little monastery run by German monks, and they had invited Patrick to stay with them and rest for a few days. He had developed an intense pain along the front of both of his legs and could barely sleep at night because it was so bad, so he gladly accepted their invitation and was there for his second of three days, hoping the rest would bring some relief.

He walked me to my hostel, an old Swiss-looking chalet of a place, and waited while I checked in. Cheater had not yet arrived, but I was assured he soon would. We then agreed to meet at the 6 P.M. pilgrim mass in the monastery church. I invited him to have dinner with me, but he said that he was having dinner with the monks and didn't want to disappoint them. I understood, so we sat down and had a beer and talked for over an hour before I told him that I needed a nap and would see him in an hour for the mass.

By then Cheater had arrived and I hauled him to my room, which was on the third floor. Suddenly he didn't seem as light as he had two days ago. I eventually made it upstairs, settled in, changed clothes, and relaxed. I couldn't really nap because I was afraid I would sleep through the mass, so after a half hour I went back downstairs to have a Coke.

There I saw three more pilgrims I had walked with along the way. The first were Victoria and her son, Eric. She was faring well, but he had torn a muscle in his ankle somehow and refused all manner of remedies offered him, preferring to tough it out naturally. She was exasperated with him, and he was annoyed with her. I offered him my remedies, but before I could even let him know what I had, including natural ones, he refused. Clearly his was a Camino of penance and he did not want anyone to interfere.

His mother rolled her eyes and snapped at him, "You are such a control freak! I can't stand it."

I tiptoed away. This was clearly not a conversation for me.

I talked with some of the others until it was time for mass. There I listened to the most eloquent German priest say mass in English, with certain parts in five other languages. He ended by wishing all the pilgrims a "Buen Camino," then said if any of us wished to speak to him after mass he would make himself available. I decided I did.

We talked about my marriage ending and my desire to move on in peace. He listened and then said, "Just let go and love him. That is what you promised to do when you married him. Try that and give the rest to God."

I promised. I would just let go and love him in my heart. I felt I could do that now. I would also love me. That would be the new part. I thanked him, and he blessed me and gave me a hug.

I met Camino Patrick, who was waiting for me outside the church, and wished him well. I told him we would meet in a few days, and we came up with a plan. The next thing I knew I was in bed, having skipped dinner in favor of a PowerBar. I was peaceful and just wanted to go to sleep. Tomorrow I was walking to the highest point of the Camino, Cruz Ferro, where I would leave the big rock I had been carrying and the burdens it represented. I was ready.

Day 25
(32 km; 20 mi)

Rabanal to Ponferrada

I woke up early this morning, ready to begin the long ascent up to Cruz Ferro.

I knew it was going to be a long, rigorous walk, so I layered up and stuffed two of my six remaining PowerBars into Pilgrim, just to be prepared for what lay ahead. I then packed up Cheater and headed down to the first floor. I managed to get Cheater down to the second floor when an Argentinean biker saw me struggling, so he took him from me and carried him down. It was a good start to the day.

After a quick breakfast of coffee and toast and a glass of fresh orange juice, I asked for a stamp for my passport and went back up to my room to grab my poles, Gumby, and Pilgrim. I then pulled on my wool cap and gloves, pulled my headscarf over my ears, and stepped out into a stiff, frigid wind under dark, cold skies. I was ready to go.

> *Holy Mother God,*
> *Please let me release _all_ my burdens at the top. Even the*
> *ones I still want to hold on to.*
> *Amen, and thank you in advance.*

The steep walk challenged my knee from the first step, but I just kept going. As I climbed, one slow step at a time, I reflected once again on just exactly what was burdening me, as I really wanted to be sure I didn't forget something. I had come too far on this pilgrimage to miss the opportunity before me.

The top notes of my thoughts cited the usual complaints: too much work, responsibility for what was not mine, years of what I felt were unfair experiences, not feeling loved and appreciated as I had wanted to be. It was nothing new.

Yet, the more I walked, the more apparent it became to me that while those were things that made me unhappy, they were not at the root of what burdened me.

What burdened me most had been my own fear and anger, even rage over these things and more. I'd been burdened by not trusting others to be good to me. I'd been burdened by the belief that I could trust only myself to be responsible and then made choices to support that belief. I'd been burdened by the false belief that I had to work and never stop because I was taught that working hard is what love looks like. I was burdened by the belief that I had no right to the full range of my feelings or to healthy boundaries. I was burdened with resentment and bitterness over things past. These were the real burdens in my life and what I wanted to unload from my heart. It wasn't what had happened, or who made it happen, that burdened me. It was my own emotional confusion and lack of forgiveness toward all that pained me, which weighed so heavily on my heart and kept me from being happy and peaceful today.

The climb was intense, and I was shocked at how cold it was outside. But I didn't mind. After a few hours I came across a small café and decided to stop and warm up. My fingers were freezing and I was getting very hungry, my breakfast longed ago burned off.

When I stepped inside, I was surprised to see so many familiar pilgrims standing around a roaring fire in the fireplace in the middle of a large room. Clint and Dean were there. So were Hans and Peter, and Linda. I also saw Victoria from last night, but I didn't see her son, Eric, anywhere. I asked about him and she rolled her eyes.

"I left him behind this morning," she said. "I had to. We have been fighting since we started the Camino. In fact, I think that is what I am here to unburden myself from today. His control and neediness are strangling me. I needed to get away, so I told him I would meet him in Santiago if he makes it."

I applauded her decision and wished her a "Buen Camino" as she stepped past me and out into the cold once again. I looked around before I sat down. It was an old hippie establishment, complete with peace signs, incense, and tons of Camino T-shirts and memorabilia for sale—all of which I wanted. But I knew that I couldn't take this experience with me, so I didn't buy any of it. Then my eye was caught by a small deck of cards called *The Way*, made up of insights from previous pilgrims who had walked to Santiago, offering advice from the Camino for the journey through life. I pulled a card from the deck. It said, "Don't fear the criticisms of others."

That piece of advice made me think. I have been severely criticized all my life for being intuitive and making it my vocation. I have been criticized for being an outspoken and strong woman, accused of not being feminine enough. I have been criticized for being playful when I taught my workshops, told I was not worth being taken seriously. For most of my life, I was criticized just for being me, and while it hurt me, it didn't stop me. Rather than collapse under all that criticism, I just fought back. Now, I didn't even want to do that. I just wanted to ignore the criticisms of those who didn't like me, or approve of me, or "get" me and carry on in peace. That would be wonderful. That was what I would pray for today.

After drinking a cup of hot chocolate and eating my last PowerBar of the day, I put my gloves and hat back on, reached for Pilgrim and my poles, pulled my poncho back over my head, and headed out. I was being called to the top.

Today marked a turning point in my pilgrimage. For over three weeks now, my walking had dredged up the deepest wounds from my past and shaken them free from both my psyche and my bones, along with the long-held pain, sorrow, and grief that they had trapped in my body. Today was my opportunity to release all of it, from my body and from my life. This was the day to leave the past behind and open my heart to living fully and freely in the present.

The fog became thicker once I was back on the path, the cold intensifying along with it. I finally reached the summit, and through the fog I could barely make out the huge iron cross that stood at the top of the mountain. But it was there. I had arrived at Cruz Ferro, the place to unburden myself and ask for forgiveness.

Approaching the cross, I was taken aback by the massive amount of small stones and talismans, prayers and pleas, piled high all around it. It was surreal to see the world's prayers and pain all symbolically left behind in these offerings. There were photos, teddy bears, letters, little shrines made of stacked stones, shoes, rosaries, and more, each item representing someone's heartache.

Looking at everything reminded me of how painful the human experience is and how we, as humans, cannot avoid this pain. There is no way around the human condition. We can only experience it as bravely as possible.

We cannot feel love unless we open our hearts, and yet, when we do open them, they can and do get broken. It just works that way. If we close our hearts off, however, as a means of protecting ourselves, and cover them over with anger and rage, we break our hearts from the inside. If we look to others to give us the love we are not giving ourselves, we become frustrated and disappointed and often feel rejected, creating even deeper wounds than before.

Only when we love ourselves fully and forgive all the people and experiences that have caused us pain, both inside and out, can we truly heal and find inner peace. There is no other way. We cannot avoid the pain of life, no matter how spiritually awakened we are. Life involves loss. It is impermanent and messy and causes suffering. Only when we feel our pain, feel our losses, and allow our feelings to move through us, and then onward, are we able to heal and live as fully empowered beings in the moment.

Looking at the mountain of grief left behind by so many others, I realized I had no need to feel ashamed for hurting. I had no need to feel like a failure because I got angry and scared. As spiritually conscious as I was, I was still human, and still had to experience loss and suffering like everyone else.

It was not allowing myself to freely feel my losses that caused me to get stuck. It was denying my pain over and over again that made it explode. In walking the Camino I had now felt it all, and because of that, my pain was moving on. It wasn't stuck inside me any longer. I could honestly say I was leaving my pain and my karma behind, while at the same time, as I walked, they were also leaving me. We were done.

I placed my huge rock on the pile and thanked all the people who had touched my soul, now and in lives past, for the lessons and the love they brought me. I released my rage, my hurt, my emotional pain, and underneath it all, my fear, and asked for and offered forgiveness for everything in my past. The minute I placed my rock at the foot of the cross, I could feel my last bits of pain tumble out of me and onto the ground. All that was left in its place was gratitude.

Just before I left, I took Gumby from my pocket and sat him on the rocks. He had been a good touchstone for me, helping to keep my spirits up and my humor alive when all I felt was lost. I took a few pictures of the two of us together so that I could leave everything behind with a smile. I then got on my knees and prayed for everyone in my life, thanking their spirits for their contribution to my human experience. I stayed a few minutes longer, but it was bitter cold and I felt there was no need to linger. I picked up Gumby, put him in my pocket, and got ready to go. It took a moment or two to find the path in the fog, but I did and slowly began the steep descent.

As I started down, the icy wind blew in my face with such relentless ferocity that it felt personal. And yet, rather than fight it, I let it scour off the remaining barnacles of hurtful beliefs and behaviors that I still subconsciously clung to.

"Go ahead!" I screamed to the spirit of the wind. "Do your work. Blow it all away."

I felt as though I were being bathed in pure love. In spite of the cold, a gentle, warm energy was now touching those deep places of hidden sadness and terror in my heart that for so long had held on to the harsh and frightening experiences from my past, both in this life and long before. I was healing.

The cold was refreshing. The flowers along the side of the path were magical. My heart was becoming free of some old and very ugly and painful stuck energy. I finally descended below the cold and fog and emerged into a vast mountain valley. It was incredible. The past was behind me. I was now free.

Day 26
(23 km; 14 mi)

Ponferrada to Villafranca del Bierzo

I woke up early in Ponferrada, still absorbing all that had happened yesterday while walking from Rabanal to here. Once I emerged from under the cold cloud on the top of the mountain after stopping at Cruz Ferro, I walked for miles and miles through the most exquisite mountain valley, filled with every imaginable kind and color of flower. It was breathtaking.

My heart sang and I felt as though I had just shed several thousand years of karma. Words cannot capture the bliss I felt. It was like I was stoned. Every one of my senses was amplified. The colors surrounding me were so brilliant and complex I had to stop every few hundred feet or so to stare at them. The sky was crystal clear and the birds were singing so loudly I wondered if I were hallucinating. Maybe I was. Or maybe this is how the senses work when we are not buried alive in the stale energies of past experiences and the grievances that often come with them. The sweetest fragrances from the flowers washed over me, and that, too, made me marvel, as I had long ago lost my sense of smell. Not on this day, though. I could smell everything.

I was so present and alert it felt as though every cell in my being were turned on full volume. Yet I was peaceful, quiet, and relaxed. *Is this how we are supposed to feel all the time?* I wondered. *Is this the kind of feeling we have when we are very young and uncomplicated?*

All I knew was that I was at one with my surroundings and nothing came between me and the beauty and calm of the glorious present. While I had a long way to go to my next stop, I purposely walked slowly so I could savor this incredible experience. I wanted it to last.

A few hours later, I wandered into the small village of Molinaseca. I was suddenly starving and had to stop and eat. When I entered the café, it was standing-room only. I patiently waited my turn to order, not really wanting to talk. I was afraid if I spoke to anyone, even if only to order my egg bocadillo, I might slip out of this serene state I was in, and I wasn't ready to leave it.

The waiter at the counter, a young kid of no more than 15 or so, understood this, as I held up the menu and pointed to what I wanted when it came my turn to order. He smiled and gave me a thumbs-up. Then he asked if I wanted something to drink with a motion of the hand. I pointed to Coke on the menu. He nodded and disappeared into the kitchen.

I looked around. Some people were talking animatedly. Others, like me, stared into outer space as they reflected on the experience of the morning. A young woman got up from a table nearby and left, so I set Pilgrim down and took a seat. It felt good to rest. I didn't realize how tired I was until my butt hit the chair.

"Ahh," I sighed, relieved, relaxed, and ready to eat. Two minutes later my sandwich was presented at the counter. I got up, grabbed both it and my Coke, and sat down once again. I didn't want to think. I didn't want to go back down that rabbit hole that had brought me to the point of such pain in the first place. I just wanted to rest and be.

I sat for some time, yet I knew I had another eight kilometers to go before I arrived in Ponferrada, so eventually I forced myself to get going. I grabbed Pilgrim, got my passport stamped, and headed out. The sun was shining so brightly by now it was hard to believe that only a short while ago I was inching my way through freezing cold and dense fog.

The lower I descended on the path, the brighter and warmer the day got. Soon I had peeled off all of my layers and was drenched in sweat. What a day of contrasts. As I walked I could feel something else peeling off of me as well. Old karma from those soul experiences I had as a Knight Templar. I could feel the heaviness and rigidity, that somber dark energy, with its stifling intensity, lift off my bones and drift into the light. With it I could sense guilt and judgment and all the other negative emotions in my soul disappear. In their place was a lightness of being like I had never before experienced. I had somehow burned off my karma and was now free to live fully and happily in present time.

The path wound down the mountain for miles before reaching the city below. Finally the road turned abruptly and revealed the magnificent Templar Castle, built in the 12th century. I had no idea it was there, and seeing it made me gasp. It was like something out of a fairy tale. It towered over everything, and the minute I saw it I recognized it with every cell of my being. I just stood and stared. I was spellbound.

I wasn't sure what to do. Should I first find my hostel then come back to visit inside? Should I just go in right now? I was confused. Looking up at the massive structure, I decided that I would cross the moat and drawbridge and enter right then. Only to my surprise, once I crossed the bridge, and approached the entryway, I discovered the castle was closed. I was strangely relieved. I was not to go in, not then anyway.

I walked away and looked at the castle from down below once again. I then walked across the plaza and went into the tourist office and asked what time it would open tomorrow.

The woman inside shook her head and said that it was closed tomorrow as well, and would not reopen until the day after. I walked out, shaking my head, taking this all in. I then walked to a café just across from the massive structure and sat down. I knew the doors where closed to me because my energetic attachments to the Templars were now over. I was not supposed to go backward, not even to visit the castle. I was to keep moving on. It was perfect.

I closed my eyes and felt the warm sun on my face. The cold and gray had disappeared as well as all the heavy energies that I had carried with me for all these lifetimes. I ordered a glass of red wine and sipped it slowly. It tasted so good. I then ordered a pepperoni pizza and ate the whole thing. Finally I had an ice-cream cone. It was time for a graduation party.

After that I decided to walk around the medieval town. Everything was closed as tight as a drum, and I figured out it was Sunday. The cafés were open, but not the shops. That meant I couldn't even buy Knights Templar memorabilia, which was on display in the window of every shop surrounding the castle. The past was over; my new holy adventure was in the here-and-now.

A bit farther into town, I found the cathedral. I walked in and sat down to say a rosary in thanksgiving for closing this heavy chapter of my past forever. It was dark and sad, and hard to see anything. But then another pilgrim placed a coin in a slot to one side of the altar and it lit up, almost like at a movie theater, revealing a magnificent multilayered, carved tableau filled with ornate versions of saints, surrounding Mother Mary in the center. Soon a frail, old Spanish woman came out from the sacristy and lit the candles on the altar and left. Shortly after this, bells rang and a mass began. I looked around and saw about ten very old Spaniards in attendance, as well as a sprinkling of pilgrims. I stayed through the mass and then lit candles for everyone in my family.

Afterward, I wandered back outside and made my way toward my hostel. It was a simple, old hotel just up from the castle and located on the plaza. I walked into the lobby, only to find a soccer match was blaring on TV with no one watching. In the corner stood Cheater, waiting patiently for me to pick him up.

No one was in sight, so I walked to the receptionist's desk and rang a small bell sitting there. Moments later, a young woman came rushing from the kitchen to help me. After checking in, I went upstairs to find a comfortable room, with a fairly new bed, warm blankets, and heat, although today I had to turn it down. It was too warm in the room. Exhausted, I lay quietly on the bed. What an incredible day. I could hardly believe all that had transpired in the expanse of only seven hours. It felt as if I had just been in a time warp, as lifetimes had passed before my eyes.

I was spent, so I promptly fell asleep.

The next morning the town was still quiet when I woke up. I took a shower and started to get dressed when I noticed that sitting on top of my hiking gloves was a bright shiny American penny, the kind my father used to give me as a child. I heard his voice, "Remember, Sonia, in God we trust." I burst into tears, as I knew my father had placed that penny there while I slept. There was no other way it could have gotten there.

"Dad, thank you," I cried. "Thank you for walking with me. Thank you for all the lessons. I love you so much." I had to sit down and regain my composure, as I was overwhelmed with my find and the love that had just poured down from heaven and throughout my body.

"Okay, Dad," I finally said as I finished getting dressed. "Let's go."

I had a quick breakfast and got under way. After only ten minutes of walking, I left the surreal realm of medieval Ponferrada and entered into a very different reality. Modern Ponferrada was gray, dreary, and took forever to get out of. I yearned for the calm beauty of the Camino more than ever before as I inched my way out of town.

After about an hour, I encountered a Brazilian man of around 25 years old named Paolo, who could barely walk his feet hurt so badly. He stopped and showed me why. He had so many blisters on his feet they looked like shredded wheat. I offered him some of the many Band-Aids I still had, and he grabbed them all. He covered his feet with them and then decided he would walk in his socks, as his shoes didn't fit with all the bandages covering them.

I wished him a "Buen Camino" and carried on.

Eventually I freed myself of the urban sprawl that was modern Ponferrada and headed back into more pastoral territory. This part of the Camino is known as Galicia and was once populated by ancients Celts, so the music playing in little cafés and shops along the way was filled with bagpipes. I hadn't expected that, but it was delightful.

There was a big winery just off the path at one point, and I stopped to grab a snack. Inside I found many pilgrims having a very drunken good time, which they heartily invited me to join. Since it was only 11 in the morning, I took a pass. I knew if I started drinking now I wouldn't make it the rest of the way.

While the walk was not as long as it was the day before, because I was so spent from yesterday's experience, it seemed as though I would never arrive. I could barely trudge along for the last ten kilometers.

"Please end!" I screamed in my dramatic fashion to the Camino, as it kept going and going and going. "I'm tired of walking today. Let it end!"

So much for bliss, I thought. While I was free of my past, the present was getting on my nerves big-time.

It was just plain fatigue. I had walked an average of 29 kilometers (18 miles) for the past 25 days in a row, and it was just too much today. *I guess what goes up must come down,* I thought as my irritation flared. It was not realistic or possible to expect that I could drift on a cloud indefinitely. In my heart I was still light, still peaceful, still feeling free. My body—especially my feet and now knees—on the other hand, was miserably aching, and I was tired of pushing myself. I had not taken a day off since I started and today I felt it.

Still, I kept walking. What else was there to do? To waste energy fighting the path was silly. I knew that much by now. I prayed instead.

> *Holy Mother-Father God,*
> *I'm tired. If you have a few angels to spare and can give me*
> *some wind under my wings, I would very much appreciate it.*
> *Thank you, and amen.*

No wind came. I kept going.

Finally, finally I wandered into Villafranca del Bierzo. It was charming, filled with little cafés and restaurants all situated along the lovely plaza running the length of the town. I sat down and promptly ordered a large, cold beer. I had arrived.

I took my time drinking it before I set out to find my hostel, but had no luck. I traversed the town three times before I decided to stop and ask for directions. Good thing I did because it was located down some hidden steps at the end of the plaza, something I would never have found on my own.

The hostel was in a medieval stone building, so it was cool and dark inside, a very pleasant relief from the bright sun I had walked under all day. I rang the bell and waited for five minutes. I could hear someone talking, but he didn't come out. I was impatient. Why was he making me wait?

I had not had a bitchy day in a while, and was surprised to see nastiness descending upon me like the flu. I rang the bell again. A minute later, out walked a man from the back.

"Why are you ringing the bell again?" he snapped at me, in perfect English. "I heard you the first time!"

Whoa! He was bitchier than I was.

I took a breath. He was so stern he scared me.

"I'm sorry," I said. "I wasn't sure you did."

He was curt and handed me a key without looking me in the eye.

I asked about Cheater, and he said that he was in the back hallway. He led me to retrieve him, and then pointed to the stairs.

"You are on the third floor," he said dismissively. He started to walk away, then stopped.

"Dinner is at 7 P.M.," he barked up at me.

"Okay," I said.

I went back down at 7 P.M., starving.

I must have been the only guest staying there, as there was only one table setting in the entire place. Moments after I sat down, the surly man came out and nearly threw a bowl of soup in front of me, then left.

I was annoyed that he was still not very nice as I took my spoon to taste his fare.

Then—oh my God! The soup was outstanding. I couldn't believe I was served something so delicious by this troll of a person. I licked the bowl clean.

Moments later he came out again, removed my soup bowl, and slammed down a plate of roasted pork, garden vegetables, and stewed fruits. Again, I was blown away by how delicious it was. I ate every bite, forcing myself to slow down, as I didn't want to finish too fast. Surly Man was a fantastic chef.

When he brought out dessert, an orange flan with homemade whipped cream, I nearly died.

"Wow! This is so good. Thank you," I said. He just looked at me and grunted, then left the room.

I ate all my dessert and had two glasses of wine. My dinner was gourmet from beginning to end.

As I sat sipping my wine, I wondered why I was having this experience on the Camino right now.

I had been so high and felt so transcendent yesterday, only to face this paradox of mixed messages sent by a grump today.

I listened for guidance and heard that I was to be happy inside no matter what was going on with others around me.

As an empath, I've often been affected—even controlled— by the energies and moods of those around me, having my good mood or happy feeling snatched away by someone else's bad mood before I could even try to stop it.

What a great lesson—and served with such a delicious meal.

When Grumpy inquired as to whether or not I wanted some coffee, I just smiled and said, "No, thank you, but thank you for a lovely dinner. You are a magician in the kitchen."

He stopped and looked at me and almost smiled. Then he turned and left.

I decided to get up and do the same, heading for my room, now exhausted.

I looked at Gumby as I was falling asleep.

"Get that, Gumby? It is time to stop allowing others to dictate how I feel."

He smiled as usual.

Day 27

(28 km; 17 mi)

Villafranca to O Cebreiro

I woke up praying to God to keep my heart open and my ego quiet. Yesterday while walking I kept thinking of ways in which I could further unburden myself. I knew in my heart that it was time to forgive, to let go, to release, and to give up all attachment to and control over everything in my life and turn it over to the Universe and God.

I was still in grief about my marriage ending, but I knew I had to trust that God had plans for me and that I would be okay. It was now time for me to accept what was happening and simply send Patrick love. It was difficult. Yet, I just had to believe that the things I needed—such as healing with my daughters, good friendships, and peace in my heart—would show up. I had to release everything in absolute faith that all would be well.

Physically, I felt surprisingly good. Of course, my feet still hurt like hell, but the rest of me was raring to go. I quickly packed up Cheater and went back down to breakfast. Surly Man was nowhere in sight and in his place was an attractive woman who said she was his wife. She served me a lovely breakfast of bacon, eggs, toast, and fresh juice and coffee.

I went to my room, brought Cheater down, left him at the front desk, put Gumby under the front strap of Pilgrim, and said, "Okay, Gumby. It's time to go."

Holy Mother-Father God,
Please close the door to my past so I never return to that
misery.
Amen, and thank you.

The day was gorgeous. The sky was blue, the air was crisp, and flowers were exploding everywhere. I took my time walking, as I knew I had another very steep climb up a mountain today to O Cebreiro. The early part of the walk was peaceful, and not too far along the path I ran into the same French people I had seen all the way back in the Pyrenees, complete with their wagon, having a picnic in front of a small church on the outskirts of the village.

I waved to them, and they recognized me. They invited me to sit and join them for a snack. I wasn't hungry yet, but I sat down anyway. They offered me fresh figs, smoked salami, slices of hard cheese, dried apricots, toasted almonds, pieces of dark chocolate, and slices of fresh bread. It was sublime.

We conversed in French for a while, which was nice because I had rarely spoken on the Camino other than a few sentences, at least until I arrived in a town at the end of the day.

I found out that the French people were not going all the way to Santiago, but rather were quitting in O Cebreiro, and then were headed back to France, as one of their sons was getting married. They decided they would return next spring to finish the Camino. I thought it was a shame, as they had put more than three weeks into the journey so far and had only a week to finish, but they were okay with it.

I sat for a little while, then was called to keep moving. We wished each other a "Buen Camino," and I got up and left. I started singing my old favorite, "I'm Off to See the Wizard."

My journey did feel like Dorothy's journey to Oz. I, too, wanted to come home to me, come home to peace, come home to a place in my heart and spirit that felt safe and grounded and welcomed me with love. I longed to cast aside all the demons that took me away from the blessings life had in store for me, and I especially wanted to face my fears and be done with them.

Only I knew that the fears would keep coming. That just goes along with being human. Fear of the unknown is something all people have and there is nothing we can do about it. But I also knew that it wasn't fear that was causing me pain. It was hiding my fear and allowing it to control me, rather than simply acknowledging it and then putting it aside as I moved through each day.

I wove my way through a small town, noticing a pilgrim talking in Spanish rather animatedly on a cell phone to someone while he twirled his walking stick like an extra-long baton. He didn't seem very fearful. He was having fun.

I thought about what I was afraid of. Then I started naming my fears out loud, like the Cowardly Lion on the way to Oz. That led me to singing "Lions and tigers and bears, oh my! Lions and tigers and bears, oh my!" I picked up my pace as I did this, getting faster and faster until I was almost running, then spontaneously burst into a rousing rendition of "Somewhere Over the Rainbow" with a hop and a skip and a twirl of my own walking pole, laughing all the way out of town.

The path slowly started to climb, and with it the air got much colder. There was a lot of mud and rocks and deep grooves in the path, and walking was not easy. Still, it was one foot in front of the other. I had to go slowly but I kept moving.

Eventually I came to a small village, where I noticed a group of horses by the side of the road and several men standing near them, talking to a few pilgrims. As I approached them, one turned to me and asked, "Would you like to ride to the top of the mountain on a horse today?"

I stopped. I knew it was at least an eight- to ten-kilometer climb straight up the mountain, and the idea seemed appealing.

"We need three people to ride and we only have two, so if you join us, we can go," the Spanish cowboy continued.

It was tempting.

"Come on," urged one of the women. "I read that it counts as walking."

"It's not expensive," said the man with the horses. "Only 20 euros to the top."

Looking up at the steep climb ahead, it didn't sound expensive.

"I'm not sure," I said. "I have only ridden a horse once in my life, and I wasn't good at it."

"No problem," the Spanish cowboy assured me. "I show you how to ride."

The other two pilgrims looked at me imploringly.

"Please," said one of them. "I do not want to walk to the top. My feet are so sore today. You can do it. I'll watch over you. I know how to ride as well."

I looked at Gumby. He was smiling.

"Okay," I said. "I'll do it."

Two minutes later, I was wearing a helmet and sitting on top of a large gray mare, first in line behind our guide, ready to take off. I looked down at Gumby stuffed in the front of Pilgrim and said, "Ready?"

I did my best to follow instructions, but my butt was slamming up and down on the saddle so hard it rattled my brain and I couldn't hear what my guide was saying. Oh my gawd! This was far, far worse than walking. What had I gotten myself into? I had lost so much weight since starting out I had absolutely no padding on my rear end to take the bumps, and as much as I tried to get in the rhythm of riding, I was clearly not succeeding. *Ow!*

The guide didn't seem to notice.

"So-knee-yahhh! Let's go. Let's go," he kept urging. I'm not sure why he did this, as I was going. Just not as fast as he wanted. The path was so steep and narrow at times that my horse could barely find his footing between the rocks and the mud, and slipped and slid a lot, causing him to lunge and lurch as we made our way up the very steep path.

It was sheer torture to bang up and down on the saddle and I laughed because now I would have a huge pain in the ass as well as two destroyed feet. *Why not?* I thought. *Might as well completely destroy myself before I'm finished.*

While it took all my concentration to guide the horse and not fall off as we trotted and half galloped straight up to the clouds, occasionally I was able to peek out over the valley, which was absolutely breathtaking.

I was finally getting the hang of it, and doing okay, cheered on by my more experienced riding partners, when all of a sudden a dog jumped at my horse from out of nowhere and started barking viciously.

Startled, my horse took off like a bat out of hell, with me holding on to the reins for dear life. We were flying at high speed, headed for the hills. I miraculously managed to stay calm. I did not want to have come this far only to be thrown by a horse.

I kept my head about me and gently pulled on the reins while I held the horse with my legs, saying, "Whoa, Nelly!" even though the horse's name was Guida. She seemed to get the message. After three frightening minutes, she broke into a trot, the two other riders and my guide chasing after us.

"Great job, So-knee-yahh!" they screamed. "You held on!"

I thought the same. And I was done riding. I wanted to get off—now! But I couldn't. I had to ride for another half hour before our guide pulled over. "This it! The end," he announced.

Everyone wanted to take pictures with the horses, so we passed our cameras around and took several shots. We laughed and hugged and wished each other a "Buen Camino" and started back on the path toward the summit, which was only another 300 feet.

Just as I entered the town, I looked down and noticed that Gumby was gone.

Oh no! He must have fallen off during the wild ride!

I was so sad I almost started crying. Gumby—my muse. My buddy. The toy I had had since I was a kid, lost somewhere on the Camino. I felt terrible and ridiculous at the same time.

"It's a toy, Sonia. You can get another one back home," I reasoned. It was true, I could. But still, it was a loss. I talked to Gumby the entire time I had been walking the Camino. I laughed with Gumby. He watched over me. I shook my head. I did say I wanted to let go of all attachments.

I guess he needed to bail ship and cheer up some other pilgrim now. I knew he would, as he was such a silly-looking toy. Someone would find him, and maybe it would be someone who really needed encouragement. I went into the church at the top of the summit and lit a candle. It was time to have a funeral for a friend.

"So long, Gumby," I said, praying in gratitude. "You were good company!"

As I left the church I said, "Note to self: When you get home, order another toy Gumby."

I walked into the small village at the summit. It was charming. I looked at the time. It was barely past noon, which meant it was time for lunch. Now that I was in Galicia, and nearer to the sea, the menu was entirely different from the pork and beans of the last three weeks, and I welcomed that.

I found a café near the hostel and ordered a delicious vegetable stew, grilled octopus, corn bread, and a big glass of wine. I was celebrating that I didn't get taken out on the trail earlier, as well as having a post-funeral meal for Gumby.

After lunch I poked around at the several gift shops in town. They were filled with Camino and Celtic memorabilia, all of which I loved. I bought the St. James Camino Cross of Forgiveness for both of my daughters, and then at the last minute, I bought one for Patrick, as well, although I wasn't sure why or even how or when I would present it to him.

Then I wandered over to my hostel and checked in. As I was escorted to my room, I saw Cheater sitting in the hallway, waiting for me. "Hurray, you made it! I hope your journey was less challenging than mine," I said to him as I picked him up and carried him to my room.

I took a long nap, and then went back outside to look at the surroundings. I was at the top of a beautiful mountain and the valley below was breathtaking. Looking out I saw vast forests, fields of wildflowers, and in the distance, more snowcapped mountains. It was freezing out, and the rain had started up again, but I loved every bit of this foggy, soggy Camino. "Thank you, God! I am so grateful to be here. I surrender more and more. I let it all go. You take over from here. And thank you for keeping me on the horse today."

I took a few photos and went back to my room and fell asleep. I slept till morning, dreaming all night that I was riding a wild stallion like a champ, across fields of wildflowers and butterflies.

Day 28
(21 km; 13 mi)

O Cebreiro to Triacastela

Today started out with the sun shining brightly, but it was really cold. I was so happy for my pillow and sleeping bag last night, as there was no heat in my room and what they offered for a pillow was more like a thin towel. It didn't matter. I slept like a rock.

My butt hurt from riding the horse yesterday, making walking a bit more painful than usual. I looked around my room. I missed Gumby. Silly as he was, he kept me company on the Camino. "Oh well, Gumby. Rest in peace," I said. His disappearance was just another Camino lesson. For me this one was about how, in the end, we must let go of everything we are attached to, because nothing remains except for how much we chose to love in our lives. I was just sorry Gumby had to be sacrificed for me to learn this lesson.

I was moody. Part of it was pure fatigue and the fact that I was now certain that my feet were permanently trashed. I was sure I would never wear high heels again. Even the thought pained me as I shuffled across my minuscule room to get into the shower.

The water was steaming hot and took the chill out of my bones. Being at the summit, the walk ahead was downhill all day. I wasn't sure if that was good news or not for my knee. I looked over and saw my walking poles. Thank God Camino Patrick let me have them. They turned me into a four-legged walking machine and helped stabilize my knee on tricky terrain such as I would be facing today.

Next I looked at my walking gloves and the penny my dad gave me sitting on top of them, where I had placed it last night. "Morning, Dad. Ready to go soon?" I asked him out loud. I could feel his loving presence with me now so strongly.

As I dressed, I wondered what it was like in heaven and how my brother was. I had been feeling his spirit, as well, off and on over the past few days. "Say hi to Bruce Anthony for me, Dad, and tell him I love him," I said.

Two seconds later a beautiful butterfly landed on the ledge right outside the bathroom window. I felt it was my brother's spirit saying, "Thank you."

Breakfast was okay. The croissant was not fresh, but the toast with jam and butter tasted good. And they had fresh-squeezed orange juice for one euro more, so I asked for two glasses of it. My strep throat was long gone, but a chest cold had settled in and I welcomed the juice to help fight off my cough.

After breakfast I reached into Pilgrim and pulled out my little purse with my passport and got it stamped before I set out for the day. Just as I was dragging Cheater up front, the man who was to transport my bag walked into the hostel, took it from me, and carried it to his van.

I was happy to see Cheater settled into his ride, as it made for one less thing to worry about today. I stuffed my little purse back into Pilgrim, verified that I had two of my remaining four Power-Bars with me, then pulled on my hat and gloves and set out.

The sky had clouded over already and it looked as though it was about to rain again. *Whatever,* I thought, long used to the rain and accepting that it was probably going to follow me all the way to Santiago.

> *Holy Mother-Father God,*
> *Please keep my moods from settling in and weighing me down.*
> *Help me stay present to this moment and the beauty and power of this day.*
> *Amen, and thank you.*

As I descended, I was flooded with beautiful memories of times going back to childhood. I remembered how my father taught me to drive by taking me to the mountains outside of Denver, where we lived. I had just gotten my learner's permit and showed it to him one Saturday morning. He took one look at it, then spontaneously said to me, "Get in the car." He then drove us about 30 miles outside of Denver to the top of a mountain, and parked. Next he turned to me and said, "Now you drive us home."

I freaked out and said I couldn't, but he just said, "Quit your whining. Let's go."

So that's what I did. I got behind the wheel of our 1967 VW Bug, turned on the ignition, engaged the clutch, and with a sharp jerk, we took off. He didn't say much to me except, "Take your foot off the brake. Slow down by shifting." I did as I was told. Occasionally he said more sternly, "Don't ride the brakes, or you'll burn them out."

"Okay, Dad. I won't."

If he was scared, he didn't show it. Finally, I made it home. It was one of the happiest experiences of my youth. "Thank you, Dad!" I screamed as I hugged him, relieved and proud that I had succeeded. He just smiled and walked into the house.

I hadn't thought about this occasion since it happened, but I could see now that on that day he put his complete faith in me. What a vote of confidence that was! Since he trusted me that day, I learned to trust myself and have ever since. That is probably why I have been so brave and so willing to try things I've never done before all my life, including this pilgrimage.

As I walked, even more positive memories from the past came flooding into my consciousness, most of them now concerning Patrick and all the fun we had when we were married.

I remembered some of our solo trips, including one across from Spain to Tangier on a day when the seas were so rough nearly every passenger on the ship got seasick. I was so grossed out at all the "yuck" all over the place I was miserable. Patrick pulled from his backpack a pair of rubber covers for his shoes, which he always carried with him, and gave them to me to put so I wouldn't have to stand in it. He was so chivalrous.

I also remembered the time we were in Assisi, Italy, with our daughters, who were only five and six at the time. It was foggy and cold, and we pretended we were transported back to medieval times. After a while we ducked into a hole-in-the-wall restaurant, where we had the best pizza in the world while listening to local musicians playing a lyre and dulcimer.

Remembering all of these great times together, I composed a letter to Patrick in my heart, acknowledging all that he had brought to my life. I could suddenly see how the pattern my father had of ignoring my gifts had been passed on to me. I didn't acknowledge Patrick's gifts as much as I could have either. I felt sad about that. It would have been so easy to celebrate him more, and I failed to do it enough.

The longer I walked, the steeper the descent.

The path was spectacularly serene. It wound through farmland, where I shared the path with herds of cows. I also saw grazing horses looking at me from behind the fences along the way, checking me out.

At times the path followed sections of the busy road, then wound back into fields of flowers and trees. I didn't see a soul for most of the morning and was free to reflect only on nature and my own thoughts.

In these past three and a half weeks of silence and solitude, it became more and more evident that while my life circumstances had been challenging, my thoughts were what caused me the most difficulty. Letting go of the thoughts that didn't serve me and taking away only love from all that passed was what mattered now. It was all I wanted to do and hoped that I could.

I looked back over my marriage and only wished I had been able to love both Patrick and myself more while in it. I could see how not having the space and time I needed to take care of myself contributed so much to our problems.

Having all this time now to be alone, to be in nature, to review my life from a place of quiet, deep reflection made it much easier to find my way to peace, to compassion, to acceptance, and to love.

We both needed more time and space to find our way back home to these things. Both Patrick and I had come from large families living in small quarters, so private time and space to be alone was not an option when we were young. It was something neither of us knew we needed. It would have made a difference if we had.

I knew now that I would never give that up again. Simply being alone to work through my grief, feel my feelings fully, and move the energy through my body while walking this magical path had healed so much in me. The more I walked, the more freedom from the past I felt.

About halfway to Triacastela, the path turned upward again, and the climb was steep. I huffed and puffed my way to the top under the bright burning sun, but this time I felt supported by my angels. I could also feel both my father and my brother championing me. Every 500 feet or so I heard, "Good job, Sonia. Well done. Keep going. You'll make it." It was so loud in my head that I thought I was hallucinating.

I have always strongly felt and sensed and heard my spirit guides in my heart, but nothing like this. I was surrounded, some pushing from behind, others pulling me forward. If anything, it felt a bit crowded on the narrow rocky path.

"Okay, okay," I finally said, bursting out laughing. "I'm doing it!"

At the top I happened upon a little oasis of a café overlooking the valley below.

I went in and ordered an egg bocadillo (yes, I know, it's pitifully unimaginative, but I'm a creature of habit) and a big, cold Coke. Then I stepped outside to find a seat in the warm sun while I waited for it.

Next to me, I overheard a young woman sitting with her father saying she had a sore throat, so I offered her the lozenges I had carried with me since Carrión, which she gladly accepted.

Turning around to sit down, I then saw Clint and Dean emerge from the steep climb, looking as delighted as I had been to see the café right there. They plopped down next to me and caught their breath.

Just then the waiter brought out my sandwich. It was huge. I looked over at them and said, "Would you two like to share this with me?"

They needed no convincing, going inside to fetch Cokes of their own while I managed to cut the sandwich into three parts. Still piping hot, it was delicious.

At that moment I was filled with gratitude for simply being alive. The Camino had stripped away all that was unnecessary, all that was superfluous, and left me knowing that we have all we need, all the time, if we can only recognize it.

Refreshed, one by one, we got up and started on our way again.

We had a ways to go and the steepest descent was still ahead. Walking got trickier, but at the same time, the path got even more beautiful. As I walked, the Camino started talking to me again.

Love is always here, it said. *You don't have to fear not having it. You are in the flow of love, and it is in and around you all the time.*

Listening, I realized that while I had resigned myself to my divorce and felt very sad about the failure of my marriage, I also carried a big fear that I would never experience or find love again in my life from here forward. I had never felt confident in my love life to begin with, and the fear that I would never experience love again was now bubbling up from deep inside me.

"Will I find love again in my life?" I asked the Camino. "I sometimes doubt it, you know. I surely don't want to look for it, or even want to feel I need it, but I wonder."

We all need love, it answered. *You don't need to look for it, though. It is right here. Look around and feel it. Just receive it.*

"But what about that 'in love' feeling?" I asked. "You know, that feeling you have when you are with someone you really love to be with?"

You are the one who gives you that feeling, it answered.

"Are you suggesting that I settle for being okay not being in a relationship?"

Whether or not you are in a relationship with another, feeling love for yourself and being filled up with the love of the Universe is what you truly seek.

"I believe that, but I will still face life alone when I get back. Or at least I'll most likely live the rest of my life without a partner. I can't deny that."

The Camino was silent. Then finally it said, *You are never alone. Your mind tricks you into believing things that aren't true.*

"But I will be unmarried."

The Camino listened but didn't answer.

Soon I wandered up to the most ancient, gnarled, huge tree I have ever seen. I felt compelled to sit at its base and rest. I closed my eyes and leaned up against it, very gently. I asked it, "Do you mind if I rest here, leaning up to you?"

It seemed to say, "No, go ahead."

As I sat against it, I felt my heart being fed and grounded by its strength and pure, unconditional love. It calmed and quieted not only my mind, but also my entire nervous system. It took away my anxiety and yearning for anything or anybody.

I sat and meditated under the tree for a long time. I was in no hurry to get where I was going. I was happy to be right where I was. Being at the base of the magnificent, ancient-looking tree erased all of my worry for the future. Sitting there, I knew I would be okay. I knew we all would.

I'm not sure how much time passed as I sat there, when suddenly I was awakened out of my reverie by a cool breeze telling me it was time to continue.

An hour later I arrived in Triacastela. I had made it one more day.

Day 29

(21 km; 13 mi)

Triacastela to Sarria

I woke up this morning and saw that it was raining again. Resigned to continuing on my wet, soggy Camino, I got dressed for the day. I bundled up and had breakfast, got my passport stamped, then headed out.

> *Holy Mother God,*
> *I am open to learning all that serves my spirit and helps me*
> *better serve you today.*
> *Amen.*

The walk was quiet as I strolled along, but about two miles into it I realized that, even though it was raining, it was actually quite warm outside. With all the layers I had on under the big plastic bag called my poncho, I was suddenly so hot I almost passed out. It was like walking in a sauna.

I stopped and began to disrobe, almost down to my underwear. I took off my wool shirt, and down vest, and headband, then rolled up my pants into shorts and took off my poncho. I didn't care if I got wet. I was dying.

Stripped down to a more comfortable level, I resumed walking, and as I did I began to notice huge black, slimy, gooey slugs all over the path. I looked ahead. They were everywhere. The Camino was giving me a very important message by placing these in my path today.

My mind started saying, *Slugs and leeches. Slugs and leeches.* The more I saw, the more I began to reflect on people in my life who had been—and were still—slugs and leeches.

These were people who didn't take responsibility for themselves. People who were deadbeats and didn't pay their bills or tell the truth. These were people who promised what they didn't deliver and didn't think they had to. People who were more interested in what they could get from others than what they could offer.

I could see how I had entertained so many of these slugs and leeches because I didn't have strong enough personal boundaries to say, "Go away. I'm not interested."

I carried these people way too often and way too far. Who knows why, really? I just did.

As I walked, I knew it was time to stop hosting such people in my life. People who were not really interested in showing up with integrity, for example. Or people who were more committed to drama than to creative solutions. Or people who felt sorry for themselves and expected others, like me, to rescue them from their own emotional BS. I knew that I had allowed way too many of that kind of person to take my energy and drain my spirit. It clearly was time to let go of the slugs and leeches in my life.

"Thank you, Camino. I get it," I said out loud, dodging the gross, slimy creatures as best I could without stepping on them, which wasn't easy, as they were everywhere.

But the longer I walked, the more I began to realize that the real slugs and leeches in my life were not people, but rather my own unexamined thoughts dragging me down and draining me of my joy.

I thought of how these negative, self-condemning thoughts and beliefs just rode on my energy, contributing nothing, while stealing away my life force, my joy, my peace, and my sense of self-love. They sucked my spirit dry.

The message was clear. It was time I paid closer attention to what I was allowing in my life, whether people or thoughts. It was time to be rid of what did not uplift my spirit. It was time to love myself that much. No more slugs and leeches, on any level.

Eventually I came across a sweet little place along the path that looked like a church but wasn't really. The door was open, so I walked in. It was very small inside. There were a few chairs, some small paintings of nature on the walls, and several lit candles, but no one was around. At the front of the single room, on a small stand, was a Bible opened to a highlighted passage that said, "Trust in the Lord."

I read it several times, then sat down and prayed for a while. I realized that this passage was what the Camino was about. It was a journey away from fear and wounding and into healing and trust in the Lord.

A short time later a man entered the room and introduced himself, saying his name was Ernest. He then asked me if I would pray with him, to which I happily agreed. Then he took both of my hands and said a prayer of gratitude for my being there. I was so touched and surprised that he would do this, and felt honored and loved in his presence.

After our prayer he shared with me that he had come to the Camino from England ten years earlier, so troubled and saddened by his life that he almost wanted to end it, and when he had finished the Camino he was healed. After that he realized that he had the means to walk away from his old life and came back in search of a way to serve future pilgrims. So he found this place and began doing his artwork and receiving pilgrims along the way. It was his bliss and he was serene and peaceful ever since then. I gave him a hug and he wished me a "Buen Camino," and I was soon back on my way.

Shortly after, I entered a section of the Camino where everything seemed strange and magical and out of this world, and I found myself totally turned around. I couldn't find the arrows anywhere. I was lost. I continued on a bit farther and came to several forks in the road, a heavy mist in all directions. I was confused and didn't know where I was or which way to go.

There was not a soul around, so following my instincts I took the path to the left, where eventually I came upon a clearing with what appeared to be a work shed of some sort.

As I got closer, I could see that the shed was attached to a house with an open door, so I called out. Then I boldly walked in, hoping to ask for directions back to the Camino. Inside was an older, scruffy, Spanish-speaking man with sparkling eyes, wearing a red bandana for a headband, who invited me into his kitchen to have a coffee. I don't know how, as he was speaking mostly Spanish, but I understood every word he said.

I thanked him and declined, saying I just needed to get back to the Camino, but he shook his head and said that I was brought to him by the Camino for a reason and should stop and rest. Seeing the light in his clear dark eyes, I knew that it was true. So I took off Pilgrim, set my poles down, and sat at the table.

He prepared a very strong coffee for me and then said, "Antonio, your brother, brought you here."

My heart lurched when I heard that. "He wanted you to come because he wanted you to know he is happy you are here on the Camino."

My eyes filled with tears hearing this. There was no way this man knew about my brother or his name, and yet it was the first thing he said to me. He continued, "Antonio is helping you with your worries and wants you to know this. He also wants you to know he is with your father and very happy."

I was so surprised to be hearing this from him that I was speechless. Then he said, "Please enter my meditation sanctuary." Then he walked me from the kitchen to an incredible meditation room, with gorgeous works of art that he had made out of crystals and stones all over the walls.

"This is a healing room," the man said. "Please relax and allow the earth to heal your body and heart. Stay as long as you want." Then he left.

I sat down, feeling a bit stunned that I had been brought here by my brother. I could feel his presence and knew it was true because my brother had loved stones all of his life. I could also feel how happy he was to be here with me at this moment.

I heard my brother singing, "May the good Lord shine a light on you," and felt his love surround me.

I sat and prayed for some time, reflecting on what a powerful day it had been so far, and thanked God and all my guides, and especially my brother for bringing me here.

Eventually I walked back to the kitchen, where the man told me he was a shaman and wanted to give me my animal totem. With that he pulled out a deck of very old, worn cards wrapped in some sort of animal skin, and put them before me, asking me to shuffle, which I did. He then asked me to pull a card. The one I pulled was of a spider. He smiled and told me that my feminine self was whole and healed now. I no longer needed to be a warrior and it was time to be creative and be at home in my spirit.

"Walk with spider wherever you go," he said. "She is the protector of your spirit. She is your helper."

He then said, "Peregrina, as you are walking home on this Camino, your brother is walking with you."

I just cried and cried when I heard this. It was true. I had run away when I was younger. Now I was walking back home.

He put the cards away and then gave me a beautiful raw crystal, saying that the Camino's wisdom and power would go with me in this crystal because it was from this mountain we were on.

I put it in Pilgrim and thanked him with a big hug.

He said, "Go in peace. All is well. Buen Camino."

I believed him.

I walked out his door and started walking, failing to ask him which way to go to get back on the Camino. Ten minutes later I came to the same fork in the road I had seen earlier, only this time there was a huge yellow arrow clearly pointing the way.

Two hours later, I arrived in Sarria.

Day 30
(23 km; 14 mi)

Sarria to Portomarín

The next morning I got off to a somewhat late start. I woke up and had a delicious breakfast and two great cups of café con leche before I set out. I then went back to my room and packed up Cheater. I left him with the front desk and got my passport stamped at around 9:30. I put it in my little purse strapped around my neck, then stepped outside. Right across from the hostel was a gift shop and, being a shopper, I was immediately drawn inside. There I found Camino tchotchkes of all sorts, including walking sticks, ponchos, postcards, St. James crosses, pens, notebooks with yellow Camino arrows and blue and yellow Camino shells, and more. I decided to get a few small mementos for my daughters, knowing as I purchased them that they wouldn't hold any significance for them and I was wasting my money. Still, I had to have them. This journey would soon be over and maybe this was my feeble attempt to hang on to the Camino magic a little longer.

Then I walked farther into town and was surprised by how charming it was. I had missed this last night, as I had stayed close to my hostel and hadn't ventured out to have a look around.

I started taking photos of the beautiful church before me when I met a guy from Ireland named Allen, a chatty fellow, who had just arrived and was just setting out on his first day. He was traveling with a friend named Johnny, and was excited to get under way. They were as different as night and day. Allen was outgoing and chatty, while Jimmy was dark and surly and barely said "Hello."

Allen offered to take a few photos of me in front of the Church of Santa Marina, a huge edifice with a Gothic feel, and I returned the favor. Afterward, we chatted for a minute and I gave him lots of encouragement and wished him a "Buen Camino."

Before leaving town, I stopped in the church, which was now open because I had lingered so long taking photos. I said a quick rosary, looked around, and then got another pilgrim's stamp in my passport from a woman in the back of the church who took her stamping job very seriously.

Once that was done, I headed out of town and was about 15 minutes into my walk when I realized I had only one PowerBar and no money. So I turned around and went back into town to find a cash station. By the time I did that and got under way yet again, it was almost 11:30 in the morning.

Still, it was a bright, sunny day, and I felt no need to rush. My mind and heart were happy and all I wanted to do was sing. So I did. For hours and hours.

Eventually I came upon a man who was sitting by a tree with a sign that said "Free fruit." It looked good, so I stopped and asked if I could have an orange. He was so friendly and happy to offer it to me that I felt blessed.

I noticed that he had a guitar right next to him, so I asked if he would play and sing a song. He turned bright red and said he was shy, but with a little encouragement he finally agreed. At first he sang so quietly I could barely hear him, but I heartily applauded anyway and thanked him profusely. It seemed to be all that he needed because after that he started playing and singing louder and louder until he was singing at full volume, song after song. Before I knew it I had just been given a 30-minute private concert.

"Wow! Thank you. That was beautiful," I said. And it was. Beaming, he laughed. Thanking him once again for his lovely song, I asked him what his name was.

He smiled and said, "Patrick."

Of course it is, I thought, shaking my head. *Wow Camino, are you making sure I don't forget about someone?*

We laughed and hugged, and then he stood up to give me a gift, just like the shaman had yesterday. He reached into his bag, which was hanging on a tree branch, and handed me a wooden cross that he had carved himself. I tried to give him money for it, but he refused. "It is a present from the Camino because you bring joy to my day," he said.

I graciously accepted it and after he wished me a "Buen Camino," I was once again on my way. Soon I came across a café and stopped for lunch. There were so many pilgrims sitting there it was shocking. I wondered where they had all come from since not one had passed while Camino Patrick #2 was serenading me.

I was now convinced that the Camino was a magical vortex where multiple realities were going on at the same time. Either that or a bus just dropped the entire crowd off across the street right before I arrived. I ordered a Coke and a tortilla, made of eggs and potatoes. I was down to my last days now and I hadn't eaten much of anything besides egg sandwiches and octopus, and lots of pork and potatoes. It was time to spread my wings a little and sample some new things for a change.

Minutes after I sat down, I saw Allen and Johnny from this morning rambling up the path, both looking pretty challenged. Huffing and puffing, they nearly flopped down on the ground as they walked into the garden area of the café.

I remembered how I had felt the first day after walking over the Pyrenees and how torturous it was. I had compassion for them. It isn't easy to do this, especially if you are not used to walking this far.

We chatted a bit, but not for long, as they ran into some other pilgrims they had evidently met along the way, so I was left to my peace once again. My tortilla was brought to the table where I was sitting, so I was able to relax and watch the crowd as I lingered over lunch.

My feet were so sore I wondered if I would have to do something drastic to heal them when I got home. I decided just to ask God to heal them and trust it would happen as soon as I stopped beating them to death on a daily basis.

After lunch I got back on my way, grateful I'd had the good sense to get money before I set out. My PowerBar was long gone, and I am sure I could have eaten another tortilla and an egg bocadillo had I the time.

The path twisted and turned, went into the woods, followed the road, went up and down hills, and eventually came to a huge river. Walking across it with speeding traffic alongside me was a little nerve-racking, as I do not like heights and the drop down to the river was very long. The wind was blowing so hard directly in my face that at times I feared I would lose my balance and topple over the low guardrail into the water below. I seriously considered dropping to my knees and crawling across.

Concentrate, Sonia, I told myself. *Stop thinking about falling into the river. You're just freaking yourself out unnecessarily. You are safe and will get to the other side.*

I just kept walking, my head down and my feet forward, taking one focused step at a time while looking away from the guardrail. It seemed to take an eternity to get all the way across, but in reality, it was only five minutes.

Finally, I made it. Whew! I felt as though I had really dodged a bullet on that one. Except the truth is I was never really in danger. My mind was just messing with me.

Safely back on solid ground, I looked up. Right before me was a steep, high, wide staircase leading to the city above, and at the top was Clint, sitting peacefully and waving down to me. I hadn't noticed him before. I was glad I hadn't crawled across the bridge now. I would have been so embarrassed to have had a witness to that.

I waved back and starting climbing up. It seemed a bit much of the Camino to ask pilgrims to make that steep climb after walking all day, and especially across that bridge, but then again, we were burning off our sins. Maybe we pilgrims needed this extra effort to make sure our karmic slates would be completely clean by the time we arrived in Santiago a few days from now.

Huffing and puffing, I finally made it to the top and plopped myself down next to Clint. "Waiting for Dean?" I asked.

"Yes, have you seen him?"

"He's not that far behind. I saw him not too long ago with his shoes off, smoking a cigarette."

"I just love that guy," Clint said, and I knew he meant it. Bonding on the Camino had to have been special, as it strips away all that is artificial and ego-centered and leaves you only in the vibration of the heart. At least it has the potential to if you come at it with the intention to move in that spiritual direction.

"I'm happy you found such a great friend, Clint. Our relationships are the most important thing in the end, aren't they?"

"That's for sure!" he answered.

I then got up and wished him a "Buen Camino." I turned to look at the river one more time and saw Dean waving and approaching fast, as at ease as ever.

I wandered another half a kilometer into town and came straight to the town's church. I walked inside and said a prayer of thanksgiving for having had yet another glorious day on the Camino. I hadn't felt any anger or upset or fear or resentment from my ego for days now. I was peaceful and happy to be me and ready to face anything life brought to my door with love and compassion for all involved. What a miracle that was.

After I left the church I walked out onto a plaza lined with cafés and saw Camino Patrick #1 sitting right in front of me, a cold beer in his hand and a big smile on his face.

I immediately walked over and joined him. "Patrick, I'm so happy to see you!"

We laughed, and I ordered a large, cold beer mixed with lemonade and sat down next to him. Patrick asked how my day was, and I started to tell him about it, when I stopped. The minute I tried to explain all the wonderful things that I'd experienced, they seemed to lose some of their magic and I didn't want that to happen.

I quickly summed it up by saying, "It was a Camino kind of day."

He smiled and said, "I understand. Enough said."

We sat and relaxed, mostly in silence, as we were both too tired to talk at the moment, sipping our beers and watching other pilgrims show up. After a while we got up and went our separate ways. I had a pilgrim dinner waiting for me at the hostel and he had made plans to have dinner with some other pilgrims from the albergue where he was staying. We hugged and wished each other a "Buen Camino," and dragged our tuckered-out selves back to our respective spots for the night.

As I was falling asleep, I reflected on all that had happened to me since I began this awesome journey a few weeks ago. I came so broken and wounded, and now I was feeling strong and more peaceful with each passing day. I was even feeling deeply happy. The Camino was healing me.

Day 31

(23 km; 14 mi)

Portomarín to Palas de Rei

I woke up feeling like a little kid. My heart was happy and I was eager to start the day. The sun was shining brightly and everything was so green it seemed like the height of summer, save for the still fairly cool air outside. I took my time getting out of bed and out the door because I knew I was down to the last four days on the Camino, and I wanted to savor every minute.

At breakfast I ran into Allen and Johnny, who were apparently arguing over something. I smiled and left them alone. They acknowledged me but didn't seem to want to interrupt their conversation to say good morning.

That was fine with me. More now than ever I wanted to remain in silence as much as possible, not wanting to miss any bit of insight that might come through while I was in this clear and calm inner state.

After breakfast I left Cheater with the front desk, got a stamp for my passport, and headed out. Following the yellow arrows, I wound through town, then followed the path from the center of town at the top of the hill back down to the river, and on from there.

This part of the river was neither as wide nor as windy as yesterday's crossing, for which I was grateful, as I wasn't ready to be freaked out again so early in the morning.

Once across and on my way, I was in pure bliss. I was mesmerized as the Camino led me into a deep green forest that spilled out into several small farms. Gentle mist danced through the trees, and wildflowers exploded everywhere, filling the air with an interesting and very strong mixed fragrance of cow dung and rose petals that was so powerful that even I could smell it. Birds were singing in the trees, and bees were swarming around the flowers. Cows were grazing, farmers were working, and nature was in full bloom. Everything felt so alive, including me.

The walk starting winding uphill again about an hour after I began, and at times it was quite steep. I took my time and used my poles to support my feet and my knee, as they were both starting to hurt a lot.

Today I noticed more pilgrims on the path than in all the weeks before combined. It felt at times as though I were on the Camino 500, with groups, some as large as 10 or 15, flocking all around, leaving my private Camino a thing of the past.

I was warned this would happen, as many people chose to walk only the last 100 kilometers of the Camino. That was the minimum distance you needed to walk in order to get the Compostela, or the certificate of completion of the Santiago pilgrimage, and be granted a plenary indulgence, or forgiveness of the past, by the Catholic Church.

It took extra focus on my part to stay centered and remain undisturbed by this sudden shift in the Camino energy. I didn't want the crowds to take away from my inner peace. I decided this was just another opportunity to prepare for reentering life after the Camino, where life would be as demanding and intense for me as it ever was. Maintaining my inner peace through the crowds here was good practice for life back home.

The path was very muddy, no doubt from all the rain over the past few weeks, and at times it was more like gum than anything else. It reminded me of the muck I had to fight my way through in the Pyrenees way back in the beginning, leaving me with the sense of coming full circle. I figured it was just a reminder for me not to get stuck in the mud—not here, nor in my life.

A little farther on, the air smelled so strongly of acrid cow dung it almost knocked me out. *How can these people stand this smell?* I wondered. *Do they even smell it all anymore, or is it such a part of their lives that it doesn't bother them at all?*

I knew that fertilizer was necessary to help everything on these farms grow, which led me to see it, too, as a metaphor. *I guess I have to view the past pain and suffering in my life as the fertilizer I needed to help me grow, as well,* I decided.

I was grateful for it all and would not have wanted my life to be any other way. Everything that had transpired in my past life brought me here, to this beautiful and peaceful point in my being, and without life unfolding as it had, I wouldn't be here at all, inside or out. Looking around, I couldn't imagine missing this experience for the entire world and was grateful for everyone and everything that made this possible, including the deaths of my father and brother, and my split from Patrick.

I happened upon such an inviting tree stump that I didn't want to pass it up and sat down. As I did, I looked at Pilgrim. Inside I had been carrying my lightweight shoes as well as my Tevas every day, just in case I needed to take my boots off, but every time I tried to walk in either pair, the pain along the sides of my feet became so severe I just couldn't do it.

So right then, I took both pairs out and decided to leave them on the path. I had seen shoes that had been left to die on the Camino along the entire way. Maybe some of those people needed new shoes to replace their dead ones. I put one pair on the tree stump next to me and another across from it, for pilgrims behind me to find. They were brand-new and maybe would be welcomed by someone who had just had a shoe blowout. I hoped so.

This now took even more weight off my back and left me with very little to carry in Pilgrim other than my iPod, my few remaining Band-Aids and blister creams, my water bottle, and my down vest. I was dropping so much weight now and it felt great. Even my pants were falling off as I left the past behind.

Eventually, just when I was running out of steam and didn't think I could walk any farther, I dragged my weary self into Palas de Rei, where I was going to stay for the night. As I walked into the town, I could hear a band in the distance playing the most lively Celtic music, complete with bagpipes and drums. The deeper into town I got, the louder it became, until I walked up to my hostel and saw that the music was coming from there.

A big wedding party was under way; and everyone was out on the lawn laughing, singing, and dancing to the music, celebrating the happy occasion.

I took this as a sign of new love and life, and to happen upon it and enjoy the celebration vicariously was a wonderful way to end the day.

Moments later I checked in and found Cheater patiently waiting for me in the lobby. I was then shown to my room, as this hostel was spread out among several buildings and I was in one located in the back. Once I settled in, I went outside again and sat in the sun, enjoying the live band and watching the party continue.

Eventually Camino Patrick came wandering up to the hostel and said he was staying at the pilgrims' albergue a little farther into town, but came to see if I was staying here. Happy to find one another once again, we decided to have dinner together in the hostel restaurant. We sat in the sun a little while longer and shared a glass of wine while waiting for the dinner hour to come around. Fortunately, it was only an hour away, as the hostel was sensitive to tired pilgrims who needed to eat early.

Just as we were about to be seated, Johnny and Allen came strolling in, and once they saw me, they came over and asked if they could join us for dinner. Patrick didn't seem too keen on the idea, but I didn't mind, so I left it to him to answer. He hesitated for a minute then said, "Of course, please do," and moments later we were all seated around a small table in the corner of the hostel restaurant looking over the menu.

Once we ordered and wine was served, Johnny and Allen started talking. To our shock, they complained bitterly about the hostel, the menu, the weather, and the price they paid for the accommodations, and then began attacking American politicians, corporate America, England, Germany, the Church, other pilgrims, and more. This was all in the first 15 minutes after sitting down! The next thing I knew they were slamming the President, and Americans in general, causing Patrick to rise up in patriotic defense of everything they were attacking. Soon a tense argument ensued, with sniping back and forth on the part of all three men.

I was appalled at what was happening, as it shattered my Camino calm and tranquility, leaving me to wonder if Johnny and Allen had any idea this was a spiritual pilgrimage. Several times I attempted to temper the conversation by bringing it back to more neutral territory, but Johnny especially seemed to be just warming up to his assaults and was in no mood to change the subject or take notice of his effect on either Patrick or me.

Finally I attempted to stop the barrage by directly asking them to change the subject and direction, explaining that having been on this long contemplative journey I was not available to participate in the conversation at hand. But they only rolled their eyes at me and smirked.

Rather than taking this in, they turned their negative energy on full force toward me now, as they not only ignored my request, but carried on even more aggressively than before. Again I politely asked them to stop and change the direction of the conversation. I assured them that while it wasn't personal, I simply wasn't available to listen to what they were saying right now.

All the while I was thinking, *What the hell is the matter with them?* I hadn't experienced anything like this from anyone the entire time I had been walking, and it really caught me by surprise.

After my second request to change the subject, I was met with stony silence on their part, accompanied by sideways stares of resentment, while Patrick seemed to now want to not only come to my defense but also to the defense of the good American people. So moments later, off they went at it again.

It was crazy to be surrounded by this toxic energy after walking my way into such a serene inner state of being over the past month. I had just finished my soup when I realized the evening was not going to improve, and if anything, with addition of more wine, it was only going to get worse. So I suddenly got up, offered a "Buen Camino" to all, and went back to my room. I was as surprised as they were by my exit, but greatly relieved to be away from the negativity and combativeness that I had just escaped.

"What the heck was that?" I asked myself as I got back to room, scrambling for any last bits and pieces of PowerBar left in Pilgrim or Cheater. I wondered why the Camino gave me that unexpected and toxic experience. Perhaps it was to give me a chance to fully experience the devastating impact negative energy has on people.

Perhaps Allen and Johnny were two Camino angels sent to remind me to be extremely mindful of my own temptation to be negative from now on.

Perhaps they showed up to mirror aspects of myself that could be equally negative that needed to be brought to light so I could pray and meditate to clear them as I walked tomorrow.

Perhaps they were a very loud and clear warning to get away from negative people as soon as possible and not allow them to drag me into their vortex.

All three thoughts felt right, and I was grateful for the experience and awareness even if it did catch me off guard and leave me feeling a little rattled. That's how the Camino had worked for me.

I felt a little guilty leaving Camino Patrick there with them, but then I figured he could take care of himself. I didn't have to protect him. He could have left just as easily as I did. I wondered if he did.

Too tired and hungry to analyze it any further, I went to bed, figuring the sooner I went to sleep, the faster I could get up in the morning and eat. I closed the shutters to my room, which made the space pitch-black, and after praying for a while I passed out.

Day 32

(28 km; 17 mi)

Palas de Rei to Arzúa

Transition. That was what I woke up feeling today. The energy of transition. Today was one of the last three days before I was to complete my pilgrimage to Santiago, and I had so many mixed feelings rolling around in me because of that. Part of me didn't want this journey to end because it had been so incredibly life changing in every way: body, mind, emotions, and my more deeply awakened spirit. Another part of me was quite aware that today's walk was long and moderately taxing, and I was worried about my feet. They really hurt.

I also thought a lot about transitions and how uncomfortable they made me feel because they left me so ungrounded. I was not quite done here and not quite able to begin there, so had to balance between the energetic push away from what it was time to end and the pull toward the next experience, and wait.

As I ate my breakfast, I realized why transitions caused me to feel this way. It's because when I'm in transition, I am not in control of things. In transition, I must surrender control over to trust and faith.

Transition times are dangerous. If you don't stay focused, crazy things can happen. I could lose my footing, or get lost, or something else. I had to remain alert until the end.

"I also have to beware of sentimentality," I told myself. "I can easily think, *I'm so sad this is ending,* rather than embrace it comfortably, knowing as this ends my spirit is now preparing me for new experiences, which may be equally meaningful."

Who knows? I thought as I ate my toast. My mind likes to scatter shadows across my inner landscape when I'm not certain. It's all a game to distract me from the moment. Still, the thoughts were intense.

Drinking my café con leche, I thought about the changes I would be facing once this pilgrimage was over. So many questions now flooded my mind. Would I be able to hold on to the profoundly healing insights the Camino has gifted me with? Or would I fall asleep again and back into the old patterns that caused so much pain and drama? The Camino gave me these gifts. It was now up to me to call them my own and make them a permanent part of me. I wondered if I could.

I decided the best way to move through this uncertainty of what lay ahead was to stay very present to the path before me and just focus on the walk today. Ever since I began this pilgrimage, there were times when I had to climb and climb, only to crest the hill and descend just as quickly. It made me aware that it's best to set my intentions and then trust my spirit and God rather than think ahead too much. Life goes up and down and sideways and sometimes in circles, but if I just stay present, I can respond well enough to it all without playing out worst-case scenarios as a means for my ego to feel in control.

So on that note I got up, finished my juice, grabbed Pilgrim, and headed out, not wanting to stir up more anxiety than was already tumbling through my brain, shaking off those thoughts and more as I zipped up my jacket.

As I walked I intentionally noticed as much as I could with each step, asking my guides and angels to help me remember not to get ahead of myself today or in the future. I wanted to be in the moment and soak everything up in the now, trusting that the future would take care of itself.

I prayed and prayed as I walked, asking for help from the Holy Mother-Father God, all my angels and guides, my family on the other side, and especially my father and brother, so that my transition from the Camino and back to my life in Chicago would be graceful and filled with ease, and not a return to drama and fear.

Thankfully, I knew enough and had grown enough throughout my life, and especially throughout this pilgrimage, to now place my full and complete faith in God and the Universe and surrender all personal control over to God's will. I felt completely safe to do that now.

Perhaps this was because I no longer felt the old pain and grief in my body that I had brought to the Camino. I came purely on my intuitive guidance, with no expectations. But if I'd had any hopes for the Camino, how I felt today would have far exceeded them in every way. Walking the Camino had freed me of the bondage that holding on to anger and resentment had kept me in. It was gone. My karma felt cleared.

I also felt a surprisingly deep wave of love and affection for Patrick right now. I could see how much pain from his own past kept him trapped, as it had me, and all I felt for him was compassion and understanding for why he acted as he did. We came together in this life to help each other get free of this old pain and karma, and we had to jar it loose in one another so it could move on. Of that I was certain.

My healing was happening now. I hoped it would happen for him, as well. I had no way of knowing, of course, but I intuitively felt that if he was no longer fighting with me, he would be able to relax and turn his attention back to himself and his own heart in a kinder and more loving way. I wanted that for him. And I prayed for it.

As I walked, the sky went from sunny to overcast, which I liked because it made for pleasant hiking. I thought about endings quite a bit, contemplating those that are natural completions, those that I resist, those that are thrust upon me, and those that I choose, perhaps thrusting them upon others as well.

I became clear on how we cannot hold on to anything other than fear or love. We have to choose. I chose love, but fear kept trying to grab back on. I was so glad I could walk it off today. It made me aware that I would never be completely over fear. I would face it every single day. I just had to move through it when it showed up and not allow it to grab hold of me.

The path continued to be so beautiful as I walked that I felt as though I were in nature's private spa. The colorful wildflowers, birds singing, strong scent of grass and hay, and even the cow dung were all so healing to my spirit. I soaked in as much as I could, and started looking forward to arriving at a town called Melide, which was halfway to Arzúa.

Even with my hearty breakfast, after going to bed with only soup for dinner, I was now starving. I had heard there was a particularly good restaurant in Melide, which was famous for their grilled octopus, called *esquival*, so that's where I headed.

The thought of grilled octopus made the long walk fly by, and shortly before 1 P.M., I walked into the door of the restaurant. To my delight, there sat Camino Patrick, who looked up and smiled at me. I was so glad to see him, after bailing on him the night before.

"Patrick! How was the rest of dinner last night? I am so sorry I left, but I just had to," I gushed all at once.

"It was as bad as the first half," he said and smiled. "What a couple of creeps!"

"I know. It was strange to meet up with that kind of energy here on the Camino, wasn't it? It's good to be made aware of just how potent negativity is before we finish this pilgrimage, don't you think? So we won't be guilty of spreading it around ourselves once we leave the Camino."

"That's one away of looking at it," he said. "Still, I hope I don't run into them again because if I do, I plan on ignoring them."

"I understand," I said, setting Pilgrim down next to me. "Been here long?"

"Only for an hour," he answered, winking, "waiting for you."

"How did you get here so fast? I'm not racing, but still I am not going slowly either."

"I leave early. People are up so early in the pilgrims' albergues I just get going, too."

"Well, then you must be as hungry as I am. Let's eat octopus!"

Afterward we wandered through the town. It was Sunday and there was a huge market going on, with every kind of dry goods and food imaginable. We strolled around and looked for a place to get our passports stamped. We were told to go to the church for that, so we did. A mass was going on as we entered, so we felt obligated to stay until it was over, as everyone there turned and glared at us as if to say, "How dare you interrupt."

After the mass was over, I walked around the church. It was a particularly intense place, with a statue of Christ dressed in purple robes in one corner, looking very much like a statue of Dracula, blood dripping all over. Whoa!

There were some other statues, including of Mother Mary and some saints, looking equally ominous, and I wanted to see them all.

Looking up, Patrick seemed far less taken by this place and stood in the back waiting for me, so I quickened my pace and headed toward him so we could go. I could tell Patrick was a bit agitated. I asked him if he was okay, and he said he was just worried about finding a pilgrims' albergue that night. So we abandoned the stamp idea and continued on our way.

The path was all over the place and so was the weather. It went from warm and overcast to cold and rainy every 30 minutes. We put our rain ponchos on, took them off, put them back on, decided not to put them on, got soaked, then put them back on, and then off, for hours.

It was frustrating, but we laughed about it rather than let it bother us. Patrick was also experiencing serious pain running down the front of his legs and said he could hardly stand it.

I had brought some painkillers along with me that I never used, so I offered him all of them. He took them, hugging me with gratitude.

The afternoon walk dragged on and on. Talking and walking made it go a little faster, but the more it dragged on, the more worried I became about making it to Arzúa, as my feet were now in agony. Between the two of us we were a mess, and we laughed at ourselves because of it, two old geezers crawling to the end.

Eventually we arrived in a town called Ribadiso, which was a welcome sight. That meant we were getting closer, as Arzúa was only three or four more kilometers away.

As we entered the town, we saw many pilgrims we had both met along the way sitting around a small terrace drinking beers and calling it a day at this point.

There was a huge pilgrims' albergue there, and I strongly encouraged Patrick to stay, but he wanted to accompany me all the way to Arzúa, so he declined. No matter what I did I couldn't get him to change his mind, so I stopped trying. He had a beer and I had a Coke and some fries, as I was now starving again. No sooner did our order come to our table than it started to rain again, this time pretty hard.

We grabbed our stuff and ran under an awning and waited. Five minutes later it stopped.

We stayed and chatted with a few other pilgrims that Patrick knew, and then I said I needed to keep going, as it was getting late and I was worried my feet wouldn't make it all the way. With that said, we were off once again.

Those last few kilometers were torturous. Rain was now steadily pouring down as we wound our way out of the fields and forests and into a long stretch of dreary town that eventually spilled out along a highway. It seemed as though we kept walking and walking and walking without advancing a single step.

"So much for not wanting the Camino to end," I said to Patrick. "I changed my mind!" I yelled out loud to the Camino. "Please end! At least for today!" Patrick just looked at me and shook his head without saying a word.

We continued following the yellow arrows for another hour before we finally saw signs of hotels ahead, and eventually stumbled into the one where I was to stay. Patrick checked to see if there was a room there for him as well, but the innkeeper said that sadly, there was not.

I felt terrible about that. He didn't seem to mind as much as I did, saying there were several more hostels down the street, so he would keep going and find one in no time. We then hugged each other and said, "Buen Camino," and agreed that we would meet at my hostel tomorrow night, as it would be the second-to-last night on the Camino, and he wanted to walk with me into Santiago.

He then stepped back into the pouring rain and disappeared. I asked for Cheater and went to my room. Dinner would be served next door in an hour, so I had time to dry off, and change my clothes. What a long and winding road it was today.

Day 33
(23 km; 14 mi)

Arzúa to Amenal

I woke up to rain and howling wind, and only wanted to roll over in bed and continue sleeping, but this was my second-to-last day before arriving in Santiago, so instead I got up and took a long, hot shower. I couldn't believe I was almost at the end of this incredible pilgrimage. It felt as if I were slowly waking up from an epic dream.

I looked over at Cheater. He was one lightweight fellow right now. Since I began this pilgrimage I had given away nearly a third of my clothes, all of my shoes except for my hiking boots, and all of my bandages and first-aid supplies, and had eaten all of my PowerBars. We had both done a good job of letting go of the excess baggage we carried to the Camino. "Well done, Cheater. We are almost there," I said to him out loud. Pilgrim just smiled in the corner.

Given the weather outside, I layered up with the last little bit of warm clothing I still had with me, and then packed up Cheater. Next I stuffed my rain poncho, gloves, and headband into Pilgrim, threw my little purse with my wallet and my pilgrim's passport around my shoulder, and headed downstairs with all my stuff in tow.

Once I handed Cheater over to the receptionist and got my passport stamped, I strolled over to the small dining room. There, at the far end, Johnny and Allen were seated, doing their very best to ignore me. I wasn't sure whether I was glad about this or if it made me feel uncomfortable. At any rate, I took the hint and sat at a table at the other end of the small room. I didn't need any negative vibes today—that was for sure.

Since Johnny and Allen were the only ones besides me in the restaurant, however, I was too uncomfortable to linger, so I hurriedly swilled my last sip of coffee, grabbed my poles, and walked out the door, smiling and wishing them both "Buen Camino" as I left.

Outside, the rain had stopped, and I was greeted with a few rays of sun peeking through the still heavy clouds and a stiff, cold breeze. It woke me up and got me going. I looked around for the yellow markers, and once I saw them, I started to sing, "I'm Off to See the Wizard," this time at full volume and with gusto as I got under way. An hour later, I stopped to pray.

> *Holy Mother-Father God,*
> *Please help me keep my heart open and my thoughts present as I find my way through this second-to-last day. Help me remain available to all the lessons I must learn on this day and guide me each step of the way. Please give me the help I need to succeed today. And thank you for giving me the ability to keep on going, as I don't know how my feet are doing it, but they are.*
> *Amen and with gratitude,*
> *Thank you.*

The air was so fresh and cool it cleared my head and lifted my heart. I tried to reflect on all that I had experienced so far, but the Camino wouldn't allow it. *You can think about that later, when you've finished,* it said to me. *Pay attention and stay aware, or you will miss the gifts of today.*

The rain had by now completely cleared and though it was still cool outside, the sun was brilliant and felt good on my face. As I walked, I enjoyed the gorgeous symphony of nature coming alive. Butterflies were everywhere. Hundreds of them. Farmers were in the fields, dogs barking and running alongside them. Horses came trotting over to have a look at me as I walked by their farms and snorted as I passed, as if to say, "It's just another pilgrim!" I laughed.

"What's next for me?" I wondered aloud, giving in to the temptation to jump ahead once again. It was one thing to be serene in the middle of such a sacred and blessed path, under the Milky Way, but what would it be like when I got back home? "Am I really changed? Have I really accepted all that has happened in my life and forgiven others and myself for the pain that came along with it?" I questioned.

I certainly was no longer the broken person who showed up here five weeks and several lifetimes ago. I no longer felt chained to the past or to the feelings of grief and anger that had been for so long buried inside me. The Camino had healed me of all that, and I was profoundly grateful for this miracle. In its place was a quiet space in my heart, filled with compassion and love for all human beings.

I was also keenly aware of the difference between my ego and my spirit, and how painful and heavy my ego was to carry. It was dead weight and brought nothing good with it. Nothing. It only perpetuated stories that isolated me from life and love and everything I wanted or needed. It set up battles and power struggles with others that no one would or could ever win.

It wasn't that I was done with my ego. I knew that wasn't possible. My ego was part of who I was. It was the lower part. The confused part. The never satisfied, never secure, never trusting part of me. It was also the vain part. The scared, manipulating, thin-skinned, hypersensitive, easily offended, easily threatened, and entitled part.

It was the part of me that said, "I am right, and *they* are wrong." It was the part looking for love and not finding it. When it took hold of me, I was no longer connected to my spirit, my true and beautiful self. I became lost.

I had no illusions that I was done with my ego. I knew it would, again and again, try to run my life, as I was only human. I knew it would flare up when I was tired or feeling insecure, or felt afraid to be seen. Only now, I knew how to tame it. There was only one way. I had to love myself fully and unconditionally. I had to have compassion for myself and be sensitive and responsive to my authentic needs. I had to pray daily for guidance and give myself the time and space to nurture my spirit and enjoy my life. I had to stay present in the moment and not leap into the future or fall back into the past. That was a tall order, but I knew it would bring me peace.

I also needed to stop seeing my ego as "the enemy" and start seeing it as the "me" who needed more love. I didn't have to fight my ego when it flared up in pain. I needed to soothe and calm my ego, handing it over to the care of my spirit and to God to quiet down and reassure.

It was simple. When I loved me, I was filled with grace. When I didn't, the battles and pain began.

Please help me remember this, Holy Mother-Father God. Help me take this lesson and carry it forward from this pilgrimage back to my life. Like St. Francis, I only want to be an instrument of peace. I pray for the guidance and strength and presence of mind and heart to live with love and compassion for all.

I sat down and soaked in the beauty around me. Soon it would be over, so I was blessed to be here now. I was so grateful that words couldn't begin to express how I felt. I was whole. No longer broken and shattered.

Thank you for healing me. I pray I can carry this healing forward and touch all those in my life. Amen.

The walk was magical. I laughed, I cried, I sang. I limped along. There were no other pilgrims on the path almost the entire time, unlike the past few days. It was so quiet I even questioned whether I had missed an arrow and wandered away from the Camino. Right then I saw an arrow, as if the nature spirits were pointing it out to me.

As the sun rose higher and higher, so did the temperature, and I began to peel away the layers of clothing that I had bundled myself into that morning. It was close to noon by the look of the sun. I had been walking for at least four hours, so I decided to stop and get a snack.

Fifteen minutes later I happened upon a little outdoor café filled with pilgrims basking in the sun and drinking beers and Cokes. Again I wondered where they all came from, given that I hadn't seen a single one of them for hours. Strange how that kept happening.

I noticed a table and sat down. I took Pilgrim off my back and proceeded to reach for my little purse to get some money and order lunch, only to discover it was *not* strapped across me, as it should have been.

Not allowing myself to panic, I calmly reached for Pilgrim. *I must have stuck it in there,* I said to myself, knowing full well that I had not. Still, I looked inside, only to confirm it was definitely not there.

I took a deep breath and made a concerted effort not to freak out. That little purse had my only credit card, all my money, my passport, my ticket home, and my little pilgrim's passport with ALL MY STAMPS FOR THE ENTIRE WAY!

I burst out crying. What was I going to do? I tried to stay calm as I went into the café to ask for help, but no one there spoke English. My mind was frantic. I had already walked four hours, and I could have lost it anywhere along the path. *Should I leave now and go back? If I do, how far should I go? What if someone found it? How would they get it to me? Maybe I should run ahead and call from the next hostel.* I stepped forward then back, turning in circles and getting more upset by the moment.

I started praying. I needed a miracle and fast.

Just then, Johnny and Allen came walking into the café. They both took one look at me and Allen came right over and said, "Sonia, are you all right?"

I burst into tears all over again and told him I had lost my little purse with everything in it. I needed help and didn't even speak enough Spanish to ask for it. At that point Johnny walked over.

"What's going on?" he asked. Allen told him, because I was too numb to speak, feeling so close to the end and so out of control.

Allen said, "Sit down. I'll get you a coffee."

"I saw you at breakfast. Have you stopped since?" Johnny asked me, mobilizing into action.

"No, I haven't. I just walked," I responded, shaking my head.

Next, he whipped out his cell phone, tuned in to the Internet, and started speaking to the woman behind the counter in fluent Spanish all at the same time, asking her what cafés and hostels were between where we started out this morning and here. They spoke furiously back and forth, he barking things at her, and she barking things right back, then both now barking things on the phone, while he nodded at me and told me to keep drinking my coffee.

I let it sit there. I couldn't even drink a sip I was so stressed out. All I could do was pray.

Fifteen tense minutes later, he started talking to someone new on the other end of his cell phone. "¡Sí, sí, sí!" he said, then hung up.

He then turned to me and said, "I found it."

I was shocked. "Where?"

"Someone saw it on the trail about four kilometers past where we started out today and took it back to the hostel because you had the name of it written on a piece of paper inside."

"Oh, thank God!" I cried in relief. "I have to go back now and get it."

"No need," he said. "I told him to send it along with your bag to the hostel where you are staying tonight because your bag was still there."

"You're kidding! What a miracle!"

Johnny continued, "He said not to worry. Everything is still there. No one took anything."

I was stunned.

"Oh my goodness. You are my Camino angel, Johnny! I can't thank you enough. You saved me."

He laughed out loud very hard when I said that.

"No one has *ever* called me an angel before."

"But you are. You are my angel, and I am so grateful for you in every way," I said, giving him a big hug. He seemed uncomfortable.

Allen then took out five euros. "I bought your coffee. I hope this is enough to get you to the hostel tonight."

I took the money and gave him a big hug, as well. They looked at me and said, "Okay, then. Well, buen Camino," and left.

I just sat there, speechless. My dark angels of two days ago just saved my trip.

Who knew that would be my experience today?

Thank you, God. Thank you, Camino angels. Thank you, Dad. Thank you, Bruce Anthony. Thank you, knights, and anyone else looking after me.

As I resumed walking, I started singing the old song "Johnny Angel," and thought about how little we really ever know anyone. The worst two pilgrims of the entire Camino just became my most beloved today. That goes to show you should never judge anyone because you never know who they really are and can be. I knew this before, but now I *really* knew this.

"Thank you for this lesson, Camino. It is one I am sure I won't forget."

I walked the next two hours feeling blanketed by angels. The walk was long and wound in all directions. I walked through farmland, across roads, and past long stretches of forest. As I did, the weather got worse and worse, rain coming down so hard now it was scary. I even saw a cloud that looked eerily like a tornado from afar. It made me run.

Finally, finally, I arrived at my hostel. Once inside I was told that someone was coming to pick me up and take me to a second location belonging to the same owner.

"Is my little purse here?" I asked anxiously.

"No," was the answer. "No little purse."

"Is my bag here?"

"No, no bag either."

"Stay calm, Sonia," I said, keeping myself grounded. "It'll be at the next hotel."

In five minutes a man drove up and put me in the car. He spoke very little English but was kind and friendly. I relaxed a little. When I got to the hostel, I asked him for my little purse. He said he did not have it. Then I asked for Cheater. He took me into a room near the desk and, whew, there he was.

I explained about my little purse, and he got on the phone to the hostel that had delivered my bag. He then said that he would get a call back in 30 minutes.

I sunk to an all-new low.

What if it doesn't arrive? I worried. *What then?*

There was no use staring at him while he stared at the phone, so I grabbed Cheater and, with Pilgrim and poles in hand, I went to my room.

I sat on the bed and wondered what to do if my purse didn't show up.

Coming up with no ideas, I decided to take a shower and just have faith. I let it all go, knowing everything had worked out this far, and would till the end.

I unzipped Cheater. Surprise! My little purse was inside.

"Hurray!" And true to their word, everything was inside as promised.

What a roller-coaster ride this day had been. I couldn't believe it!

I threw myself on the bed and nearly screamed, "Thank you, Jesus, Mary, and Joseph, and all the angels in the world," relief surging through my every cell.

As I feel asleep that night, I thought about my lesson today. I realized how much goodness is all around, sometimes hidden right before our eyes. We only have to have faith in others and in life, be patient and stay grounded when the unexpected occurs, and remember to pray and have faith that we will always receive the love and support we need if we let go and allow it.

"Wow! Camino," I said, falling asleep. "I wasn't prepared for this lesson today, but I really needed it before I got home. Moreover, it's one I'll never forget. Ever. Thank you."

I then set the alarm for 4 A.M. I had another 15 kilometers to go to get to Santiago, and I wanted to make it to the 10 A.M. mass at the cathedral. I was excited to complete this pilgrimage, and yet sad it was coming to an end. What an adventure! My mind danced all over the place. It was difficult to fall asleep, but eventually I did.

Day 34
(15 km; 9 mi)

Amenal to Santiago de Compostela

When the alarm went off, it was pitch-black outside and I didn't know where I was. I had been dreaming that I was taking part in a religious ceremony, celebrating my arrival at a new land after being on a ship for years and years. In my dream a bell was ringing as part of the solemn ceremony. Now starting to wake up, I realized it was my alarm clock going off. I turned it off and sat in the dark for quite a few more minutes before I remembered I was walking to Santiago today.

"How appropriate," I said out loud, turning on the light, thinking of my dream. "At least I hope I'm arriving in a new land." I looked at my watch: 4 A.M. Time to get going.

My feet were so sore today that I had to step very gingerly as I walked to the shower.

"Feet, don't fail me now," I said, recalling one of my favorite disco songs, "One Nation Under a Groove," as I stepped in and let the hot water run down my face and back. *Ahh.* It felt good. "I can't believe I will arrive in Santiago in only a few hours. How surreal is that?" I continued talking to myself.

Once dried off, I got dressed quickly. I had laid out everything I was going to wear the night before, along with my poles, gloves, and headband; the penny my dad gave me; and the crystal I received from the shaman, as well as my wooden cross from Patrick #2, the singer, so it only took a minute.

I packed up Cheater and looked at him, saying, "Can you believe it? I walked and you rode across an entire country, Cheater. I'm impressed. Aren't you?"

Then I looked at Pilgrim. "You, too, little friend. We are almost home."

Then, as hard as it was, I shoved my painfully sore feet into my boots. "Ow!" Somehow at this hour of the morning, it was more painful than usual. "Almost there," I said to my feet encouragingly. "I promise you both a long and well-deserved rest after this. And when my toenails grow back, I'll get you a pedicure, too."

"Yeah, sure," they answered, unimpressed. "Just finish this already, will you?"

I patted them gently. "I know. Hang in there. Today is the last day."

Then I gathered up everything and headed downstairs. I had to be extra careful not to make noise in the hallway, as it was still so early in the morning, and I didn't want to wake anyone up. I had three floors to descend so it was tricky, but I managed.

When I got downstairs, it was pitch-black, save for a light in the coffee shop next to reception. I walked in and saw the woman who served me dinner last night. She was waiting to take me back to the other hostel where the Camino left off yesterday so I could resume my walk. She said I could get some breakfast there as well.

I loaded Cheater into the backseat, along with my poles, and before I left, I unzipped Pilgrim and looked inside to make sure my little purse was there. It was. We were good to go.

The other hostel was only minutes away, which was good because I wanted to eat breakfast before I left and it was inching toward 6 A.M. If I was to arrive on time for the pilgrims' mass in the cathedral, I had to start walking by then, and no later.

Once back at the hostel, I left Cheater with reception, got my passport stamped, and then sat down to a delicious café con leche and a warm chocolate croissant. Just then I remembered I was to have met Patrick last night at the hostel. I wondered where he ended up and if I would ever see him again. He had been such a blessing and champion for me as we walked. I loved him dearly and prayed that I would get to see him. Then I grabbed an apple and set out.

The sky was clear and filled with stars. I looked for the Milky Way. I am not much of an astronomer, but there it was, lighting my way and guiding me home.

As I walked, I didn't know what to think, so I prayed instead.

> *Holy Mother God,*
> *I can't believe I am taking the final steps toward Santiago. This has been such an incredible journey to the center of my soul and back; and because of it, I am now going home forgiven, whole, healed, and at peace. I had no idea it would heal me like this. I am so grateful. Thank you for all your blessings as you guide me the rest of the way. I can't even find words to express what I feel in my heart, so for the rest of the way, my prayer will be in silence.*
> *Amen . . . and thank you, thank you, thank you.*

As I walked, I sensed the millions of pilgrims who had traveled The Way before me and knew they were escorting me to Santiago. My heart was quiet, listening to God, filled with humility and gratitude, my spirit completely at ease.

In time the sun rose and the sky exploded with brilliant rose and orange colors. The birds burst into song, greeting this beautiful day. Clear to the end, it couldn't have been more perfect.

As I walked I contemplated the power of forgiveness. It actually transformed everything in my being. But I also knew it wasn't something that just happened unintentionally. Forgiveness, at least for me, came about in increments. I had to feel and honor my wounds and traumas before I could release them. For years I had tried to forgive through spiritual platitudes, but in spite of my ambitious ideals, I only managed to bury my wounds even deeper into my bones. Walking with my pain freed me from it. I always wanted to forgive, but it was only through the act of being with my pain fully, walking with it day after day, that it began to ease up and leave my body, allowing me to open up to greater understanding of how people hurt one another, myself included. In doing this I found compassion and could forgive, and hope to be forgiven.

It didn't bring me any peace to hide from my anger or deny it. Nor did it bring me peace to self-righteously hold on to it. It didn't bring me peace to hide in shame for the pain I caused, nor did it bring me peace to justify my behavior.

The only thing that brought me peace was to fully feel my human experience and accept that no matter what had transpired, in this or any life, underneath it all people do what they think is right or necessary at the time, and because of that, we are all both victims and perpetrators. We are all wounded, and wound one another because of it. And we are all innocent, too. And for that I had compassion for all of us.

I also learned you can't force-feed forgiveness either. I actually felt more wounded by those who seemed to shame me for not forgiving quickly than by those who hurt me. I could not forgive simply because I was told that was how I should feel. That wasn't how forgiveness worked for me or for anyone else, ever. Forgiveness could not come about with a spiritual bypass that ignored my feelings or by having others tell me what to feel. I had to walk through it all in order to forgive.

Nothing is too big to forgive. I was injured and injuring. And still I knew I was a beautiful spirit who was loved by God. We all are. That brought relief.

Now I fully understood what Christ meant when he said on the Cross, "Forgive them, for they know not what they do." In my wounded state, I didn't know how deeply my behavior affected others. In forgiving everyone else, I knew I too needed to be forgiven. This pilgrimage really was The Way of Forgiveness. I prayed in silence and gratitude for my release, and asked for release from pain for everyone in my life, and in the world.

The path was intoxicating, layered in shades of green among the trees and the moss I didn't even know existed. The sky was crystal clear, which was another blessing given how dark clouds and rain had accompanied me almost all the way from St. Jean.

My heart was clear, as well. I could feel my dad walking with me, as well as my brother. I also felt my beautiful spirit guides. There were my ancestors, the knights, my guardian angels, and the pilgrims gone before me. The veil between this world and the subtle realms had parted, and my spirit communed with the gentle spirits surrounding me. I was feeling more like me than ever before. Not just my temporal me, in this body in this life. I was connected to my true self, walking in the wholeness of my divine nature. I was no longer struggling or wounded or afraid of anything. All I needed to do was continue to walk in love and all would be well. Of that I was completely certain.

A few hours later, I entered the outskirts of Santiago. My heart skipped a beat, and I became overwhelmed with emotion. As I crossed the river and made my way to the center of the city, I began to sob uncontrollably. I looked ahead and saw the spires of St. James Cathedral in the distance. It was my Emerald City. I made it.

Soon I saw a sign that said "Welcome to Santiago" at a very busy roundabout, with a yellow arrow pointing to the historic center of town. Still in disbelief that I had finally arrived, I paid close attention to the yellow markers, not wanting to get lost in this now big confusing city at the end point of my journey. I walked steadily, as I still had 20 minutes to get to the mass. I was going to make it. In spite of the pain in my feet, I quickened my pace.

Ten minutes later I found my way into the historic center of town, drawn in by the sound of bagpipes playing under an arch leading to the cathedral. When I got closer, I saw that the man playing them was dressed in full medieval regalia. Farther on I saw more people dressed in medieval-period costumes pointing the pilgrims toward the church. It was touristy, but I loved every moment of it. I used the medieval people as my new markers until I walked into a great plaza, and there before me stood the cathedral, the most magnificent I have ever seen in my life.

I stood in awe of it and the fact that I was finally here. I took a breath. "We made it, Sonia," I said. "We are here."

A few moments later I climbed the stairs, walked inside, and found myself among throngs of people, including many of the familiar faces of those I had walked with along the way. We laughed and hugged and laughed some more and hugged some more, in between wandering around in awe of where we were.

The church was packed, and I realized that if I wanted to get a seat before mass, I had better find it now. I started walking toward the altar, trying to get as close as I could in spite of the crowds, when I heard a whisper next to me. "Sonia, sit here." Surprised, I turned and saw Sarah, one of the women who had ridden a horse with me to O Cebreiro.

"Sarah! Thank you!" I answered, delighted to now be seated right on the aisle, looking straight at the altar. Moments later the mass began. It was moving to be among the pilgrims from 165 countries around the world who were there that day.

The priest who said the mass was fantastic, and his sermon spoke straight to my soul.

"Now that you've walked the Camino, you can carry on in God's grace. Your heart will be lighter as you are free of the past." At the end he said, "Buen Camino, dear pilgrims. It means, 'Have a good way.' Take the Camino blessings forward, and don't let it stop here. Forever, buen Camino."

Before the mass was over, 12 more priests came out and then raised the great Butofumeiro, a huge incense burner filled with frankincense, used in ancient times to fumigate the pilgrims and remove the stench of their journey.

It took all 12 to raise it far above the crowd and begin to make it swing from one side of the cathedral to the other. It was an incredible sight to behold and one we were all blessed to experience, as it is not raised every day. I had wanted to see it and couldn't believe my good fortune.

The smoke filled the cathedral with its sacred scent, burning this moment even further into my brain and the cells of my body. We received communion and a blessing at the end. I sat for a while after mass ended, then lined up with the others to touch the statue of St. James.

I walked out of the church in a daze, and wandered over to the Compostela office to get my Compostela, my official certificate acknowledging my completion of the pilgrimage. As I stepped up they asked for my name and wrote it out in Latin. "Congratulations," they said as they put my certificate into a special tube to protect it from damage while I traveled.

"Thank you," I answered, proud to hold it in my hands.

I then wandered back to the front of the cathedral. There I saw so many more fellow pilgrims. There were Kate and Alice, and Linda and Clint and Dean. There were Hans and Peter, and even Eric, whom I had given my coat to weeks ago. It was wildly fun to see everyone. Then, from out of the crowd, running toward me, with a huge smile on his face, almost in slow motion, came Camino Patrick. We screamed and hugged and twirled around.

"We made it, Patrick!" I cried. "We two old geezers made it!"

He laughed. We took photos. We danced. We hugged some more. Then it was over.

It was now up to me to carry the flame of forgiveness back home to Chicago.

I hugged and kissed everyone I knew one last time, and then Patrick and I decided to have lunch. Afterward, on a whim, we decided to get tattoos of Camino symbols, his on his forearm, mine on each foot.

"I don't want to forget this, Patrick," I cringed through this final pain inflicted on my poor feet when it was my turn. "This will remind me not to."

Then it was time to part ways. Patrick was walking on to Finisterre, so he had another 150 kilometers to go. I was going to take a flight in the early morning to meet my daughters in Vienna for the workshop I was to teach in a few days, barely able to take another step.

Standing in the pouring rain, we just looked at each other and smiled.

"Buen Camino, Patrick," I said, giving him a final hug. "Have a good way."

"You too, Sonia," he answered. "Buen Camino."

AFTERWORD

Two months after I returned to Chicago, I received an e-mail from my husband, Patrick, saying he would be in town and asking if I would be willing to meet him while he was here.

I agreed, and we arranged to meet at the lakefront several blocks from the house.

My feet had healed enough to walk over, and it felt more personal that way. As I approached our meeting point, I wondered how I would feel once I saw him. Looking up in the distance, my question was immediately answered. I saw Patrick walking toward me—not the monster I felt he was the last time we were together, but just a guy who seemed vulnerable and scared. A guy I actually loved.

Moments later we came face-to-face, and he put out his hand for me to take, which I did. We started walking and didn't say a word to each other for a long time. Finally we made our way over to a park bench and sat down in the shade.

"How are you, Sonia?" he finally asked.

"I'm peaceful, Patrick. My pilgrimage healed my heart."

He was quiet for a long time.

Then he said, "That's great. I'm so proud of you for doing that."

A few minutes later, I asked, "How are you?"

He was again quiet for some time.

"I'm sad," he finally replied. "I miss you and our family."

I listened. I could tell it was true.

After a while he said, "Do you want to try it again with us?"

I looked out at the water, feeling for the answer. It came easily.

"Sure, Patrick. I'm willing."

"We've had so many difficulties before. We hurt each other so much."

"Yes, we did," I said, "but I've forgiven all that. I hope you can as well."

"I can."

He paused, and then asked, "Do you think we *can* work things out?"

"I don't know," I answered.

"How should we even begin?" he asked. "It seems like a lot."

I took a breath and thought for a long while.

Then I said, "I have an idea. Do you want to walk the Camino with me?"

Walking home alone after our conversation, I thought about what lay ahead between us. I've always been a big believer in happy endings and worked so hard to bring them about, so the thought that we might be able to reconcile was seductive. But now I knew in my heart that even if things between us did come to an end, I would still be happy. And that gave me freedom and peace.

ACKNOWLEDGMENTS

I would like to thank my beautiful daughters, Sonia and Sabrina, for holding me in love when I fell apart and for convincing me to take this pilgrimage. And to my beloved siblings and father, as well as Camino Patrick, for encouraging me to make it to the end.

And finally, to all my fellow pilgrims and unseen helpers who helped me remember and love who I am today and leave the rest behind. I am grateful beyond measure to all for my newfound and unshakable inner peace.

ABOUT THE AUTHOR

Sonia Choquette is celebrated worldwide as an author, spiritual teacher, six-sensory consultant, and transformational visionary guide. An enchanting storyteller, she is known for her delightful humor and adept skill in quickly shifting people out of psychological and spiritual difficulties, and into a healthier energy flow. Sonia is the author of 19 internationally best-selling books about intuitive awakening, personal and creative growth, and the innate leadership capabilities that reside within, most notably with the *New York Times* bestseller *The Answer Is Simple . . .*

Sonia's work has been published in over 40 countries and translated into 37 languages, making her one of the most widely read authors and experts in her field of work. Because of her unique gifts, her expertise is sought throughout the world, helping both individuals and organizations dramatically improve their experience and abilities to perform at optimal levels through empowerment and transformation.

Sonia's extensive background in uplifting guidance began as early as 12 years of age; she established her unwavering integrity at this young age, and continued following along this guided path to help other people find their truest selves through intuition. Sonia's legacy is continued by her two daughters, Sonia and Sabrina, who both have their own careers in spiritual coaching and guidance.

Sonia's philanthropic work has brought her to workshops in South Africa, through her publisher Hay House, which helped her set up organizational collaborations with Nurturing Orphans with AIDS for Humanity (NOAH), in addition to extensive charity work and fund-raising throughout the United States.

In 2012, Sonia was awarded the Leader of the Year by the Global Holistic Psychology Association and the award for Exceptional

Human Service by the 1st Global Parliament of Human Spirituality in Hyderabad, India.

Sonia attended the University of Denver and the Sorbonne in Paris, and holds a doctorate from the American Institute of Holistic Theology. She is a member of the Transformational Leadership Council, and is the host of her own weekly radio show, *Six Sensory Living*.

When not globe-trotting, Sonia can be found in Chicago, Illinois. She is an avid traveler and prides herself on her passionate pursuit of learning and growing every day. In her spare time, she enjoys dancing, playing the piano, fashion, art, and design; and she practices yoga and Pilates to stay in shape. She also loves everything about Paris and spends time there every year! To learn more about Sonia, please visit www.soniachoquette.com.

Hay House Titles of Related Interest

YOU CAN HEAL YOUR LIFE, the movie, starring Louise Hay & Friends
(available as a 1-DVD program and an expanded 2-DVD set)
Watch the trailer at: www.LouiseHayMovie.com

THE SHIFT, the movie,
starring Dr. Wayne W. Dyer
(available as a 1-DVD program and an expanded 2-DVD set)
Watch the trailer at: www.DyerMovie.com

I CAN SEE CLEARLY NOW, by Dr. Wayne W. Dyer

*IF I CAN FORGIVE, SO CAN YOU: My Autobiography of How I Overcame
My Past and Healed My Life,* by Denise Linn

LOVE, GOD, AND THE ART OF FRENCH COOKING,
by James F. Twyman

*MARRIED TO BHUTAN: How One Woman Got Lost, Said "I Do,"
and Found Bliss,* by Linda Leaming

*PEACE FROM BROKEN PIECES: How to Get Through What You're
Going Through,* by Iyanla Vanzant

*YOU CAN HEAL YOUR HEART: Finding Peace After a Breakup, Divorce,
or Death,* by Louise Hay and David Kessler

All of the above are available at your local bookstore,
or may be ordered by contacting Hay House (see next page).

We hope you enjoyed this Hay House book. If you'd like to receive our online catalog featuring additional information on Hay House books and products, or if you'd like to find out more about the Hay Foundation, please contact:

Hay House, Inc., P.O. Box 5100, Carlsbad, CA 92018-5100
(760) 431-7695 or (800) 654-5126
(760) 431-6948 (fax) or (800) 650-5115 (fax)
www.hayhouse.com® • www.hayfoundation.org

Published and distributed in Australia by: Hay House Australia Pty. Ltd., 18/36 Ralph St., Alexandria NSW 2015 • *Phone:* 612-9669-4299
Fax: 612-9669-4144 • www.hayhouse.com.au

Published and distributed in the United Kingdom by: Hay House UK, Ltd., Astley House, 33 Notting Hill Gate, London W11 3JQ • *Phone:* 44-20-3675-2450
Fax: 44-20-3675-2451 • www.hayhouse.co.uk

Published and distributed in the Republic of South Africa by: Hay House SA (Pty), Ltd., P.O. Box 990, Witkoppen 2068 • *Phone/Fax:* 27-11-467-8904
www.hayhouse.co.za

Published in India by: Hay House Publishers India, Muskaan Complex, Plot No. 3, B-2, Vasant Kunj, New Delhi 110 070 • *Phone:* 91-11-4176-1620
Fax: 91-11-4176-1630 • www.hayhouse.co.in

Distributed in Canada by: Raincoast Books, 2440 Viking Way, Richmond, B.C. V6V 1N2 • *Phone:* 1-800-663-5714
Fax: 1-800-565-3770 • www.raincoast.com

Take Your Soul on a Vacation

Visit www.HealYourLife.com® to regroup, recharge, and reconnect with your own magnificence.
Featuring blogs, mind-body-spirit news, and life-changing wisdom from Louise Hay and friends.

Visit www.HealYourLife.com today!